James P. Mackey

D1743535

Jesus of Nazareth:
The Life, the Faith and the
Future of the Prophet
(A Brief History)

the columba press

First published in 2008 by
the columba press
55A Spruce Avenue, Stillorgan Industrial Park,
Blackrock, Co Dublin

Cover by Bill Bolger
Origination by The Columba Press
Printed by Athenaeum Press Ltd, Gateshead

ISBN 978 1 85607 601 2

Acknowledgements

The author and publisher are grateful to the following for permission to use material in their copyright: Cló Iar-Chonnachta for quotations from Cathal Ó Searcaigh; Faber and Faber for quotations from T. S. Eliot; Bloodaxe Books for a quotation from Brendan Kennelly; The Trustees of the Estate of the late Katherine B. Kavanagh, through the Jonathan Williams Literary Agency, for a quotation from Patrick Kavanagh.

Jesus of Nazareth
The Life, the Faith and the Future of the Prophet:
(A Brief History)
James P. Mackey

Jesus of Nazareth is a life of Jesus researched and written with the central purpose of discovering the true kind and content of the faith for which he lived and died, and which has come down to us as the Christian faith by which so many still profess to live. A second and equally important purpose in this research and writing is to estimate just how loyal, and how disloyal the main churches that claim his name have been over almost two thousand years. The findings are radical, in the best sense of the word, going back to the roots to revive the full and true vision of the faith of the Nazarene in churches that badly need reform at the present time if they are not to continue to haemorrhage even more members.

James P. Mackey is Emeritus Professor of Theology at Edinburgh University and Visiting Professor at TCD.

That a Systematic Theologian of the stature of James Mackey should turn his attention to the historical Jesus is a welcome change from the current plethora of non-religious Jesus-figures to which we have been subjected by critical historical scholarship. This is a radical – in every sense of that word – treatment, that will inspire and challenge its intended readership. For Mackey's Jesus is no mere liberal thinker but a prophet and son of God who lived and died to restore the true reign of God in the world.'

— *Seán Freyne, former Professor of Theology, TCD, and Visiting Professor of Early Christian History and Literature, Harvard Divinity School.*

In James P. Mackey's *Jesus of Nazareth* his invocation of 'the idiom of imagination' enables him at once to relate faith and reason across the many dimensions and disciplines of human life and thought and to open up the biblical accounts of Jesus to truths and practices too frequently neglected. In method and substance, the study of Jesus is a truly remarkable achievement by the author and an equally remarkable source of nourishment and delight for the reader.

— *Enda McDonagh, Emeritus Professor of Moral Theology at St Patrick's College, Maynooth.*

James Mackey's previous book on Jesus, *Jesus the Man and the Myth*, went through two editions in German translation, *Jesus der Mensch and der Mythos*, and received impressive reviews on both sides of the Atlantic. Elizabeth Johnson, Professor of Theology at Fordham University, New York said of it: 'Back in the 80s he wrote the definitive book in Christology that everyone was using in classes: *Jesus the Man and the Myth*.' John Bowden of SCM Press, London, wrote: 'With power, learning, wit and poetry, James Mackey has written a book on Jesus perhaps unequalled, for all the recent competition, since Schweitzer's famous *Quest of the Historical Jesus*.' Yet *Jesus the Man and the Myth* was written largely in the jargon of professional theology, whereas *Jesus of Nazareth* is more accessible, in that it is written in the story-telling language of works of history.

Jesus of Nazareth is a companion volume to Mackey's recently published *Christianity and Creation: the Essence of the Christian Faith and its Future among Religions*. The latter is a fuller up-date of *Jesus the Man and the Myth*, but it is even heavier with theological critique of Christian doctrine and practices that developed over the ages, whereas its essential contents are once again more accessible through the biblical style story-telling forms employed in *Jesus of Nazareth*. Of *Christianity and Creation* Elizabeth Johnson wrote: 'Mackey has crafted a sage and passionate reflection on the core beliefs of Christian faith that reconnect human beings both with nature and with God in a beautiful, holistic vision. This is a creation theology that does not neglect sin, a Christology that places Jesus Christ at the hub, all the while honouring indigenous and world religions, an eschatology shot through with scientific learning yet replete with hope for eternal life. A powerful legacy to spur reflective persons of the twenty-first century into new appreciation of their tradition and action in its light.' John Bowden has also written: 'In this brilliant new book, written with inspirational vision and no academic paraphernalia of notes, but simply relying on the Bible, James Mackey presents God's grace and truth in the natural history of the only world we know to exist, reinterpreting creation, fall, salvation, revelation, faith and grace in a sweeping theology of creation.'

Table of Contents

As With The First Jesus Book, So With The Last
For Noelle
The Closest Mortal Source To Me
Of The Love That Moves The Sun And The Other Stars

Preface

This book, as its title indicates, offers a history of Jesus of Nazareth. Since Jesus is of historic interest because he was the founder of a faith that came to be known as Christianity, what is offered is the history of the faith that emerged as a result of his life's work and, to some minor extent, a history of that faith as his followers, early and late, understood and promoted it. By his life's work is meant, not merely the formulation of that faith in words and the ways in which he evinced the evidences for its truth and rightness for the human race, but also his living out of that faith and the way in which he died for it.

It is often said that the Bible is not a history book but a book about faith, and so there is a Prologue in which I argue for a revision of that basically false dichotomy between history and faith. But people who do not have either the interest or the philosophical and theological background to engage in such abstruse argumentation can simply skip over the Prologue and read the rest of the book. And then the only test they will need to apply to the history of Jesus of Nazareth is that of reading the Bible, or at least those sections of it that are called in evidence in the course of the book's argument, in order to see if the picture of the historical founder of a faith rings true to all the evidences therein discovered.

The quoted authorities for my reconstruction of the original faith of Jesus of Nazareth then, and hence for any suggestions I make about distortions of that faith from the beginning by self-proclaimed opponents and followers alike, are the authors of the various documents that make up the Bible. I find no need to supply the book with references to any larger list of author-authorities, although I freely acknowledge that I have greatly benefited from a great range of biblical scholars in my own reading of the Bible over the course of my professional life. These are fully acknowledged where occasion called for it in most of the other books I have written. But these were then books in which philosophers and theologians talked to each other, that is to say, talked to themselves. And as a consequence most of our books then came to be about other philosophers and theologians, and only in this indirect fashion were we producing a philosophy or a theology for our time. I simply want, as I play my own endgame, to be more direct.

Jesus of Nazareth was designed as a companion volume to *Christianity and Creation: The Essence of the Christian Faith, and its Future among Religions.* The difference between the two books is this. The theme of *Christianity and Creation* is laid out in alternating sections. Sections in which the coinage of communication is the philosophical concepts and logic of which all theology strictly so-called is composed, alternate with sections in which the coinage of communication is that of literature, story, poetry, myth and history. The latter is the coinage of communication in which the entire Bible is entirely composed: there is no theology, in the strict technical sense of that term, in the Bible.

This is neither the time nor the place to discourse in detail on the relative advantages and disadvantages of these two modes of communication, often designated respectively as the abstract concept and the concrete image. But this one point might well be made: the language of imagery has the advantage of instant and universal intelligibility, composed as it is of the elemental images of earth and sea and sky, of living and dying. Synge's *Playboy of the Western World*, set in a shebeen in the western seaboard of Ireland, is just as accessible to people who live in the suburbs of Los Angeles. Whereas the concepts of which philosophy and its outreach, theology, are composed inevitably present us with somewhat artificial mental constructions that are then tied to their time and place, and have to be learned by potential users at other times and places. You do not need to be proficient in philosophy or theology; indeed, you do not need to know Hebrew or Greek in order to get the messages of the Bible, although people who do know these languages are necessary in order to translate the Bible as transparently as possible into whatever language you do speak.

The history of *Jesus of Nazareth*, as distinct from the account contained in *Christianity and Creation*, is wholly pursued and presented in the idiom of imagination. It is, through and through, an account of the contents of the Bible, focused upon Jesus of Nazareth, his life, his faith and his future as son of God and prophet. This account is taken straight from the (hi)story and poetry of the Bible, and then summarised, discussed and explained in that same literary form. An odd reference is made to some theological formulae that have been made into doctrine and are therefore likely to resonate in the minds of the faithful, but only in order to prevent these from obscuring what is revealed in the other currency. Therefore this book should be intelligible to any who read, say, historical novels, and enjoy them.

At the same time, those who do have some acquaintance with the philosophy of the West from ancient times, for that is the philosophy in which Christian doctrine is largely cast, and who would like to check more closely the implications of this Bible reading for our traditional Christian theology and doctrine today, both positive and negative implications, could usefully read at least the theological sections of *Christianity and Creation*, before issuing their verdict on the whole. Just as those who have read *Christianity and Creation* and would like much more discussion of the biblical data on which its theological judgements are based, would find such extended discussion in *Jesus of Nazareth*.

What the two books have in common is this: both belong equally to the 'essence of Christianity' genre, a genre much criticised by devoted Christians, quite commonly on grounds allegedly illustrated by such 'essence of Christianity' practitioners as Nietzsche, Feuerbach and Harnack, on the grounds that these people and their many imitators simply read the faith of the historical Jesus through the heavily coloured spectacles of the rationalist enlightenment or, worse still, the enlightened materialism of the modern era.

There is, of course, much that is true and fair about such criticism. Yet it must always be balanced by the following considerations: first, there are many of the aspects of the faith of Jesus that those masters of suspicion and critics of late Western Christianity saw much more clearly than did the authorised theologians of the main Christian churches. It would not be the first time, nor the last, that those we consider our enemies see through us, far more clearly than those we consider our lovers and friends. Look for instance at Nietzsche's poetic description, in *Thus Spoke Zarathustra*, of the nature and process of divine creation. Or consider Feuerbach's powerful emphasis on the immanence of the divine. Or Harnack's account of the way in which the commandment of love of God and neighbour does indeed sum up the new Torah handed down from the Mount of the Sermon by the new Moses, the prophet Jesus. And then notice, for this is really the case, how intimately connected are those three insights. So Christians can learn a lot from those they regard and so regularly denounce as their cultured despisers. If only because philosophies change with time and culture, and a

Christian theology and doctrine that has been expressed for too long in ancient and somewhat obsolete philosophies can become unintelligible or misleading, or both.

Second, most Christian churches in their better moods proclaim: *ecclesia semper reformanda*, the church is in constant need of reform. Yet most churches most of the time, being human both in construction and composition, prove reluctant to put this proclamation into practice. And it is then the duty of those whom God has called to be theologians in the churches, to jog these churches into some recognition of the reform required for the time that is in it. A bit like common or garden-variety prophets in this, although, with very rare exceptions, without either the latter's inspiration or their moral authority. The humble theologian has no authority whatever other than the intrinsic persuasiveness, or otherwise, of the case set out and argued. And the worth of any such case where Christianity is concerned, must be weighed primarily on the scales of the faith of the unintentional founder of Christianity. Only so can one see how much the present forms and practices of Christianity the religion diverge from the faith for which the historical Jesus, quite literally in the end, gave his life. Hence the need for historical studies of the life, the faith and the future of the prophet and son of God, Jesus of Nazareth.

Prologue: The Bible as History and Literature

Not many decades ago, and then for quite a few years, theological literature was dominated by a debate about the relationship of history to faith. This was no doubt due to the fact that an enterprise known as 'the quest of the historical Jesus,' and then 'a new quest of the historical Jesus' had been pursued by that time for very nearly two whole centuries. And if one impression remained constant throughout all of the differing portraits of the historical Jesus that were painted over the long years of the quest, it was this: despite all the differences between the historical figures made to stand up in the name of Jesus by all of these modern historians, they were each and all quite easily distinguishable from the common portrait of Jesus painted in equally graphic detail by the devotees of the Christian religion who regarded Jesus as the founder of their faith. To define this distinction as that between a thoroughly human and a thoroughly divine Jesus might be thought a trifle excessive, but it could also be regarded as a pardonable excess for the sake of an acceptable effect.

With the inestimable if also always-too-late benefit of hindsight, it is now possible to see that the debate about history and faith was bedevilled by a false assumption from its big-bang beginning to its somewhat whimpering end. The false assumption concerned the nature and incidence of faith in the course of human knowledge and conduct and, odd as this might seem, it actually crossed the divide that both historians and believers seemed otherwise and equally anxious to maintain between their warring camps. Both sides assumed that faith is the proper and indeed the only response to positions put to people where they have no way of arriving at these positions by dint of their own intelligence and enterprise, and no ever-present possibility of independently verifying these positions when they are accepted 'on faith'. Naturally enough, in the *soi-disant* Age of Science such intelligent enterprise and verification became the near monopoly of science. So that history had to be a science, and historians had to be scientists, instead of the good old storytellers they always had been and in the latter capacity had served the race so well, as the saying goes, from time immemorial. In this ambient cultural conviction, it should cause no surprise to note, faith very frequently attracted to itself the adjective, blind.

The religious side in this confusion tended to be less uniform and absolute in their contrasts between faith and science or reason in general. The more Catholic ones promoted very odd entities called proofs of God's existence. The more Protestant ones, aware that their Bible did suggest quite frequently and indeed insistently that a rational being could know God from the creation, still insisted that an inherited sinfulness had from the origin of the species blinded human intelligence to this knowledge; so it was human reason that was blind, not the faith that God required to greet the special divine revelations then purposefully designed to relieve that blindness. But then, on the Catholic side also, the view prevailed that from the very origin of the species sin intervened in God's otherwise good creation, and it spread to all of human kind. So that the knowledge of that sin and, more especially, of the manner in which God alone could and would save us from its effects and penalties, must be quite beyond our natural ken, and needed to be conveyed by special divine revelation, and accepted in pure faith. In effect, that leaves Christian believers, on both sides of their divide, distinguishing reason from faith. And it explains how the two sides of that other divide, the two sides of the divide between the historians and the believers, both hold to that same distinction between reason and faith, if with differing valuations placed on faith and reason respectively, and for different motives and reasons.

This is not the time or the place to broach the arcane discipline of epistemology, the science of human knowledge. Enough needs to be said only to break down any solid wall epistemologists might wish to build between faith and reason. So as to see human faith for what it is, an integral part of human knowing, and then to add some sentences in order to assure the modern historian that storytelling is still of the essence of her particular science – for science is merely a transliteration of the Latin word for knowledge.

We know the world through our interactions with it. These interactions are of the essence of the existence of all things that in their inevitable inter-relationships and inter-dependencies make up the unified entity we call the cosmos. The continuous play of these inter-relationships shows us, from our mother's womb, a world in continuous creation, or as we would say nowadays, in continuous evolution. Each entity strives for continued and ever better existence, and has to adapt to the others as they must adapt to it for the overall success of what is and must of necessity be a process as extensive as the cosmos itself. For to some extent each advance in existence and life is at the expense of others. The foetus that has taken its very substance from the mother's body gains its individual independence very gradually, and at first by being expelled from the womb, at great pain to the mother. But if any entity takes more from those on which it is dependent, more than it needs to become a contributory member of the community of entities that make up the cosmos, then the delicate balance is broken. This is the balance for which Heraclitus long ago coined the phrase: 'living each other's deaths and dying each other's lives.' So that if an evil selfishness spreads sufficiently, a selfishness that consists in taking from others more than we need to live and thereby threatening their lives unjustly, then the cosmos itself as a harmonious unity of interdependent entities is threatened; or at least that part of it that one species or another calls home.

The knowledge we have then, from our first conscious moments in the womb, is a knowledge of what to do with the entities that surround us and with which we are so interdependent, just as much, if not more than it is a knowledge of what these entities are. It is a knowledge the most basic feature of which is imagination – the ability to imagine the best outcome for all from the interactions in which all the agencies operative in the cosmos must engage. From the smallest particle that moves in the infinitesimal depths of minutiae, to the greatest agency that sources the cosmos as such. So that every move in such vitally necessary knowing engages trust and hope, in short, it engages faith. Faith in my own imagination and its configuring of all constantly co-creative things, for imagination is the prime heuristic faculty that works the moving images of the surrounding world into movies of what is and is to come. Abstract conceptual or mathematical analysis comes later and makes its own valuable but subsidiary contribution. Faith in the entities and especially in the other persons that surround me, that they might construe our joint evolving cosmos correctly and might act for the best for me also. Faith in the cosmos itself, for the sun to shine tomorrow morning, and the rain to come and water the crops. Faith in the end and above all in the creator of the cosmos. Not a blind faith. Never that, but a faith based on all the evidences of my life-experience, and as open both to development and correction as a knowledge so based must always be. For as imagination is, as someone said, reason in its most expansive mode, then the truth possessed at any given moment, and even the certainty that people may express about such truth, always takes the form of reasonable belief. And for us mortal creatures in any area of knowledge and life in the cosmos, there can seldom if ever be anything other than reasonable belief.

The historian then can never distance herself in the least degree from the believer. For what she writes is always a history of human faith, whether that might be in the form of a history of what certain people believed about their world, or a history of the little worlds they created, or destroyed, or re-created, in the belief that these were good or evil, or an improvement upon what they knew before. And the very writing of that history itself is of interest to writer and reader alike because, and only because of the light it throws on human faiths now being realised or as yet unrealised, but always open to critical comparison with those that have been realised before and the outcomes of which are now largely known. The historian therefore has a pivotal role to play in the on-going self-criticism of human systems of belief, *aka* human philosophies of life in the world, human *weltanschauungen*. The historian has a pivotal role to play in the critical discrimination between religious and secular humanist faiths, as much as between different religious faiths, if only once again by weighing in the scales of history and then comparing the crucial outcomes of each in turn. It is true of all human faiths what Jesus said of his: by their fruits you will know them.

Nor need the modern historian worry about being called an old-fashioned storyteller, despite the awesome peer pressure, especially amongst academics, brought to bear on every possible discipline to describe itself as a science. These days, virtually every practitioner in academia needs to be seen as a scientist of one sort or another – a social scientist for instance, whatever that might then be taken to mean in each particular case. And least of all need the historian worry if it is a scientist from the department of physics that refers to the historian as an old-fashioned storyteller.

In the first instance, history writing always has been, still is and always will be a form of fiction. What the historian does, as every historian knows all too well, is to examine all that is left by the ravages of time of the human journey during some past age within the natural history, as it is still called, of the cosmos. The job of the historian is to contemplate critically these fading pictures of humanity's past, through intelligent lenses that are always already imprinted with the images projected by her present world. Imprinted images of what agents are operative in the cosmos, or at least in the part of it that most nearly concerns the human species; images of what these agencies, and most especially the human species itself, are doing as much as what they are. Images of what can be done with them in order to prevent mutual destruction, and in order to be enabled to hope instead for mutual advancement of existence and life.

Contemplating the details of such fading pictures of the past with such crucial and critical intent, enables the historian to see what is common and constant, what changes and what changed or can be changed for the better or the worse. An overall exercise in images and their linking together into stories – an exercise of intelligent imagination or of imaginative intelligence. And bearing the most striking of family resemblances to the novelist, let us say, who fashions out of the mere facts of the lives of herself and of others, present or remembered, a story that corresponds fully neither to any one of these experiences and events factually recorded, nor to all of these put together in such a purely factual manner. And yet, if it is well done, it can turn out to be a story that reveals to the reader in a new and clearer light the common experiences contained in the raw facts, the loves and hates, the beliefs and despairs that accompanied them, and the overall and usually mixed outcomes that can be expected for the enhancement of human life, or its degradation. A moralist can be detected in all such fiction, but a moralist who never, ever moralises – a type whose common self-portrait can still be viewed in Andre Gide's *The Immoralist*.

In the second instance, in the case of science and the scientist, even in the case of the hardest of the sciences, physics and mathematics, and especially in the areas of astrophysics, cosmogenesis and cosmology in general, the presence of imagery and the need to weave stories out of this imagery seems unavoidable, and even in the most abstruse and advanced reaches of contemporary science it still retains a quite substantial presence in any account of the coming to be of the cosmos. It is true that the earliest physicists of the West, the *physiologoi* as they were called, preferred to work out the abstract forms of what they then called philosophy, rather than use the plentiful supply of concrete cosmological imagery supplied by contemporary myth. Yet they did this largely because of the way in which they felt contemporary mythologies had sadly betrayed the second and inseparable aim of their profession, namely, the effort to envisage how the pullulating entities and processes that make up this cosmos-in-becoming could work together for the better ultimate outcome for all. *Philo-sophia* means the loving quest for wisdom, where wisdom, as distinct from mere factual knowledge, refers to knowing-how rather than knowing-that. That is to say, knowing how to live in this cosmos for the best outcome for all. And that is still quite palpably the goal of modern science, and of all who devote their lives to its pursuit. And it reveals the same panoply of measured beliefs in the present results of scientific investigation of the entities, events and agencies operative in the cosmos that science with increasing acceleration reveals. Together with the same hope that existence and life in this cosmos can be advanced, in an advance that seems unbounded by any perceptible limit. And the attentive reader of the first philosopher/physicists will observe that, despite their persistent attacks upon the poets and their myths, never in the course of the succeeding centuries did they rid themselves of the substantial use of imagery until, with Plato, the greatest of these, the myths turn up regularly and take some of the best seats at the symposium table.

So science is simultaneously an exercise in imaginative perception of what is and what is going on, and an exercise in creative imagination that attempts to figure out what to do with it for the best. The scientist works with images; the images that come to her, not in a series of stills, but in the form of a movie that through moving images tells the story of the constant creation, the perennial evolution of the ever new. Science is the story of the agencies that are creatively involved in the evolution of all that has come to be in the creation so far. A history to which some of our more adventurous scientists add an extrapolated story of the grand denouement of it all, a Big Crunch that will parallel an originating Big Bang; or an infinitesimally weakening Whimper? Nothing but the final fizzling out of whatever it was that originally exploded? Or did not explode, but began in an originally inaudible moan? It is all imagery. All metaphor, metaphor being the application to something that still puzzles us, of the image of something that is known and familiar, in the hope that the familiar image will throw some light on what is still dark and seemingly impenetrable. And in the larger hope that the entities and processes that lie at the deeper and higher levels of the cosmos that our earthly inspection cannot reach, will show at least such similarity in all of their sometimes vast differences from what is near and familiar, as to allow these glimmers of light to reach us, so that we can imagine and speak of the otherwise unthinkable and unspeakable.

Perhaps the most persistent imagery that has dominated the modern science of cosmology up to quite recently, although it goes back in more primitive form to the Greek Atomists, is the image of the cosmos as a great conglomerate of hard, tangible and very visible stuff called matter. The scientific imagination that came to be dominated entirely by that image, then went on to imagine everything that existed and every agency within the cosmos, as a series of clusters of lumps of this hard matter that, from the macrocosm down to the microcosm were successively made up of smaller and smaller lumps of hard matter until, down at the last level of the sub-atomic world, one came upon, or would certainly one day come upon the tiniest of all particles, of which every other level, up to the level of the cosmos itself, could then be seen to be made up.

The reader at this point might quite reasonably feel that this talk of endemic imagery in the hardest of the hard sciences, however interesting it might be in itself, must surely be irrelevant in a book that presumably concentrates on seeing the history of Jesus set in a broader story of the creation of the world by a divine being, a kind of creator and creation story with which science in itself can have nothing whatever to do; and a story moreover that a great many scientists today vociferously reject as an over-credulous challenger to their reasoned cosmology. But this is not so, for there are more similarities than one might expect at first blush between religious accounts of creation and accounts of the evolution of this cosmos offered by hard scientists of the crudest materialist kind: all that exists is matter, and there is nothing that is not material or produced by matter. Just one essay, 'A Free Man's Worship', by the renowned mathematician-physicist, Bertrand Russell, would convince one of this fact. It is an immemorial and universal convention of religious faith to understand the term, god, to refer primarily to the source-creators of all that has come to be. And that comprehensive and source creator of all that comes to be, Russell names as 'matter'. And he cannot but hint at divine status, even if he does so unconsciously, sometimes by capitalising the first letter, Matter; sometimes by talking of the entity that brings all things into existence and successively annihilates them as 'omnipotent matter rolling on its relentless way'. But most graphically of all, Russell illustrates the relationship between traditional religious imaginings and the way in which he imagines blind, reckless matter by describing the effect on human beings who, out of fear and trembling, worship such an arbitrary arbiter of life and death, as people who then exercised such cruelty on themselves and others, in religion's characteristic fashion, as he would see it. So yes, this thoroughgoing materialism is a dogma; and it is still maintained as such even by contemporary scientists who have still to realise, apparently, how much of modern physics has undermined it with much more mysterious stories of the ultimate components of our universe.

In any case, Bertrand Russell's crude materialist picture of hard matter exploding to give rise, blindly and sequentially to all the types of things and the living species that continue to come and go in the long making of the universe, found itself increasingly challenged by the very advances of the science to which he made such a fine mathematical contribution. (Although his description of religion as the self-destructive worship of a cruel god still comes uncomfortably close to more operative religions than one would care to name.) The most elementary sub-atomic particles known, instead of allowing themselves to be broken down into the most elementary particles of all, seemed instead to disappear into, and to re-appear out of 'fields.' (If you never recognised a metaphor before, you must surely realise that you are looking at one now.) At the same time, according to a dominant school of scientific cosmology at the moment, particles also lose their foundational place in physics. According to this school of thought, the most basic elements in the making of the cosmos are 'one-dimensional strings'. They are not at all like your shoe-strings, which are three dimensional, as all particles must be. They are one-dimensional, like a line that has length but not breadth and depth, and is actually a mental abstraction from hard matter as we know it. Still, mysterious as they are, these cosmos-generating strings must have something in common with our shoe-strings, in order to make the metaphor yield some knowledge of that even more mysterious process. They are vibrating strings, incidentally, and the different modes in which they vibrate, 'represent' all of the different particles that come and go in the on-going formation of the universe.

However, that word 'represent' would seem at first blush to evade rather than answer the question: out of fields of what do the most elementary particles emerge? A possible answer comes from a recent account of cosmogenesis known as inflation theory. In the words of a physicist colleague, Michael O'Keeffe: 'According to this theory the universe began – without particles, without matter – as a zero-valued Higgs field. This represented the presence of a very high energy density in the universe … a highly unstable state of affairs … (and) led to an extraordinary brief, but stupendous, accelerated expansion of the universe, ending with the energy being converted into a spectrum of exotic particles.'

So our familiar particles are back again? They and their familiar touchy-feely, good old thoroughly material cosmos have not disappeared into the primeval depths of insubstantial vibrating one-dimensional strings, like the phantom waves of a dark, impenetrable abyss without water? But no, we are by no means back at the hard, not to say crude materialism of Russell and his era. For the simple reason that energy, the term now suggested for the primordial 'content' of the 'field' from which particles fleetingly emerge, is another metaphor, and it is not, as a matter of fact, a metaphor for another region or type of that matter, or mass, that is the common and sole currency of your pure and simple materialist's account of the make-up and the making of the cosmos. It is true that all ordinary people probably think of it as a material entity, in the common sense of the word, that comes in gusts or blobs, close enough to particles to confirm the similarity with hard matter. But, as Richard Feynman, the boffin friend of the layman in matters scientific, puts it: 'In physics today, we have no knowledge of what energy is … it is an abstract thing … In reality, energy is part of a set of mathematical relationships that connect together observations of mechanical processes in a simple way.'

Energy in our common vocabulary is our name for something we experience that seems to enable us to get things up and running, to get things done. Whether it is mental or physical, both or neither, it is difficult to tell. And the speed, efficiency and standard to which we get things done is for us but one measure of it; for we also sense it to wax and wane in what appears to be a more subjective means of measurement. So the image we have of our energy becomes the metaphor for whatever it is in the cosmos that enables things to get up and running. *Energia* in Greek refers to activity, activating, actualising. Something like our energy must be operating out there, but how like our experience of what we call energy we do not know. Yet this is the very metaphorical insight that allowed the Jewish philosopher-theologian, Philo of Alexandria to picture God continually creating the cosmos through his twin *energeia*, his twin activities of creativity and overlordship, *ktisthes* and *kurios*. We may not have come that far from Philo after all.

Mathematics then corresponds to the imagery of particles, energies and so on, just as the ancients knew, and as philosophy corresponds to the wider poetic imagery of what to do with it all for the best. Mathematics is the language of the physical cosmos, an abstract analysis and expression of the measurements of the number, shape, size and mass of the distinguishable elements that make up the cosmos; of their distance and speed with respect to each other; of the forces (another metaphor) they exert upon each other; of the changes that are brought about in the course of their mutual interdependence and interaction in the course of the consequent evolution of the cosmos, and of what are called certain constants in the cosmos as a whole. Mathematics thereby discovers the regularities that govern the myriad interactions of these pullulating entities at the different levels of the cosmos – the laws of nature, as they are called. But these mathematical regularity-regulations are always abstract accounts of the mutually adaptive behaviour of all of the agencies operative in the universe, and as such they must always suffer from two different sets of limitations. First, the perception of them will always depend upon our necessarily anthropomorphic imaging of the kinds of agencies actually operative in the cosmos: strings or particles; mineral, vegetable, animal and/or human agencies, and so on. And second, the very idea and operation of regularity-regulations will differ in the course of the cosmic-creative advance of existence and life, with the advent of creatures that can become aware of these 'laws of nature', to the point of creative insight and ability at which they are freed to simply obey the laws of nature as they stand, to put them to more creative uses than as yet envisaged, or to break them and take the consequences; any or all of the above.

For as the story of the continual creation or evolution of the cosmos proceeds, the pullulating particles and the more and more complex entities that they construct by means of the creative formulae or 'laws' of nature working in and through them, give rise to life. And latterly, in this corner of the cosmos at least, they give rise to intelligent life in the form of *homo sapiens* (humanity the wise), so named no matter how often that self-congratulatory species acts as *homo insipiens* (humanity the stupid). This creative coup came about, according in this instance to practitioners of the biological sciences, by having clusters of particles known as genes develop a code by which information was not merely passed on, but adapted and developed from generation to generation of living species. Until there emerged from this otherwise wonderful cosmos this species that named itself *homo sapiens*, because they could so easily see that the cosmos itself was intelligently designed to evolve intelligent life. And they could then at least glimpse the responsibility that fell on their ape-like shoulders, to continue that cosmic creativity on its upward *élan* for the benefit of all living things. Yet they chose instead to live lives of conspicuous consumerism, treating the cosmos, or at least as much of it as they could get their greedy little hands on, as a means to their own self-aggrandisement, thereby setting themselves well on the way to destroying the cosmos, or at least as much of it as they can currently inflict with their stupid, destructive and death-dealing ways.

The point of telling just so much of this story of science here is manifold: to illustrate the lingering but accelerating and well-deserved death of the kind of crude materialism that is still so robustly alive in Bertrand Russell's day and after. To open the prospect once again of the sight of mind-like agencies, great and small, that conspire in the continuous co-creation of the only cosmos we know. But most of all to show that the story of science is the story of a story that continually has to go through series of revisions. And the story in question, like the stories that historians tell, or the great cosmic story of both the natural history and the human history of the cosmos that the Bible tells, is made up of imagery and the weaving of that imagery into a movie script.

To which is then added the mathematical physics that assigns measurable values to agencies imagined as balls, strings, explosions, implosions, vibrations, bubbles, energy, mass, and certain cosmic constants, as they are called, and so on, and so on. For by doing so the mathematics of the physical cosmos reveals the regularities, the 'laws' by which all of these agencies, so imagined, interact to inform and transform each other; and to deform each other also in the course of that process of continuous transformation or creation that is called evolution. Like Einstein's equation for the interactive relationship of energy and mass, $E=MC2$. This gives the rule that in any transformation of mass into energy, or vice versa, the equivalence will be found to be the 'amount of energy' to the 'amount of mass multiplied by the speed of light squared.' In this way the story is given abstract mathematical expression just as, some six centuries BC, the stories of cosmos were given abstract conceptual expression in what came to be called philosophy. But it is always the story, woven out of moving images, that is given such abstract expression, in order to inspect and see more minutely what is going on and what could yet emerge. And the great leaps forward in science are therefore always likely to involve initial leaps of imagination, as when Einstein imagined time to be an integral dimension in what we had normally understood to be a three-dimensional physical cosmos, and the theory of relativity was born.

Once it dawns on the reader who is about to take up the Bible to read it through on its own terms, that both the natural history of the cosmos and the history of a species, *homo sapiens*, that seems destined to play an increasingly important role within it, is and must be written first and foremost in the fictive form of imagery woven into a cosmic story – then and only then will that reader be in the least likely to be able to see what the Bible really says about Jesus of Nazareth, the story of the significance of whose person and the faith for which he lived and died the Bible sets fairly and squarely in the context, not merely of the history of Israel and the history of religion in that time and place, but of the natural history of the cosmos from creation to consummation. And only then will the reader of the Bible be able to form a personal assessment of the credibility of the man and the worldview that he promoted as a reasonable and true belief, by setting what it says against humanity's universal and perennially practical knowledge of that same cosmos. Whether that knowledge be otherwise expressed in general literature, or in the literature of the academic discipline of history, or in the practice and literature of science, or simply in the short experience of everyman's conscious existence.

At this point it might be necessary to offer a number of summary assurances to prospective readers of this book whose minds have been confused or perturbed by recent designer wars between science and faith or history and faith. First, to read the Bible as history, as belonging to the genre of the literature of that discipline, is in no way to impugn its character as the documentation of a historical and historic faith. Indeed anyone taking up the Bible and determined to see for themselves what it has to say for itself, while ignoring any forced presuppositions about it, would certainly see that from first page to last it is the history of a people and a faith by which they lived, set within the history of a world they believed to be created and controlled by named agencies, natural, human and divine. Second, to read the Bible as history does not in itself incur any denial whatever of claims to the effect that the Bible enjoys a certain inerrancy with respect to the true faith by which all people in the world should live, for the best outcome for all. Nor does this incur any denial of claims to the effect that the writers who composed all of the documents that over many centuries finally accounted for what is now called the Bible, did so under the inspiration of the Spirit of God.

But it does need to be said that the documents that were finally admitted into the canon of Scripture, as the Bible is called, were admitted to that canon on the grounds that the judges of these documents recognised in them the true faith, first, of the God of Israel and then of the version proclaimed by the prophet and son of God, Jesus of Nazareth. It was as, if not after, this long-drawn-out company of leading Jesus-followers drew up the list of documents in which they felt they recognised the story of the true faith, that they said, or others said, that the resulting 'canon' of documents was divinely inspired. However, this divine inspiration was thereafter analysed and explained in more detail then and in succeeding centuries.

Nor does this claim for inerrancy preclude the possibility of the writers of these documents presenting false faiths and even falsifications of the true faith by which people, including their own people lived. The Bible frequently and stridently portrays the false and death-dealing faiths of other peoples that its own people only too often were tempted to adopt, and to which they succumbed. With depressing regularity the Bible records the prophetic denouncement of the falsifications of their own faith in which the Israelis indulged. And in the part that Christians call the New Testament, although it is simply the renewal of the oldest testament of all, the Bible shows the prophet Jesus ascend a mountain, like Moses did, and quite deliberately and radically reform the faith that his fellow Israelis understood Moses to have bequeathed to them. 'You heard that it was said to them of old, thou shalt not kill … But I say to you, you may not even mock your brother.'

And the Bible also records, dutifully and persistently, the resistance to certain defining aspects of the faith of Jesus in which from first to last even his closest disciples and would-be leaders of his community after him persisted. It records certain ways in which these followers altered the teaching of Jesus in order to suit their own designs, a process that continued in Christian churches to this day. And yet in spite of that the Bible does, from first page to last, advertise the true faith, for the true and faithful preaching and practice of which the true followers of his to this day can commend Jesus the Jew. So that the patient and perceptive reader can find that diamond there in all of its blinding truth and terrible glory, all the better set in defining relief by the contrasting dross with which its practitioners, preachers and publishers, including the scripture writers, have surrounded it in every age. That, for anyone who really reads the book without the blinkers of self-serving dogma, is what must be meant by the inerrancy of the Bible.

Finally, it must be clear from all that has been said already, that the most common currency in literature, including the literature of the 'science' of history and much of the literature of the science of cosmology, is stamped with imagery, and the images are then arranged in groups and woven into the forms of the story. Stories of cosmic depth and extent, or of historic origins and importance, are commonly called myths. And myths, of course, like any other attempted expression of the truth of things, may be true or false or, as is mostly the case, they may fall short of the full truth, or be mixed with varying degrees of falsehood. The Bible is one great myth, construed from many lesser myths. And so the only way to get at the truth of it is to learn to interpret the images in their arrangements and weaves. Not difficult in most cases, since it is in images that we perceive the world first and last, and it is in imagery that we habitually express whatever understanding of it, and hope for it, that we may have gained. A literary critic of note, treating the Bible according to his own *metier*, that is to say, as a remarkable instance of literature, entitled the book that ensued: *The Great Code*. That was his metaphorical way of saying that interpreting the woven imagery of the Bible was just like deciphering the ciphers in which an otherwise secret code is written.

This book is focused upon Jesus of Nazareth as a historical figure of note, his origins, his role in life, the life's work in which his role and mission was fulfilled, and his succession, in the dual sense of the historical success of his mission, and of those who succeeded him in the leadership of that mission. The book must then focus on the larger story of creation only in so far as this is reflected in the life-work of Jesus himself. Now the dominant images that form the warp and woof for the story of Jesus are easily and quickly picked out from these short biblical documents called the gospels. Whatever he was beforehand, a carpenter or something else, and in any case a nobody, these gospels picture him easing himself upon the public stage of a backwater province of the Roman Empire, on the banks of the river Jordan, to experience at the hands of a prophet (some claimed) called John, and through the symbolism of a cleansing baptism in the said Jordan, a change of heart from a life of sin to a new life now lived under the true reign of the one, true God. Yet the same gospels simultaneously depict him as one who was (already?) a greater prophet, indeed a son of God, who was now coming to devote his own life to changing people's hearts, so that the reign of God would come amongst them and enter into their very hearts (the king of hearts), and they would be worthy and blessed members in that kingdom of the Eternal King forever.

That cluster of images from which the opening of the story of Jesus is woven, would have been familiar to his fellow Israelis, and most especially familiar from one particular historical context. In the case of the first image, the image of prophet, it seems from the gospels that it was disputed in the case of Jesus by the leaders of his nation and religion, as it had also been disputed by these same people, it would appear, in the case of John. But it is otherwise relatively unproblematic both because the title of prophet in Israel is well defined throughout the Bible, and because it is the title for Jesus that both he and his close disciples and inspired authors accepted without qualification.

In the case of the second image, the image of the reign or the kingdom of God, the historical context in which that image of the kingdom of God would be heard would make these same leaders fear as much as question the image in the case of Jesus. The historical context is that in which a King of Creation (a piece of cosmic imagery) ruled the creation through appointed earthly kings. The paradigmatic example for Israelis of the time, as for some modern Israelis, was that of King David who, through his son Solomon also, ruled over the richest and most extensive kingdom the Israelis had or have ever known. And the three other images that completed this particular cluster, for they accompanied the title of King David, were: Lord, Messiah or Christ, and Son of God. And these three titles, being at the head of the list of the most common titles used of Jesus in the Bible, are also the titles most frequently applied to Jesus from the time in which the Christian additions to the Jewish Bible were being written and circulated, and down to the present day.

Indeed the title, Christ or anointed one, seemed over time to have become part of the proper name of Jesus: Jesus Christ. So that for those who expected that the kingdom of God which Jesus said he came to restore would be something like the kingdom that David and his son secured for God's own people, the continuity of a royal blood-line could be quite as crucial as the titles that might be borne by the occupants of the earthly throne of God's expanding kingdom on earth. Genealogy, to put the matter bluntly, could clearly be thought to constitute a crucial part of an individual's claim to be the king appointed by the Cosmic King to reign on earth as plenipotentiary, and as such to bear titles such as 'the anointed one' (christ), 'the Lord' or 'the son of God'. Little wonder then that so many down the centuries, from writers of the gospels of Matthew and Luke down to the present day, have answered in terms of a royal genealogy or, better still, an imperial succession the question implicit in the title of this book: the question as to the historical role of Jesus in his lifetime, of the kind of faith it assumed and promoted, and of the succession in both senses of that pregnant term.

I: The Genealogies of Jesus
The Story of the Virginal Birth

Two genealogies are drawn for Jesus at the beginnings of two of the gospels, Matthew's and Luke's. (Matthew 1:1-17; Luke 3:23-38) Both trace the genealogy of Jesus through the male line, as was *de rigueur* for his time and culture. Matthew traces the genealogy forward from Abraham through King David: 'The Book of the Genealogy of Jesus Christ, the son of David, the son of Abraham', and down to Joseph. Luke traces the genealogy backwards from Joseph, again through King David and Abraham, but now as far as Adam, 'the Son of God,' and thereby to God. And the full significance of this cipher, the genealogy of Jesus? Clearly, at face value, the pivotal position of King David in these genealogies would suggest that Jesus is recipient and transmitter of royal blood. But there may be more, much more than this. The genealogical cipher might be sufficient of itself to account for the fact that the three most common titles for Jesus in the Bible are Christ, Son of God and Lord. Christ, from the Greek, or Messiah, from the Hebrew, both mean 'the anointed one', for the kings in this line of David were inaugurated by anointing. Then Son of God was also a common title for kings in this line, as was finally, and unsurprisingly, Lord.

The two latter titles are explained by the fact that in that ancient ideology the king was considered to be God's plenipotentiary on earth, whose whole *raison d'être* was to work to dispense the gracious rule or reign of God over God's good world. Hence the consistent meaning of the title, Son of God, throughout the Bible is something like 'the spitting image of his father', in that the one who bears the title is seen to act in and towards the world in order to promote in time both existence and life, to nurture the people and to defend their lives and prospects from all who would do them evil – just as God does, eternally. Similarly, the title Lord is a cipher for the one who rules the world by that same process and in that same manner, towards the end of eternal *shalom*, a term that means more than a bare peace in the absence of war. In fact the term refers to nothing short of the unthreatened happiness of the ultimate enrichment and fulfilment of all existence and life.

There was nothing surprising, then, about Jesus being conferred with the titles of Son of God and Lord, or about his acceptance of them. He opened his public mission by calling on people to have a change of heart and to promote the reign of God that, as always, was upon or within them. (Mark 1:14) Adam after all, a name that in the earliest biblical stories functions as a cipher for humanity, already according to Luke's genealogy bore the title Son of God, and with that he bore, as do all of his race, the responsibility of promoting God's especial reign as much as any king could do. But there was something almost inevitably problematic about the third title, Messiah or Christ, when applied to Jesus, or to any human being. It could imply that only kings, or queens, could be entrusted with the task of promoting God's reign in the world. Or conversely, and especially in the place and time of the mission of Jesus, the Christ title might only too easily suggest that anyone going around proclaiming that the restoration or promotion of the reign of God in God's good world was his divinely appointed vocation and destiny, was equivalently issuing a claim to royal status, and with that, naturally enough, a claim to a kingdom of his own in which he could enjoy such status. This in turn might well excite a certain kind and level of expectation in the hearts of any who threw in their lot with his movement and cause. And it might equally evoke a certain level and kind of suspicion and hostility from those who felt they had good enough reason to think their own rule and power threatened, at least over the areas affected by this messianic pretender's mission.

Both of these things happened in the course of the life and death of Jesus of Nazareth.

He was executed as a messianic pretender by the Roman overlord of his land, Pontius Pilate, at the instigation of the puppet native rulers, the temple priesthood in Jerusalem. The crime for which he was executed was nailed to the instrument of his execution: Jesus of Nazareth, King of the Jews. Readers of the so-called passion narratives at the end of the four gospels may well detect a sense that Pilate did not really believe that Jesus posed a challenge of this kind to Roman imperial rule, and could not see him as a credible pretender to an Israeli throne. Yet in cynical but politically requisite conspiracy with the puppet native ruling faction of that segment of the Roman Empire, the court of the High Priest of the temple of Jerusalem, who seemed to want very badly to have Jesus executed, Pilate had the fellow hanged anyway. But however all of that may be, that messianic title did have something quite significant to do with the execution of Jesus.

On the other side of the same coin, his closest and most faithful followers and promoters of his movement seem to have thought that the reign of God that Jesus had called them to help re-instate and promote would be something very like the restoration of the kingdom and kinship of Israel's most glorious era under the reign of David and his son, Solomon. To them the very title, Christ, seems to have held out the alluring promise that Jesus had come to replicate, if anything more amply, that past glory, and that they would rank very high indeed amongst those who enjoyed it all. There is the incident in which James and John, men high on the roster of the leadership group of The Twelve, send their mother to ask that they be Jesus's right and left hand men when he comes into his kingdom. (Mark 10:35-45) There is even a story at the opening of The Acts of the Apostles that recounts how, on one of Jesus's return visits after his death to his old stamping grounds, in this case Jerusalem, his closest cohort of disciples are still asking him, 'Lord, will you at this time restore the kingdom to Israel?' Some people never give up.

To this day there is a man sitting in state in a tiny sovereign statelet in the centre of Rome, in the sumptuous architectural and artistic surroundings that befit such monarchy, and ruling the millions of Catholics who are then called Roman with an absolute power that any monarch or emperor would envy. All of these, each in their own way, envisage a royal dynasty, if not indeed an imperial power, as plenipotentiary of God's reign on earth. And a consequently clear line of succession, with the single difference between these that the papal succession had to be engineered for purposes of the self-propagation of a celibate ruling caste, who could not avail themselves of the normal means of having wives with whom to beget successors.

The Bible has a number of ways of dealing with what appears to be this fundamental but persistent misconception of the role and status of Jesus as scion and further source of a royal dynasty, and of the nature of the reign of God so envisaged. First, Jesus simply deflects the question about places of power in his royal court for his faithful followers, saying in effect that the restoration of Israel's traditional kingdom is simply none of his business or theirs. As he puts it in the little scene at the beginning of The Acts of the Apostles: 'It is not for you to know the times or seasons which the Father has fixed by his own authority.' (Acts 1:7) And in the meantime they should get on with their witness to Jesus's own mission to spread the reign of God, in the power of the Spirit that will be given them. To the request by the mother of James and John for high places in the kingdom, Jesus responds that the only thing they need to ask is whether they can die for the reign of God; it is the Father's business as to whether or when there may be actual kingdoms and places of power. And furthermore, in the case of the reign of God as he sees and shows it to them, the form and shape of leadership will be as different as chalk from cheese in contrast with the leadership forms that characterise earthly kings and their imperial ambitions: 'You know that the rulers of the Gentiles lord it over them, and their great men exercise authority over them. It is not to be so among you; but whoever would be great among you must be your servant, and whoever would be first among you must be your slave; even as the Son of Man came not to be served but to serve, and to give his life as a ransom for many.' (Matthew 20:20-28)

Another way in which the Bible handles the attribution of the title, Messiah or Christ, to Jesus appears in Peter's famous confession to the effect that Jesus is indeed for him 'the Christ, the Son of the living God'. There is first the same kind of evidence just seen, to the effect that Peter's confession also envisages a gloriously powerful reigning king of Israel. For when Jesus talks of dying for the cause, Peter rejects all thought of such a thing, and is promptly reduced by Jesus to the status of a follower of Satan rather than a leader of Jesus's merry band. But then there is a strict caution issued by Jesus that they 'tell no one that he was the Christ' (Matthew 16:13-23). Now this is an instance of a note of extreme caution against saying that Jesus was the Christ, a note that sounds quite frequently in the gospels, and especially in the gospel of Mark – to the point at which a mini-literature in biblical exegesis can be entitled, *The Messianic Secret*, and a mini-industry grew up around the problem of deciding what this repeated cautioning against being heard to confess publicly that Jesus was the Christ could be all about. It would seem clear enough from all the contexts and considerations covered above, that the very title of Messiah of itself tended to mislead even the closest followers of Jesus in their understanding of the nature of his role and mission. It is therefore very likely that the use of this title so misled the followers of Jesus and others on the very nature of the reign of God that he and his followers were supposed to be restoring and promoting, that it really was prohibited by Jesus, at least on occasions on which he saw recent enthusiasts for his cause apparently moved to proclaim it indiscriminately all over the place. For Jesus was not a king, and not even a royal pretender; and the reign of God that he did proclaim and promote was poles apart from the kind of reign customarily exercised by monarchs and emperors, both at his time and before and since.

There is one further scene from all three synoptic gospels, as they are called, that implicitly but no less powerfully refute the royal genealogy case for the mission and succession of Jesus. (Mark 3:31-35; Luke 8:19-21; Matthew 12:46-50) In Mark's version the scene takes place when Jesus is at his own home, to which crowds had followed him in such numbers and with such persistence that he (and The Twelve he had just appointed 'to be with him'?) 'could not even eat'. Add some scribes who came down from Jerusalem to accuse Jesus himself of demonic possession and you see a situation that is volatile indeed. 'When his friends heard of it, they went out to seize him,' fearing for his safety and also, it seems, for his sanity. And then 'his mother and his brothers came' – clearly to his home, not theirs – 'and standing outside they sent to him and called him. And a crowd was sitting about him; and they said to him, "Your mother and your brothers are outside, asking for you." And he replied, "Who are my mother and my brothers?" And looking around at those who sat about him, he said, "Here are my mother and my brothers! Whoever does the will of God is my brother, and sister, and mother".'

Can there be any doubt in anyone's mind that instead of turning his metaphor of family relationships sideways, sideways towards siblings, and backwards towards his mother, he might as easily have turned it sideways and forwards? Sideways now towards some woman who might well have been his wife in his home, and forwards towards their son already old enough to accompany his mother now in this altered scene coming home to this same hullabaloo, and wanting to extricate him from it somehow? In this altered but equally credible scene is it not clear that he would have used the same kind of metaphor to the same effect: 'Who is my wife and who is my son? Whoever does the will of God is my wife and my son and my successors.' In short, the whole issue of Jesus's natural family relationships, any and all of them, is in his own stated view of the matter entirely irrelevant to his role – primarily, as we shall see the role of prophet and Son of God. So the blood bonds that link families down the generations are simply irrelevant to Jesus, to his mission, to the movement he started, and hence to his true succession.

That should be quite enough then to show that issues of royal blood lines and of genealogies in general are irrelevant to the matter of the status and avocation of Jesus and of his true successors, as he stated quite strikingly in the short scene with his mother and brothers. Indeed as he constantly made clear to those who took the Christ title rather too literally, this use of the genealogy cipher would lead disastrously astray the very ones he had chosen to succeed him in the business of spreading the true reign of the one, true God. Yet some close and careful readers of the biblical text of the genealogies presume to find further proof of the irrelevance of the genealogies. These readers of the biblical genealogies of Jesus point to certain phrases in both genealogies that actually serve to undermine, from within as it were, this whole impression of a master narrative that seems otherwise designed to present Jesus as a *bona fide* blood relative and legitimate descendent of the royal line that goes back to David, and a transmitter of that line to future ages.

Here are the two allegedly undermining phrases. First, in Matthew's genealogy, when it comes at last to Joseph and Jesus, the formula used consistently up to that point, X was the father of Y, is suddenly abandoned. And instead of concluding the genealogy with the formula, 'Joseph was the father of Jesus who is called the Christ,' the following relatively cumbersome formula is found: 'Jacob (was) the father of Joseph the husband of Mary, of whom Jesus was born, who is called the Christ.' The highly unusual strategy of naming the mother in the succession, as an addition if not a substitution for the required place of the father is, at the very least, a quite subtle means of raising some suspicion of Joseph's fathering of Jesus. Second, in Luke's genealogy Joseph's fatherhood of Jesus seems to be called in question with equal subtlety, but by a different strategy. For once again, instead of being aligned with the consistent formula now used in this second genealogy, X the son of Y the son of Z, we read 'Jesus ... the son (as was supposed) of Joseph, the son of Heli.' It is the parenthesis here that seems to call in question Joseph's fatherhood of Jesus. But with that, and in both of these unexpected phrases, there is also and inevitably called in question the whole point of the genealogy, which is surely designed to prove that the royal blood of David flowed in the veins of Jesus of Nazareth. For in that time and culture the royal blood-line was patrilinear, not matrilinear. If Jesus was the son of Mary, but not the son of Joseph, then he had no claim to the royal blood and lineage of David and both genealogies are fatally undermined.

Yet it is difficult to conclude that someone, either the original author of Matthew or some later redactor of the text, deliberately undermined the whole logical and natural point of the genealogies. Not at least without looking to the broader context in which these genealogies in their present form are set. Particularly since these broader contexts presume to tell us more about Jesus at his conception and birth. For just as Matthew and Luke alone offer us genealogies of Jesus so they, and they alone offer us narratives of the infancy of Jesus, narratives that are often also referred to as virginal conception or virginal birth stories. So then, as an obvious aid to correct deciphering, set these genealogies in their immediate context of the infancy narratives, and see what happens. The first thing that should strike the reader is that the narrative of the virginal birth makes use of metaphorical language from beginning to end, beginning with the overtly sexual-procreative imagery for the Holy Spirit – that is to say, God as the Creator Spirit – and ending with the familiar metaphor, son of God. A familiar metaphor that retains the same meaning throughout the Bible, whether it be applied to Adam, the king, the people of Israel, Jesus of Nazareth, or any one or any group of a host of others who prove to be as like to God as sons to fathers in so far as human beings can be like to God; most particularly in acting to advance God's good creation to the eternal benefit of all, as does God.

Those who may be reluctant to regard the virgin birth stories as metaphor can only be advised, first, to read them again and see and, second, to read other stories scattered throughout the gospels, the Acts of the Apostles and the epistles, about the Holy Spirit coming upon and remaining on Jesus of Nazareth, and note in each case the result of that coming. First, the language of the virginal conception stories is sexual-procreative language, and unmistakeably so. Particularly in Luke, who graphically describes the conception of Jesus by Mary in these terms: 'The Holy Spirit will come upon you, and the power of the Most High will overshadow you; therefore the child to be born will be called holy, the son of God.' (Luke 1:35) Matthew has the more restrained phrasing of the same episode: 'that which is conceived of her (Mary) is of the Holy Spirit,' adding with respect to Joseph, to whom the angel has just been explaining this matter, that 'he knew her not until she had borne a son; and he called his name, Jesus.' (Matthew 2:20) This is standard sexual-procreative language of the kind that is used of humans and animals alike. The stallion covers (overshadows) the mare; so that the offspring is by or of the stallion and (out) of the mare. Now since it is obviously nonsensical to say that the Holy Spirit impregnated Mary after the usual fashion, the whole language of this episode must be taken metaphorically. And the literal meaning of the metaphor as metaphor yields the idea of Jesus being, in this case, the son of the Holy Spirit, the son of the Most High. And the metaphorical meaning of that sonship of God yields the idea that Jesus, from the moment of his conception in the womb of his mother, Mary, was so overcome and so indwelt by the Holy Spirit that all his living and dying, his very human existence and character, was the spitting image of his heavenly Father, the same Creator Spirit.

The second set of texts that could convey the careful reader of the Bible to that same set of conclusions is found in those scattered contexts in which the Holy Spirit comes on or into Jesus, now long after his issuing out of the womb of Mary, and the result is always the same. As a result of this coming on and remaining in him, Jesus is declared Son of God. The scenes of the baptism of Jesus, pictured by Matthew and Luke just after the virgin birth episode, and at the beginning of their gospels by Mark and John who have no infancy narratives, are the next occasions of this kind of metaphorical language. And the last occasion, in the chronology of the life of Jesus, on which the Holy Spirit is said to make Jesus son of God is at or from his resurrection from the dead, this according to Paul in the opening of his Letter to the Romans. So it really does not matter at what point of the earthly life of Jesus, or even of his 'pre- or post-earthly life', that the claim to his sonship of God, understood in the usual biblical sense, is made. All add up to the same claim made on behalf of this historical human being, and in the same metaphorical sense and meaning. In fact John makes the same claim, using the image of God as Word, rather than as Spirit, when he says at the beginning of his gospel that this Word was made flesh in Jesus of Nazareth, a particularly powerful manner of picturing God coming and remaining in the very body and the whole life of Jesus and making of his whole life, death and destiny a life and existence in the very image of the life itself of God the Creator. 'And the Word was made flesh and dwelt amongst us, full of grace and truth; and we beheld his glory, glory as of the unique son of the Father.' (John 1:14) The coming on and remaining in, the overshadowing of Jesus was then true for all of the existence of Jesus, from its very beginning and into eternity. And each story of Jesus takes its own choice of the significant episode or episodes in his life as the occasion on which to make that matter plain.

None of this, of course, need be taken to constitute an argument to the effect that there never was a virgin birth. Such virginal conceptions and births have been claimed for other great figures of significance in the history of religions: the Buddha Gautama Siddatha, for instance, and even Plato. And Matthew is particularly specific and insistent that the case of Jesus was a case of virginal conception, a tradition that has been long and stoutly maintained in the Christian churches ever since. For Matthew, as already noted, was at pains to add quite pointedly to the story of Jesus being conceived 'of the Holy Spirit', that Joseph did not know Mary, in what is still called the biblical sense of knowing her, before Jesus was born. But what all of this does make clear is that a virginal conception, if it did take place by some kind of miraculous divine intervention, had of itself nothing whatever to do with making Jesus a son of God in the sense in which the Bible understands such sonship of human beings. Nor needless to say – or is it needless to say this? – would such virginal conceptions and births have anything to do with sonships of gods in Trinitarian or polytheistic systems in which gods really are said as a matter of eternal rather than historical fact to have 'natural' sons and/or daughters by whatever means might be thought consonant with divine being in itself.

In short, for all immediate purposes of having Jesus acknowledged as son of God in the common and consistent biblical sense of that high and distinctive title, Jesus could just as well have been the natural son of Joseph. And the virginal conception element could then simply be one other instance of a metaphorical or mythic way of pointing to that unique status of Jesus, as son of God in the common biblical sense. Pointing to it rather than constituting it, in the manner in which other religious traditions used a miraculous conception as an imaginative way of saying that their great founders or formers were fashioned in all of their human being and behaviour more by God than by men and women. Or, to put the same point in another way, what these virginal conception stories did, whether or not they were, or were only believed to be historically true, is to make the case in the most graphic form for the known fact that the resulting offspring, from the very moment of their conception and in all of their human being thereafter, were the most perfect image of the Most High that God's very Spirit could contrive and the human condition could bear. The image of God as Spirit is then quite rightly pictured as coming upon and remaining in them at conception and at any other chosen and important times of their lives. The Most High God must therefore be depicted as the true origin and source, the primary claimant to the title of Father of all that these founders of faiths were and did, and still are and do, throughout the whole of their existence.

So then, to return to our question as to the point and intent of the genealogies in this broader context. It looks as if Matthew certainly, if not Luke also, wanted to have it both ways. They wanted to have their Jesus – the name means 'he saves' – descend directly from the royal lineage of David, presumably with the mission of restoring a similar kingdom to David's, and with the possible prospect of handing that kingdom down the ages in a somewhat similar line of succession. Yet they also wanted a good old miracle, of the kind that Jesus himself clearly denounced, as a fully persuasive pointer to something divine, present and operative on the human scene. In this case they wanted the very Spirit (of) God miraculously operative in and about the very conception of Jesus, in such a manner as to strengthen their account of his role, mission and succession. Despite the fact that the particular miracle they chose in this instance militated of its very nature against the very genealogical claims that seemed central to their cause. Hence the rather confusing nature of the subtle alterations to the standard formulae of the genealogies when the conception and birth of Jesus hove into view.

It is to Paul, then, rather than to these infancy narratives, that we must finally turn in order to complete the biblical critique of the royal genealogy theme as the centrepiece of the code that, once cracked, reveals the true and eternal role of Jesus, his provenance, his mission and his succession. For Paul, in a passage from the very beginning of his Letter to the Romans, from which a quote about the sonship of Jesus and the Spirit at his resurrection has just now been taken, does indeed face fully the retrospect that Jesus may well have been a scion of the house of David. And yet he lets his readers know, subtly but quite clearly, that this genealogy of the Davidic sonship of Jesus, a sonship that is 'according to the flesh,' is an entirely separate matter from the sonship of God 'in power' that also characterises Jesus. For that latter title of Son of God 'in power' results from the kind of coming of the Spirit that is celebrated in the Bible at different occasions of the life, death and resurrection of Jesus. In these opening sentences of his Letter to the Romans Paul describes what he preaches as the gospel or good news concerning God's son 'who was descended from David according to the flesh and (a word which here has the power of 'but') designated Son of God in power according to the Spirit of holiness by his resurrection from the dead, Jesus Christ our Lord.'

In this short passage Paul has used all three of the titles of Jesus which were also titles of the Davidic king – Lord, Christ and Son of God – yet in the case of the last of these he has felt it necessary to distinguish clearly between 'sonship' of David by natural lineage, and that sonship which is conferred only by the coming of the Holy Spirit, the very factors that the infancy narratives tried so confusedly to combine and yet keep apart. Incidentally, this contrast, according to the flesh/according to the Spirit, particularised in this case of the genealogy of Jesus, we shall find to be generalised as we read further into The Great Code. For instance, and interestingly enough, when John in his gospel has Jesus himself attempt to decipher for his puzzled followers the symbolic code of his distinctive eucharistic table fellowship, John has Jesus issue the now more general principle: 'It is the spirit that gives life, the flesh is of no avail.' (From the eucharistic discourse in John 6.)

And finally, it is perhaps not irrelevant to note at this point that Paul was the one who had trouble with the leaders of the early community of Jesus-followers, amongst whom was James, the brother of the Lord (keeping the dynasty in the family?) and clearly a leader of 'the circumcision party'. The circumcision party was composed of those, and particularly those in the leadership of the earliest community of Jesus-followers, who believed that Gentiles who wanted to join the fellowship must become virtual Jews by the ritual of circumcision. The kingdom of Israel and even its temple was therefore, in one way or another, still uppermost in their minds as the locus of the reign of God. And Paul clashed with them – even Peter was once of their party, and lapsed back into it later, after an initial conversion to something more like Paul's view. In any case, Paul clashed with the circumcision party precisely because of his stand on a certain principle. This principle, which Paul believed he derived from his conversion by and to Jesus himself, stated that Gentiles could join the movement and mission inaugurated by Jesus without being circumcised, that is to say, without ritually becoming Jews and thereby becoming part of a restored kingdom of Israel, under a new dynasty restored in and by Jesus himself. (Read the second chapter of Paul's Letter to the Galatians.)

Royal Genealogies Nevertheless Abound
Yet despite all of this biblical criticism of the ideology of monarchy as the determining imagery in which the story of the origin, role and succession of Jesus is cast, that ideology continued to thrive down all the centuries between. And it thrives not least through the imagery of genealogical claims of one kind or another, in secular or ecclesiastical dynasties, or in that combination of the two that for many centuries in the West constituted what then came to be called Christendom. To this day and particularly in Roman Catholic textbooks of theology, the whole role, function and office of Jesus in history is often summed up in the triple titles of Prophet, Priest and King. And in the foundation myth of the Roman Catholic version of the Christian religion these three offices have, so to say, been rolled together into one, conferred by Jesus on The Twelve as a body, who are said to have been ordained priests at the Last Supper, and to whom popes and bishops claim legitimate succession down to the present day.

The prophetic role, the role of speaking God's word to the world (*pro-pheta*) is now controlled by the *magisterium*, the teaching authority of the Roman Catholic Church, that is to say, by the pope and the bishops in union with him. A prophetic role may be exercised by others in the church only at the discretion of this hierarchy. And the governmental role with its absolute authority, the kingly role as one might well say, is confined to that same hierarchy, to the higher echelons of that Roman Catholic priesthood. No wonder that Roman Catholic priests are called 'other Christs', the anointed ones, a title in origin of Davidic kings. No wonder that their High Priest, the Pope, 'The Vicar of Christ on Earth,' lays claim in the constitutional law of that church to a *suprema potestas*, a supreme power of jurisdiction over all Christians (in theory), over the ethos by which they live their lives and over their very beliefs – matters of faith *and* morals. Roman Emperors scarcely had more dynastic power than that; and it may be significant to note that the title, *Papa*, from which the title, Pope, derives was originally one of the titles claimed by Roman Emperors. For the Emperor was, after all, the father of his people, *papa*. Although not even a Roman Emperor would claim to be a father like the heavenly Father; satisfied with the humbler claim of apotheosis when he died, and a place amongst the stars. There was something awesome and very beautiful about all of that – a permanent pageant that might well soothe the hungry heart of the poorest peasant. Throw in some bread from the *papa*, the father who fed all his people, invite to the entertainment of the odd circus, and the poor man might well think that even he was lucky to be alive. Certainly the *papa* would think so, and expect nothing but gratitude and an ever more devoted obeisance in return.

The phenomenon of a Christian church gradually aping the ethos of the Roman Empire became lapidary with the conversion of Roman dynasts to the Christian faith, beginning with Constantine, perhaps. The most striking evidence of this assimilation emerged into the full light of day during those long centuries in which Pope and Emperor strove to claim the higher place over the other in the self-same imperial power structures. And even when Luther broke with Rome his conduct towards the peasants in revolt showed with which side of the ruled and ruling divide the leaders of a Christian church would still be aligned. Yet it was the largely unreformed Roman Catholic Church that survived the ending of the *ancien regime* in every country in which in more recent centuries that kind of rule was ended. So that to this day it is the Roman Catholic Church that still pretends to the ancient secular forms and ethos of the imperial power of ancient Rome, still extant in the continuing dynasty of a self-propagating clerical caste. It would be comic were it not also so tragic to witness the current and repetitive papal warnings against the corrosion of the Christian faith by the intrusion of a secular ethos, when the officers and the office from which these warnings emanate with grinding regularity provide what might well be the most striking example in the history of Christianity of the intrusion of a secular ethos of ruling power into the institution of leadership in some of the principal Christian churches.

The fact of the matter is that in both ancient and medieval times the practice of claiming genealogies that presumed to lead back to the divinity itself was widespread indeed. And in some cases, during the course of the early Christian centuries, the bloodline was claimed to lead back to God through the family of Jesus. It was all the fashion in those far off times, all the rage. Yet it would be facile in the extreme to imply that such genealogies served merely as fashion accessories to princely families, when in fact they fulfilled the important dual function of legitimating the claim of this particular prince and scion of this particular ruling family to rule the kingdom he now ruled, and of impressing upon him the fact that he, his ancestors and successors were God's vicars on earth, anointed in order to govern God's good world with God's own rule and justice, and so securing and advancing life for all. Anointed, in short, to be sons of God in the common biblical senses of that term. In effect, then, these 'divine' genealogies could have the same function as virginal conception stories: to point to the anointed king as the one who, in this case by his very office, was to be entitled Son of God. As the Psalmist has God say to the king, perhaps on the occasion of his inauguration: 'You are my son; this day I have begotten you.' (Psalm 2:7) Hence the confusion encountered above when these two means of securing sonship of God for Jesus, genealogy and virginal conception, are used together in the same context. Unless, of course, that the genealogical mode of asserting that sonship were to be taken as a metaphor, as the virginal birth must be taken as a metaphor for sonship of God in the biblical sense. But the metaphorical application of genealogy cannot be taken for granted in the biblical text, if only because of the persistence of the belief, even in the innermost circles of the followers of Jesus, that he must surely be engaged in restoring a true monarchy in and of this world.

This kind of claims-by-genealogies strategy was practised by the early Irish and by their linguistic and cultural cousin-peoples, such as the medieval Welsh. Already before these peoples were Christianised this kind of genealogical project had been pursued as individual royal or chieftain dynasties in pre-Christian Ireland traced their bloodlines back to God in the *persona*, for example, of that Jahweh-like divinity named Lugh. So when Christianity did arrive on the island Lugh, like other traditional divinities of the Irish, was 'euhemerised' to the status of a great saint. Although it is more than interesting to note that he, like other ancient Irish divine *personae*, kept his place in the liturgical calendar of the ancient religion intact, in this case the harvest festival. And he thereby retained his divine prerogative of bringing creation to fruition. It was quite the fashion then to trace royal dynasties back to pre-historic, legendary kings, some of whom in turn were most probably original gods of this race, like the god-king, Lugh. And always with the serious and conjoined purposes of legitimating the incumbent and reminding him that he must live by the *fir flathemon*, the divinely sourced wisdom and justice that alone would make him God's son and vice-regent on earth. Similarly there is much evidence, although this time from medieval Welsh literature, that the genealogies of royal dynasties often went back to some legendary chieftains of course, but also to the family of Jesus, whose genealogy in turn, as we have just seen, went back through King David to God.

Yes, a reader growing impatient at this point might well interject, but all of that is ancient and medieval stuff, and could scarcely expect even an attentive hearing so long after the French Revolution put an end to the *ancien regime*. Only the Roman Catholic Church has since continued to act as if the *ancien regime* should still be with us, so that its governmental structures still look like those of an empire. But that in fact is not quite true. There are other Christian churches that maintained an ethos of power that still hankered after a coincidence of church and nation long after the much advertised death of the *ancien regime*. The Presbyterian Church of Scotland, for example, whose Westminster Confession of Faith regarded the Roman Church as the very home of the antichrist, and whose governmental structures were, if not fully democratic, then at least conciliar, still maintained a distinction between teaching elders and ruling elders, rather like the Roman distinction between clergy and laity, in that only the teaching elders were ordained to the ministry of Word and Sacrament. Its highest 'Court,' The General Assembly, enjoyed the last word, on earth, on matters of doctrine and life, that is to say, on the true interpretation of the Bible in matters pertaining to both the true faith and the morality of daily living. And when in the years between the two world wars Scotland was in recession, leaders of its new-born Church and Nation Committee initiated a campaign against Irish Catholic workers who came to Scotland to seek a living. In the course of that campaign, a report of The General Assembly of 1922, invoked once more for the Scottish nation a version of what must seem very like the old Christendom idea: 'The nations that are homogeneous in Faith and ideals, that have maintained unity of race, have ever been more prosperous, and to them the Almighty has committed the highest tasks' – a statement of the messianic destiny of a nation under God that would warm the heart of George W. Bush himself.

Little wonder then that a recent work of fictionalised facts burst upon the international publishing scene, and gained the interest of millions of readers. Dan Browne's *The Da Vinci Code* undertakes once more the same kind of task of ancient and medieval genealogists: to trace a line of royal blood, in this case back to the offspring of the marriage of Jesus to Mary Magdalene, and so back further still, one must presume, to king David and to God. The book takes its name from the fact that a central clue to the existence and identity of this royal dynasty is found in Leonardo Da Vinci's masterpiece, The Last Supper, and more particularly in the identity of the rather effeminate figure seated next to Jesus at the table, traditionally thought to be John, the beloved disciple, as being instead none other than Mary Magdalene. A dynasty then that had to advertise its true status as the successors of Jesus in the secrecy of such coded images, because of the violent hostility that could be expected from the very outset, from the usurper princes of the established church.

Now it would be right to welcome *The Da Vinci Code* into the company of stories that use the genealogical method in order to identify the line of ruling personages and the ideology of kingship from the King Creator through Jesus and down to the present day, and then to learn whatever lesson all of these, ensemble, might teach us. For it would be quite unremarkable if there did exist a dynasty such as the one which Dan Browne so ingeniously traces and describes: a dynasty that traced its origins and its particular kind of claims to succession, through the coupling of Jesus and Mary Magdalene. We know of so many dynasties that made similar and, despite some dissimilarities, entirely comparable claims for themselves in ancient and medieval times. One such dissimilarity, for instance, the omission from the genealogical line-up of the coupling of Jesus and Mary Magdalene, would not have reduced the comparability of the genealogical strategy and of the ideology involved. If only for the reason that the Irish and their cousinly cultures, to take but a few examples, were wise enough not to insist on primogeniture in royal succession. Succession had to be within the *derbfine*, from amongst close blood relationships within the royal family. Hence the Welsh tracing of dynasties to close relations of Jesus within his historical family. So, strictly speaking, Dan Browne did not need that particularly strained piece of deciphering of Da Vinci's Last Supper which consists in interpreting the rather effeminate figure in the painting as a woman, and as Mary Magdalene to boot, if all he wanted was to find a dynasty comprised of royal personages or their equivalent, wielding the absolute power of monarchs in order to restore the reign of God and to extend its territory to the ends of the earth. Like King David and his son and the heirs to his throne, to whom eventually the Bible promises all the kings of the earth would come and pay tribute, and whose reign would last as long as the sun.

None of this is meant to deny outright that there is not and never was a self-styled royal lineage that insisted on tracing its descent from a coupling of Jesus and Mary Magdalene. Or indeed from Jesus and some other woman who might have been his wife. For his having a wife would have affected Jesus's unique sonship of God as little as his having Joseph as his natural father. Nothing is taken from the magnificent witness to God that is given by the monastic life of poverty, celibacy and obedience, if one were to add the fact that it was long after Jesus was dead that all of this exorbitant emphasis on the alleged superiority of celibacy and virginity became so prominent a part of the lifestyle of the fellowship of Jesus. Not even if one added that ideals of celibacy and virginity derived more directly from Platonic religious circles. And that the still later attempts to im-

43

pose celibacy on all diocesan clergy was largely motivated by the need to prevent priestly and particularly lorldly episcopal families from treating church property and emoluments as family inheritance. So what must be said instead is this: what we could learn concerning the role and mission of Jesus and his true succession, from this alleged royal blood-line from the marriage of Jesus and Mary Magdalene, could just as easily be learned from any of the other similar succession claims of similarly monarchical dynasties that have come and gone, and some of them not gone at all, down to the present day.

From the 16th century, with the imperial expansion of European powers, fragments of the once Holy Roman Empire, squabbling between secular and ecclesiastical Christian leaders as to which wielded the superior, absolute ruling power over the other, took second place to their combined efforts to spread their Christian rule over the whole wide world. Just as happened in the earlier middle ages in the course of the re-conquest of territories that had been occupied by the armies and princes of the rival religion, Islam, so in the conquest of the 'new world' of the Americas, in the conquest of the old world of 'darkest Africa,' and in the subsequent conquest of much of the East, monarchical and ecclesiastical Christian powers went hand in hand. And so, together, the soldier with the sword and the priest or preacher with his Bible, they gradually extended the now Christian kingdom of God towards the ends of the earth, as the Bible had promised would happen. And all of these additions to the kingdom of God, the new and vastly expanded Christendom, were achieved by much the same methods as had been used in the course of the conquest by the ancestors of the Israelis of the land that then formed the kingdom of God, the kingdom of David and Solomon. By armed conquest, that is to say, with all of the slaughter, rape and pillage of the peoples and lands concerned that such conquest inevitably entails.

This territorial principle in the concept of the kingdom of God, together with its assimilation of secular and ecclesiastical powers, seemed to have returned to Europe even after the break-up between Roman and Protestant churches, when the Treaty of Westphalia that ended the Hundred Years War, issued the pacifying edict: *cuius regio eius et religio*. The religion of a people should be the religion, be it Protestant or Catholic, of its governed territory. And was that a small but audible whisper of that same ideology of the kingdom of God, when the Church of Scotland (Presbyterian) Assembly of 1922 opined that it is to 'nations that are homogeneous in Faith and ideals' that 'the Almighty has committed the highest tasks,' so that the Irish who broke homogeneity by both race and religion should be sent home, forcibly if need be? Or when George W. Bush asserted that his Christian faith assured him of the messianic vocation of his country as he took it to war in Iraq, in order to share his (presumably Christian) values of freedom and so on with that doubly-misfortunate people, whose lives are now wrecked more by its self-appointed liberators than they were by its erstwhile tyrant? Or when Tony Blair, predictably, echoed Bush's sentiments about his Christian faith, if much more coyly and in muted tones?

If all of that explains nothing else, it explains how Jesus might well have had trouble, if not with the image of the kingdom of God itself – since that is the image he chose from the start in order to proclaim his whole life's purpose – then with some of its attendant cluster of images: mainly the images of messiah and lord. Yet if he was to be taken as he felt called to be, as the prophet and son of God who brought the true reign of God to people, then he could hardly avoid the perception that God now reigned through him. So that therefore he would have to accept the messianic title that the prophets of old, like Daniel, had reserved for God's human plenipotentiary, who would inaugurate in the world the 'last age,' that is to say, the age of peace and perfection (*shalom*) in which the good God's writ ran without let or hindrance. (Daniel 7:13-14)

So he did at times accept the title, Messiah or Christ, without more ado. Yet at other times he cautioned people not to broadcast it. Perhaps he knew that people, especially those who had little or no immediate experience of his words and works, would almost automatically take the proclamation of his messiahship in the meaning that the kings and other rulers of this world had given it. But Jesus also knew – he could not but know – that even the closest and most constant of his disciples, from the beginning to the end of his earthly life amongst them, resisted his understanding of the reign of God, and always, it seemed, in one particular direction. They seemed to see in the manner in which at least one earthly king, David, behaved the model for their understanding of the reign of God. Instead of seeing things, as Jesus never tired of trying to make them see, quite the other way round.

From some biblical texts that we must very shortly note, Jesus seemed to expect that, despite all of that misunderstanding and resistance, his death would bring the reign of God amongst them with full effect. And for a little while after the death and resurrection of Jesus it seemed, as we shall also see, that the kingdom of God had indeed arrived amongst these followers. But then the long history of the mode of understanding of God's reign and of spreading it abroad that has just been summarised in imperial terms, must cast some doubt as to whether it has ever really come at all. And with that particular doubt is sown another. Do we really know, has anyone ever known, what really and precisely was the understanding of the reign of God for which Jesus lived and died? And in the name of which he constantly criticised the model that 'the rulers of the Gentiles,' as he called them, offered from the dawn of monarchy and beyond the end of monarchy, in so many other forms of government, some even calling themselves democracies, to this day? In view of all that has just been said in summary, that cannot be an easy question with an entirely obvious answer.

Where to begin? No, that is the wrong question, for we have already begun with stories of genealogy and birth, where any good history of any historic personage should begin. And the genealogies and birth stories did reveal that issues of kingship and reign did bring the inquirer after the historical Jesus most immediately to the matter that constituted all that Jesus lived and died for, and upon which his effect upon the future must be judged. So then, the question is: where to go from here, in order to see as fully and clearly as possible just what is the vision that Jesus brought to the age-old question of the reign of God in this world? And the answer to that question is obvious once one remembers that the Bible is the story of God's ways with the world, woven end to end from clusters of imagery. So that, in order to decipher the whole, one begins with some image-cluster that seems indicated by one's interest; in the case of our historical interest in Jesus, with the imagery in which he himself declared his life's business and goal. And when the fullest investigation of that imagery in itself leaves questions about it still unanswered, one then looks to other clusters of imagery that always or often accompany the first cluster, or that are present, for example, at key moments of transition to new meaning. But in a book as long and complex as the Bible, it is not always easy to find and identify such helpful clusters of attendant imagery; and one should be humble enough to admit, sometimes at least, that one comes upon these by chance.

Kingdom and Feast
For example, one might well come across the attendant cluster of imagery that will help enlighten the inquirer after the full and precise understanding of the reign of God in the preaching and practice of Jesus of Nazareth, simply by the accident of having read Dan Brown's *The DaVinci Code*. In this way: as the title of that book suggests, an absolutely central clue to the kind and instance of divine dynasty in the world that Brown has Jesus represent, is to be found in Leonardo DaVinci's portrait of The Last Supper. Now anyone who knows that the figure in that portrait that Brown argues is Mary Magdalene, is known in the whole of Christian tradition as John, the especially beloved disciple, might well be driven back to the ends of the four gospels, in order to look more closely at the original pen-portraits of the last supper of Jesus with his inner group of disciples, upon which DaVinci based his portrait. And one or more of these intrepid researchers into Brown's case might then just happen to notice by the way – here's the accident – that in these gospel portraits of that last supper there occurs a most striking, intricate and revealing nexus between the imagery of kingship, with its attendant cluster of images of thrones, messiahs, lords and sons of God, and the imagery of the supper itself, the meal, the feast, with its attendant cluster of images of seating and service, of hosts and guests and servants, of sharing of food and drink.

The nexus is most clearly seen in Luke's account of that last supper. Having issued the description, common to Mark and Matthew, of Jesus breaking the bread and pouring the wine to his disciples, Luke notes that 'a dispute arose amongst them, which of them was to be regarded as the greatest. And he said to them, "The kings of the Gentiles exercise lordship over them; and those in authority over them are called benefactors. But not so with you; rather let the greatest among you become as the youngest, and the leader as one who serves. For which is the greater, one who sits at table, or one who serves? Is it not the one who sits at table? But I am among you as one who serves. You are those who have continued with me in my trials; as my Father appointed a kingdom for me, so do I appoint you that you may eat and drink at my table in my kingdom, and sit on thrones judging the twelve tribes of Israel".' (Luke 22:24-30) How very graphically does this describe a kingdom of God in which the thrones will be just the ordinary chairs round the supper table, and the guests will be each the servant of all? And how much clearer could anyone make the difference between the reign of God to which Jesus had committed his life and shortly now his death, and the kind of reigning after the manner of earthly kings that even his most intimate associates seemed hell-bent on restoring, in spite of everything he said and all that he could do?

The connection between meal and kingdom of God in Mark's and Matthew's accounts of the last supper is as peremptory as Luke's 'I shall not drink of the fruit of the vine until the kingdom of God comes.' Mark and Matthew have virtually the same formula: 'I shall not drink again of the fruit of the vine until the day when I drink it new in the kingdom of God.' (Mark 14:25; Matthew 26:29) And John's account of the last supper? Well, he has no account of breaking bread and pouring out wine to the guests. Instead, he has a scene in which Jesus at table washes the feet of his disciples. An equally graphic dramatisation of the central teaching of Jesus to the effect that those who would be leaders in the human community under the reign of God must act at all times as the servants of all, and not as lords over them. So that the same lesson on the nature of the reign of God that Luke most elaborately draws from the more conventional account of the breaking of bread and the sharing of wine at the supper table, John draws from a quite separate ritual of cleansing that is also part of preparation for a meal, but usually performed by slaves or house servants. (John 13:1-20)

This collusion of meal and kingdom imagery so fully drawn in Luke is corroborated in the Book of Revelation. Not exactly reputed for the reader-friendliness of its antique apocalyptic imagery, Revelation nevertheless presents us at one point with a fetching image of Jesus, after his death, still trying to spread the kingdom of God by coming round our doors and knocking and hoping to be invited in to share our suppers. This touching scene is painted by John of Patmos in one of his divinely inspired letters. The one to the young Christian church at La-odice'a, a place too prosperous in earthly terms to think it needed anything more from Jesus or his followers. 'Behold, I stand at the door and knock; if anyone hears my voice and opens the door, I will

come in to him and eat with him, and he with me. He who con-
quers, I will grant him to sit with me on my throne, as I myself
conquered and sat down with my Father on his throne.'
(Revelation 3:20-22) The same tantalising combination of ruling
and dining; the same link between kingdom and meal.

As soon as one recognises from the scenes of the last supper,
or from the scene of the door-to-door salesman, the crucial relevance of this supper-cipher to the unlocking of the true import
of the cipher of the kingdom of God, then images, however dim,
of other meal ciphers in the Bible may begin to flow back into the
memory. Images from as far back perhaps as that first feast in
the garden of Eden, a subversive feeding on the fruit of a certain
tree. A feast that resulted in the reign of the Creator God that
created paradise, turning humankind out of that paradise, until
they could regain paradise once more. Then images that reach
forward to paradise regained, in 'a feast of fat things' – so out of
fashion these days when the very model of womanhood is that
of a stick-insect, with small bands of them prancing about on
cat-walks like hungry locusts – a symbol and earnest of the fulfilment of life in the fully realised kingdom of God. And memories even vaguer still of other images that cluster, in the gospels
in particular, round the meal imagery: memories of feeding the
hungry of course, but also more intriguing memories of healings
at meals and forgiveness at healings. Such constant and intricate
interaction over the whole course of the Bible between, on the
one hand, the central and core symbol for the matter to which
Jesus devoted his whole life and for which alone he would wish
to be remembered, namely, the symbol of the reign of God and,
on the other hand, the symbol of the meal, together with the in-
termingling of the clusters of other symbols that accompany respectively meal and kingdom imagery. This can mean one thing,
and one thing only: the pursuit of the further understanding of
the reign of God, and so of all that is of historical significance in
the preaching and practice of Jesus, and hence of the life, death
and destiny of Jesus himself, can now proceed further through
the study of the symbolic meals of the Bible.

So the biblical place to go from here would appear to be, first,
to the scenes of the last supper at the ends of the gospels. Then
forward for a while to the Acts of the Apostles and some of the
letters, principally from Paul. Just to see what table-fellowship
was practised after the death of Jesus and in memory of him,

and how precisely his followers understood its significance at that point. Whether they were coming closer to, or drifting further from the significance of the principal cipher of the kingdom of God that Jesus felt his practice of table-fellowship clarified as nothing else could. Then backwards again over the accounts of the public life and mission of Jesus, if only to see if his table-fellowship proved to be as prominent then as its proposed position as the principal definer of his idea of the reign of God might lead one to suspect. And, finally, back to the beginnings of the Bible, if only to see if any or all of this story or of the images from which it was woven, were new to what Christians call the New Testament part of their Bible. For if so, then certainly neither Jesus nor his appointed leaders that we meet up to the end of the writing of the Christian Bible knew anything about such radical innovation. They all considered themselves Jews both by race and by faith, and never thought they were members of another religion, much less that they were engaged in founding one, even when some of them came to believe, as Jesus himself did, that the Gentiles could share in their faith in the true kingdom of God without having to take on the symbolic paraphernalia of the Jewish religion of the time.

Jumping from the genealogy and birth of Jesus to his last supper and death and beyond, and then going all the way back to the stories of the beginning of his public life, and then further back again to the story of the natural history of creation itself, might seem to some to be an odd way of writing the (hi)story of the life of Jesus, his role in history and his succession. It seems like writing history backwards. But two things might be said in its defence. First, all history is read backwards. We read the surviving records of those whose significance to their posterity was sufficient to persuade our ancestors to keep some records of them in the first place. And we do this only if we can still see that these subjects of the records still retain some significance for us today. So history writing begins when we, as we always do, try to imagine our lives and our destinies ever improved, and in that act of imagination feel we might be helped by re-imagining the lives of those who went before – lives that usually come to us as they have already been imagined and recorded for us by contemporaries or near contemporaries who have composed full accounts or partial records of them, because they already saw some significance in the people concerned. Fiction built upon fiction built on select and exemplary facts. So history is read always backwards; and the convention of writing it forwards, beginning with the genesis, physical and cultural, of the characters involved, and proceeding forwards to their deaths, followers and influences, is just that, a convention. Besides, if someone is fortunate enough to die for that for which he lived, his death can tell a great more about his life than can his birth. As this book is a record of work in progress, it has to be written backwards. And nobody can be expected to take its findings as gospel truth simply because they are recorded here. On the other hand, the only way to critically test those findings is to take this or a similar journey back through the story of the Bible that is woven throughout from an astonishing richness of imagery.

So then, if there be any merit in these foregoing meditations, we must consider ourselves invited to the Last Supper, if only in order to investigate as best we can what all was actually going on there, on that most commemorated of occasions.

II: The Last Supper and its Aftermath

The Last Supper

All four of the gospels or good news's concerning Jesus of Nazareth describe a meal that he had with his inner band of disciples just before his arrest, trial and execution. Three of these – Mark, Matthew and Luke – are called the synoptic gospels because Matthew and Luke are deemed to have borrowed much if not most of the material of their gospels from Mark, reputed to be the earliest of the four gospels to have been written. And that is also the case with the material that comprises the accounts of this famous last supper. Mark's account of the meal itself is brief enough to quote in full. Having recalled how Jesus instructed two of his disciples to find a room and prepare for their partaking of a Passover meal, for that is what is happening here, Mark goes on: 'And when it was evening he came with the twelve. And as they were at table eating, Jesus said, "Truly, I say to you, one of you will betray me, one who is eating with me." They began to be sorrowful, and to say to him one after another, "Is it I?" He said to them, "It is one of the twelve, one who is eating with me. For the son of man goes as it is written of him, but woe to that man by whom the son of man is betrayed! It would have been better for that man if he had not been born." And as they were eating, he took bread, and blessed, and broke it, and gave it to them, and said, "Take; this is my body." And he took a cup, and when he had given thanks he gave it to them, and they all drank of it. And he said to them, "This is my blood of the covenant, which is poured out for many. Truly, I say to you, I shall not drink again of the fruit of the vine until that day when I drink it new in the kingdom of God".' (Mark 14:12-25)

Matthew's account of the supper adds a few details that may or may not be found later to carry some added significance. He has Judas named in particular as one who asked, "Is it I?" And he records as the answer of Jesus the rather non-commital, "You have said so." Then when Jesus speaks his words with regard to the cup, "This is my blood of the covenant, which is poured out for many," Matthew has Jesus add, "for the forgiveness of sins."

(Matthew 26:17-29) Luke's is a rather scrambled version of the two former accounts, in which the words, "This is my blood of the covenant," are simply omitted when the cup is offered, and the sequence of cup and bread is reversed. (Luke 22:7-38) But it is only when we come to the fourth gospel, that of John, that the whole supper scene is altered substantially. First, and almost incidentally, we learn that this supper is not the Passover meal, for the scene is set, 'during supper' when 'Jesus knew that his hour had come to depart out of this world,' but 'before the feast of the Passover'. So instead of the ritual of blessing (for) and sharing bread and cups of wine, the familiar rituals of Passover meals, we watch an entirely different drama unfold. Jesus 'rose from supper, laid aside his garments, and girded himself with a towel. Then he poured water into a basin and began to wash his disciples' feet, and to wipe them with the towel with which he was girded.'

There follows a slight altercation between Jesus and Peter, who at first would not have Jesus perform for him what was the duty of a slave. This forced Jesus to decode the ritual washing of the feet for this inner core of disciples, in order to make it clear to them that it meant that all who would follow him were to live as slaves or, more gently put, servants to each other, no matter what claim some might entertain to be leaders of his other disciples after his death. Luke in effect has Jesus draw that same lesson from the fact that it was he, the one they called lord and master, who nevertheless served, as only servants were expected to do, the food and drink for their supper. John then goes on to have Jesus deal with his imminent betrayal by Judas, and then with his betrayal by Peter himself. John's account of the incident at the meal in which Judas was dealt with is quite interesting, not least in view of the manner in which the cup of the blood of Jesus has sometimes been deciphered in Holy Grail legends as a coded message about the true blood(line) succession of Jesus himself. As John sets this part of the scene the disciples at table are asking each other who Jesus is saying will betray him. But 'one of his disciples, whom Jesus loved, was lying close to the breast of Jesus; so Simon Peter beckoned to him and said, "Tell us who it is of whom he speaks." Then lying thus, close to the breast of Jesus, this beloved disciple said to him, "Lord, who is it?" Jesus answered, "It is he to whom I will give this morsel when I have dipped it." So when he had dipped the morsel, he gave it to Judas, the son of Simon Iscariot.' (John 13:1-38)

It is already quite obvious at this point that Leonardo DaVinci's Last Supper, like many another portrayal in words or in pictures, or in dramatic presentations before or since, has run together two very different accounts of a last supper of Jesus with his disciples before his death. The account by John contains the memorable love-image of the much loved disciple who lies so 'close to the breast of Jesus'. But it is entirely innocent of the imagery of a cup of blood, a cipher so central and necessary to proponents of secret bloodline legends. The other three accounts, from the synoptic gospels, combine the imagery of the Passover meal with the imagery of the sealing of covenants, traditionally by spilling and sprinkling the blood of a sacrificed animal. The cup of blood cipher is central here, but what is not central, or indeed at all in evidence is the portrait of a loving couple. In fact, in John's account of the supper, it is not the supper itself, it is not the sharing of food and drink that provides the symbolism that needs to be decoded. Rather is the meal merely the occasion for the salient symbolism that Jesus himself, due to Peter's characteristic obtuseness, then has to decipher for them, the symbolism of the slave's job of washing feet. Just as, for John, the meal is also merely the occasion for the naming of Judas, and for the heart-warming tableau of the lover whispering to the beloved so close to his breast the clue to the name of the traitor.

We are still at this point barely at the beginning of the process of surveying the whole biblical array of meal symbolism, in order to be able to decipher the meaning of this frequently used symbol in The Great Code. Yet we must already rule out of this survey John's account of a last supper that Jesus ate with some of his closest disciples, or else we court confusion from the very outset. For the simple reason just given: that for John it is not the meal as such that constitutes the salient symbolism. While, on the contrary, with the three synoptic gospels we are quite certainly dealing in symbolic meals. How do we know? First and foremost because the meal in these three cases is depicted as a Passover meal, and Passover meals are symbolic meals. A symbol, like a sign or a cipher, is a term for something that stands for something else. But it does no harm to add in this case that there is a special class of symbols, sometimes called sacraments, that are said to function most effectively as signs or ciphers by actually beginning to effect what they signify. Or to put the same matter the other way round, these symbols are said in the somewhat pompous language of poets (when they are talking about poetry rather than writing it), that they participate in the reality they represent. All of this means quite simply that some symbols, particularly of the acted-out or dramatised kind, actually begin to bring about some of the reality of life and the world that they signify. And so, acted out in such dramatised form, such symbols do enable us more effectively to imagine and understand the reality in question, to bring it within our range of comprehension and ambition, even to be inspired by it. Such dramatic symbols can even be said to breathe a new spirit into our lives.

The Passover meal to this day recalls for Jews the deathly oppression under which they once lived as an enslaved people in Egypt, the sacrifices they had to make in order to take advantage of the opportunities and aids offered in God's good world to bring about release from such suffering and death, the peaceful family meals they can now enjoy in lands flowing with milk and honey, and the sacrifices they must still make in order that all of them should continue to overcome the occasional oppression and deprivation that still is visited upon them from others and sometimes from their own, until they reach the final *shalom* of the kingdom of God. Human life is a Passover and it can, by God's favour ever shown, reach *shalom*. In this way the preparation and sharing of the symbolic Passover meal as it comes round year after year, enables the Jews to renew their sense of the Creator Spirit inspiring them to overcome the adversarial forces in the creation, and to reach and spread a kingdom in which they will enjoy, beyond their present penury, the fruits of a land and a life shared by all with all.

There are other elements, however, of the symbolic meal described by the synoptic gospels in their combined symbolic picture of The Last Supper that must enter into the full deciphering of this central cipher of The Great Code. There is, for instance, the language of blood and covenants and forgiveness of sins. But the deciphering of these and other elements that will be found to be part of this central cipher of the code must wait a little longer.

IN MEMORIAM: Table Fellowship with Jesus after the Last Supper

If nothing else, the words that Paul adds to his account of the Last Supper as described in the synoptic gospels, 'Do this in remembrance of me,' would direct this survey of supper symbolism forwards first from the ends of the four gospels, before going backwards again in order to seek out this meal-cipher in the rest of the Bible. (1 Corinthians 11:23-26) Now the next 'book' of the Bible, after the end of John's gospel, is entitled, The Acts of the Apostles. It purports to be written by the same Luke who wrote the gospel of that name. In fact it takes up the story of Jesus, of his growing band of disciples, and of the increasing success of their missionary endeavours where Luke's gospel left it. Acts, as those who want to pretend to a close familiarity with it are wont to call it, opens with the symbolic scene of a forty-day period following upon the passion and death of Jesus and ending with the ascension of Jesus into heaven, to his place at the Father's right hand. And it is already remarkable from this opening section of Acts how very much more of something you see when you are actually looking out for it, than you ever did see when you travelled over the same terrain a hundred times before. That something in this case is the meal-fellowship of Jesus and his disciples that now, as you are looking for it, jumps out to meet your eye at virtually every major twist and turn of the early story of Acts, increasingly opening up the impression that meal-fellowship is indeed a central cipher of the biblical code. So that even a brief summary of the table fellowship involving Jesus and his disciples as portrayed in Luke's second 'book,' as seen within the full context of the story of the early growth of this faith-movement, should prove to be of considerable help towards the initial deciphering of the great biblical code in full.

During this forty-day period of the post-passion presence of Jesus to his last earthly stamping ground, Luke asserts, 'he presented himself alive after his passion ... speaking of the kingdom of God. And while eating with them he charged them not to depart from Jerusalem but to wait for the promise of the

Father,' the promise, that is to say, of their baptism in the Holy
Spirit, where John the Baptist baptised only in water. For 'you
shall receive power when the Holy Spirit has come upon you;
and you shall be my witnesses ... to the ends of the earth.' The
Holy Spirit coming upon someone is by now familiar from the
conception scene in Luke, and the result there was the status of
sonship of God. So it will come as no surprise to find shortly
now in one of Peter's very successful sermons at this earliest
period in the history of this faith that, while observing that Jesus
was the prophet promised by Moses himself, he reminds his
Israelite listeners that they are 'the sons of the prophets and of
the covenant which God gave to Abraham.' (Acts 3) The Holy
Spirit coming on or in, or 'overshadowing', it is already noted,
results in sonship of God; and that obtains alike for Jesus and for
those who follow Jesus. So that these are then 'sons of the
prophets' also, or sons as the prophet is son. But they bear this
title as a result of the prophet's mission to them, and so are not
necessarily prophets themselves. At least not in the special sense
in which one can list as the Bible does the great prophets of
Israel, major and minor, with Jesus in the view of his followers
claiming the place of the ultimate prophet. And the image of
sonship conveys here what it always conveys in the Bible, namely,
that the ones so described are in the whole form and fashion of
their lives and their very being the spitting image of the parent
in question, the Creator Spirit.

Two other images are seen above to be linked, in the present
broad context now under scrutiny, with those of the coming and
indwelling of the Holy Spirit (in this context denoting simply
God, the Most High). These are, first, the images of power
(*dunamis*), the power that these followers of Jesus will receive
when the Holy Spirit descends on them in their baptism of fire.
And, second, the image of the covenant, as when they are told
by Peter that they are the sons of the prophets and of the
covenant (more specifically, in the quotation above, the
covenant mediated by Abraham). The fastest track to the understanding of these further images of power and covenant, and of
what they are about, is most likely to be found in a further link
with another image, the master image of all that Jesus himself
was about, namely, the kingdom or the reign of God. In one ver-

sion of the Our Father, Christians say: 'for Thine is the kingdom, the power and the glory'. The power is nothing other than the kingly rule or reign of the Most High in the hearts of those who acknowledge God's lordship over them in all of their living and dying, so that they all become sons and daughters of God in power, as Paul said Jesus was made son of God in power by the Holy Spirit. And the covenant refers simply to the rule of living set out in a code of conduct expected of those who acknowledged the reign of the God that Jesus called his Father, and equally invited them to acknowledge and address as their Father also.

So Matthew re-issued Peter's profession of Jesus as the Moses-like prophet that Moses himself foretold. Matthew does this by painting in his gospel (chs 5-7) a picture of Jesus handing down from 'the mountain' the renewed rule by which those who lived by the true reign of the one, true God would fashion in all the detail of their lives and destinies. For the setting of Matthew's Sermon on the Mount evokes the scene in which Moses handed down to the Israelites from Mount Sinai the law of the true reign of the true God. Incidentally, the *Revised Standard Version of the The Oxford Annotated Bible with the Apocrypha*, in a helpful observation to the Pentecost scene in Acts 2, in which the Spirit actually descends on The Twelve (now just restored to full numbers by an election to Judas's empty place) to empower them to live and inspire and spread the true reign of God, notes a Jewish tradition to the effect that the law (according to the covenant mediated by Moses) was given 'on this day, seven weeks after Passover'.

Therefore Luke's chronology in Acts, of Jesus spending forty days with his followers' doubts and hesitations after his passion and death, still trying to get the truth of God's rule in this good world, as renewed by him, into their thick heads and harder hearts, is reminiscent of Moses leading his people through forty years of trial and doubt in the desert, until Moses finally managed to bring the law of the covenant of their divine Lord into their hearts from Sinai. Jesus after his passion, according to Luke's metaphorical conceit in Acts, did the same for forty days, by eating with his renewed people, and by instructing them, until finally he succeeded a week later in fully breathing into them from his place at the right hand of God, the Spirit of Creative Fire, the Spirit of Love, the same spirit of the rule of life in God's kingdom that he had tried to breathe into them during his earthly sojourn, but with very limited success. (John 20:22, also describing a post-passion coming of Jesus to his disciples, has Jesus say: '"Peace be with you. As the Father has sent me, even so I send you." And when he had said this, he breathed on them, and said to them, "Receive the Holy Spirit".') Further confirmation, if more were needed, of the deciphering strategy of linking the images of power, sonship, kingdom and covenant, by their common link with the image of the Holy Spirit's reign, its specific character and cosmic range.

Quite enough of context there then to be going on with, especially since this whole exercise is specifically designed to facilitate an increasingly insightful survey of the symbol of the meal, so as to see what is the full import of that symbol in the Bible, and how it functions in the greater context of the seried symbols and stories that make up the Bible. In fact a careful reader of the stories of the Last Supper in the synoptic gospels might well have suspected that that symbolic meal would re-appear after Jesus had given his consummate witness to the true reign of the true God in his passion and death, and thereby breathed forth the true Holy Spirit into a dying world. For all three of the synoptics, it is already noted, have him proclaim at the Last Supper words that confirm that it would be his last in this life: 'Truly, I say to you, I shall not drink again of the fruit of the vine until that day when I drink it new in the kingdom of God.' (Mark 14:25 and parallels) But then Luke, in his account of what transpired at that last supper, after he has Jesus lay down the rule that the leaders of the new Israel under the new covenant must act like slaves who served at table rather than lords, has Jesus say to the twelve: 'You are those who have continued with me in my trials (a bit premature that, we may add with hindsight, since they would all soon run away when the real trial raised its fearsome prospect); as my Father appointed a kingdom for me, so do I appoint for you that you may eat and drink at my table in my kingdom, and sit on thrones judging the twelve tribes of Israel.' (Luke 22:28-30)

Now this surely suggests a number of very relevant things.

First, the surprising and therefore creative combination of the symbolism of sitting at the high table with Jesus in his kingdom with the symbolism of sitting on thrones to lead the renewed Israel under the renewed rule of God, surely releases a deeper insight into the symbolism of the meal. The insight, namely, that abiding by the rule of the meal is a truly sacramental symbol, involving a real participation in what is symbolised. That is to say, a real participation in the rule of living under the true reign of the true God, precisely by serving others, sharing with them the bread, the staff of life, an earnest of sharing life itself; something along those lines. Second, there is the hint that this meal fellowship round 'the table of the Lord' will therefore find a central role in the preached invitation to all to accept the reign of God, and to help spread that rule further to more and more people. And third, there is a hint in the phrase about judging the twelve tribes of Israel, that the role of the leaders of the followers of Jesus must be more like that of the judges of Israel before kings took over.

And finally, there is further confirmation and expansion of that last hint once the reader realises that the judges of the New Israel sit, not on royal thrones, but round the table of the Lord. Reminiscent of Luke's evocation of Jesus using his service at that table as a participatory symbol and example of the leadership by service that would be expected of his followers, rather than the imposition of power and authority. Further incitement to the expectation, if such were needed now, of the centrality of the dramatic symbolism of the meal to the task of instruction, more, of initiation into the distinctive ethos of the rule of the Creator Spirit, the new covenant, as a rule of leading by serving, and more specifically by serving to each other the necessities of life, and life itself in ever more abundance. That place and incidence of the natural sacramentality of the shared meal is indeed what is seen in Acts and other documents that tell the story of the fellowship of Jesus after his death. As soon as ever you look for it, you will see the meal symbolism as a central and general strategy of the followers of Jesus, especially from the point in time at which Jesus was bodily taken from them and yet, as they believed, continued still to inspire them, in the power of the same Holy Spirit that reigned over and shaped his life and theirs. That Holy Spirit seeks to shape the lives of everyone who comes into this world through the Creator Spirit's own distinctive and eternal activity of the loving creation and advancement of life.

In a statement already quoted from the very beginning of Acts, telling the story of Jesus and his closest disciples during the forty days that passed between the passion and death of Jesus and his ascension to his throne at his Father's right hand – 'while eating with them he charged them not to depart from Jerusalem' – the word 'eating' replaces the word actually used in the Bible, namely, 'staying'. For the very simple reason that, as a note in the *Revised Standard Version* helpfully informs the reader, 'The Greek words for staying and eating are the same.' Sort of bed-and-board words, you might say. So it must be legitimate to translate *sunalizomenos* as 'eating with', and if there were any remaining doubt about such a translation, it would be banished at the point at which Jesus is ascended and the story continues as follows: 'Then they returned from the mount of Olivet (a name remarkably similar to that of the olive grove in which the passion of Jesus began), which is near Jerusalem, a Sabbath day's journey away (about half a mile); and when they had entered (Jerusalem, that is) they went up to the upper room (exactly the same description as that of the room in which Mark says the Last Supper took place, 'a large upper room') where they were staying,' (and the 'they' is then named and numbered as the eleven left after the defection of Judas). (Acts 2:12-14) A clearer code for the continuity through death itself of the fellowship of Jesus and his apostles and successors in his mission, and moreover one that had a table fellowship at the centre and core of its very survival, meaning and efficacy, one could scarcely construe or even imagine.

Readers of Acts will notice in that same passage from Acts just quoted, that after the eleven are named Luke goes on immediatcly to say: 'All these (that is, 'the eleven') with one accord devoted themselves to prayer, together with the women and Mary, the mother of Jesus, and with his brothers.' And some at least might wish to draw the conclusion that, although the text does not specifically picture this larger group sharing the table fellowship, but only the communal prayer, it really must not be taken to intend in any way to exclude the larger group from sharing the table also. Then we have a picture of the Lord's supper which includes an unspecified group of women. Possibly the ones who had had the empty tomb experience followed by a vision of angels. Together with the immediate family of Jesus, who had clearly by now overcome their fear and motivation to save Jesus from what had previously appeared to his family to be a mad, dangerous path to possibly fatal confrontation with the Jewish authorities. A fear that, when you come to think of it, Peter also and the other leaders, with the exception of Judas, had to overcome.

Does any cloud of doubt still cast its dark shadow over the certainty of the reading of Acts that suggests an eating and drinking at the Lord's own table, a table-fellowship that continues through the death of Jesus, and on into the preaching and dramatic symbolising of the kingdom or reign of God, to Israel first and then to the Gentiles? If so, that cloud must surely be dispersed by a further, summary little formula which is designed to sum up all that the disciples of Jesus were doing during these first days and weeks, and would continue to do. The summary formula occurs after the day of Pentecost has arrived when, presumably in the same 'upper room', the apostles or sent ones, now restored to twelve by the election of Matthias, who had been with Jesus all during his public mission, that is to say, from his baptism by John the Baptist until his ascension, have the Holy Spirit descend upon them as wind (or breath, the origin of the image of divine spirit that breathes life into all things) and as fire (the great transformer of things and universal symbol of the act of creation), in fulfilment of Joel's prophecy that in the last days God would pour out his spirit on all flesh. After Peter has exercised his leadership role within the leadership group of The Twelve and showed how the scriptures foretold that a suffering, crucified one would be raised to the titular status of Son of God, Lord, Christ and so on, and significant and growing numbers were added daily to the followers and fellowship, the nature and characteristic behaviour of this rapidly growing community is described, simply and briefly as follows: 'They devoted themselves to the apostles' teaching and fellowship, to the breaking of bread and the prayers.' (Acts 2:42)

Almost immediately after that short summary, a slightly extended version is offered: 'And all who believed were together and had all things in common; and they sold their possessions and goods and distributed them to all, as any had need. (An early form of communism in the fellowship and following of Jesus: according to Marx's much later axiom, 'From each according to his endowments; to each according to his need.') 'And day by day, attending the temple together and breaking bread in their homes, they partook of food with glad and generous hearts, praising God and having favour with all the people. And the Lord added to their number day by day those who were being saved.' (Acts 2:44-47). Now much can and must be said about this account of the characteristic behaviour of this earliest community of Jesus-followers. But first and foremost, in the context of the present survey, the repetition of the phrase about the breaking of bread must send the memory scurrying back to a somewhat fuller formula repeated in all of the synoptic accounts of the Last Supper: Jesus took bread, blessed God, or gave God thanks for it, broke it and offered it to those at table. So that this shorthand reference to 'the breaking of bread' confirms the continuity of the table fellowship of the Last Supper scene through and beyond the passion and death of Jesus to survive at the centre of the earliest Jesus-fellowship.

Then the reference to the breaking of bread also lets us know that this is what later became known as a eucharistic meal. (*Eucharein* means to bless for, or give thanks for, recalling the second 'move' in the fuller formula.) It lets us know further that the eucharistic meal is not necessarily also a Passover meal. And it is also obvious that it need not necessarily even be a designated cultic meal that has to take place in a temple or any similarly public place of divine worship. Note the distinction between what these follower-successors of Jesus do in the temple, and what they do as a matter of course in their homes (which is to eat meals). And finally, it is perfectly clear that eating meals after the precise manner in which Jesus construed that natural sacrament, entails nothing less than a whole lifestyle, formulated here as a communist lifestyle in which all share their lives together, centrally and most significantly breaking and sharing bread, the staff of life, as it is called, as a symbol that effects what it symbolises, the sharing of life itself, even at a cost to each one's own life; a natural sacrament.

There is another picture, however, painted this time in one of Paul's letters to his converts at Corinth. (1 Corinthians 11:17-34) In this scene the eucharistic meal is not just a meal eaten at home. And there is evidence towards the end of Acts that points towards a further formalisation of 'the Lord's supper', as Paul calls it. In this second scene from Acts (20:7-12) in which Paul's preaching at this eucharistic meal bores one young man almost literally to death – he falls asleep and falls out of a window in which he had perched – it is said that it was 'on the first day of the week' that they 'gathered to break bread'. Nor is the living out of the rule of the kingdom of God which it embodies always fashioned along the lines of the creation of a communist society, in which as another summary of the practices of the earliest Christians says, 'There was not a needy person amongst them.' (Acts 4:34) One can say this without implying any criticism of the communist ideal, provided it were truly put into practice, if only because this communist ideal was fully endorsed by the appointed leaders of the followers of Jesus. So what does emerge, then, is a great deal of variety and development in the matter of the time, place and practice of the eucharistic meal in the earliest period of the history of the Jesus movement. But no change in the central symbolism, nor in the commitment entailed for those who participated in that dramatic sacrament to make the whole of life a matter of receiving as a gift life itself with all of its necessities and affordances, and then in gratitude breaking and pouring life out to others at whatever cost to each for the enhancement of life for all. It is this that Paul's Corinthian correspondence illustrates, together with the fatal consequences of living by another rule, but now for a community no longer communist.

Apparently when these Corinthians were gathered together to break bread, they gathered in some building to which there was common access, and each brought their own food and drink to the meal. And some brought plenty, especially plenty of wine, while others came and went hungry. And Paul lashes out at them: 'It is not the Lord's supper that you eat. For in eating, each one goes ahead with his own meal, and one is hungry and another is drunk ... Do you despise the church of God and humiliate those who have nothing? (Then having offered an account of the Last Supper very similar to that of the synoptics, he continues.) Whoever therefore eats the bread or drinks the cup of the Lord in an unworthy manner will be guilty of profaning the body and the blood of the Lord ... For any one who eats and drinks without discerning the body, eats and drinks judgement upon himself. That is why many of you are weak and ill, and some have died.' The full exegesis of this text would have to reckon with Paul's language of the community of the followers of Jesus as the body of the Christ, but enough is made clear here in order to conclude that what Paul means is that those who eat as these eat are serving the rule of some other god, other than the Holy Spirit that moulds Jesus and his followers into one body. Perhaps it is Mammon they serve, for a world in the service of Mammon always sees some obese and drunk while others are parched and starve. And all of this in God's good world which can support a full and happy life for all.

Does that last scenario truly decipher the imagery of profaning the body and blood of the Lord, resulting in illness and death for those who do so? There is yet another scene in Acts that might help answer that question. The particular context in Acts is one already noted: this earliest community of Jesus-followers, not yet called Christians, had made real the meal's symbolic commitment to the sharing of all the necessities of life by all to all, by forming a commune, a communist society in which 'they had everything in common'. In this latter context, the story is told of a couple, Ananias and Sapphira, who sold a piece of property, but when it came to handing over the proceeds to be distributed to the whole community, these two half-hearted philanthropists cheated the apostles by pretending that they were handing over the whole proceeds of the sale, when in fact they were handing over 'only a part' and keeping the rest for themselves. The consequences were dire. They were judged to have 'lied to the Holy Spirit': 'You have not lied to men but to God.' And their deaths followed immediately on the handing down of this sentence: each in turn 'fell down and died,' at the feet of Peter. (Acts 4:32–5:11)

When these two scenes are placed side by side it does seem as if the code in which they are cast is conveying the following message: if you do not keep faith with the reign of the eternal God who rules by gifting life and its necessities equally to all, if you do not keep faith by keeping to that rule in your own life, if instead you put your life's trust in money, even as a back-up, then your dependence upon this other power over life (Mammon once again), your service of that power will result, not in life-enhancing sharing, but in life-diminishing competition for the necessities and the good things of life alike, and with all of the self-inflicted suffering and illness, violence and death that inevitably follows. At the very least, to decipher this part of the code of the meal in this manner helps also to decipher another image that is found in Matthew's account of the Last Supper, 'This is my blood of the covenant, which is poured out for many for the forgiveness of sins.' For it brings into play Peter's appeal to would-be members of the new eucharistic community to repent, literally to change their minds and hearts, so that their sins might be blotted out. An almost exact echo of the first call issued by Jesus when he set out on his public mission: repent, that is to say, change your hearts, for the kingdom of God is come amongst you. (Mark 1:15) And the phrase, forgiveness of sins, can then be taken in the sense of the blotting out or the remission of sins, that is to say, sending sin into remission as a cancer can be said to be in remission. For as long as you turn your back to keeping faith with the Creator, by accepting all of life as gift to all, without distinction of persons, you will serve the satanic spirit of Mammon, with all that that entails in terms of deprivation and destruction for others and eventually for yourself.

To suggest that this cluster of images can be deciphered in this way is then to propose the following meaning: the sin that is the mother of all other sins of death-dealing rapine and oppression consists in placing one's life at the service of earthly wealth and the power it gives and supports, Mammon. This is the sin committed by the rich at Corinth and the pseudo-communists in Jerusalem. And the only way in which it can be remitted is to take the food and drink, the symbol of all life, at the table of the Lord; bless God, thank God for it, thereby taking it as what it is, a gift never intended as the exclusive possession of anyone; then break it out and pour it out in practical acknowledgment of its status as gift intended by God equally for all, without distinction of persons; and finally receive it from each other's hands and consume it as at one and the same time a real and symbolic support and enhancement of life on life's way to life's unlimited future. For to do this in this way is to invoke in one's life the rule of God, the Holy Creator Spirit, who holds out the hope of eternal peace and prosperity for all.

Does this suggest also a meaning for the phrases in which Peter accuses the pair of recalcitrant capitalists, that they 'lie to the Holy Spirit ... to God,' and that they 'tempt the Spirit of the Lord'? Quite probably. And does it explain the phrase about the sin against the Holy Spirit which Jesus somewhere in the gospels says cannot be forgiven? Possibly so. For as long as one worships another power, commonly called Mammon, as the supreme power that reigns over life and death, one cannot serve the Servant-Lord who is the true Holy Spirit. And for just so long one's sins cannot be sent into remission, nor can their direst consequences be relieved. But this is to anticipate too much of the survey in which these and other images of the Great Code of the Bible will gradually open up their full range of meaning by means of the poetic storytelling otherwise known as myth that creatively combines and continually re-combines these and so many other images.

So this true eucharistic meal that Acts keeps at the centre of the community life of the followers of Jesus is what Jesus was referring to when the synoptic gospels had him say at the Last Supper that he would not dine with them again until he shared meals anew with them in the kingdom of God? Apparently so. And when Luke added, also in the Last Supper scene, that this leadership group would be appointed to 'eat and drink at my table in my kingdom,' he meant that the eucharistic meal participated in the reality it symbolised, namely, it interiorised in dramatic form for those who partook of it the reign of God that ruled that all should share life and all the supports and enhancements of life with all? Yes. In short, that the meal was the meal of the kingdom, and that for the leadership group their seats at that table were the thrones (thrones paradoxically occupied by the servants, the slaves of all the others), from which they should lead the renewed Israel, to the subsequent benefit of all the families of the earth, as the covenant with Abraham had foreseen (so Peter claims, Acts 3:25)? Apparently so. And this meal is also therefore the meal of the covenant, in so far as it comprises the rules by which all those should live who truly accept the reign of the one true Creator Spirit, who creates life and all the supports and enhancements of life equally for all? A covenant sealed with the blood of Jesus who quite literally gave his life's blood for this reign when those who believed in a different kind of God and a very different kind of divine rule came to kill him? A covenant that offered a picture of the moral detail of the reign of God painted in precepts, the breaking of which would result in replacing the hope of potentially eternal *shalom* with self-inflicted suffering and death? Quite so.

The Continuity of the Lord's Table Through Death: The Meaning of Resurrection

There is one more image or cipher that in the contexts just surveyed is found connected with the images of table-fellowship or 'the breaking of bread,' and with images of the reign of God, and covenants, and that now calls for some attention. As the portrait of the early community of Jesus-followers is rehearsed once more in the early chapters of Acts (4:32-35), this time, together with the usual features of owning all things in common, and no one being in need, and no one profaning the body and blood of the Lord, or lying to the Holy Spirit and so bringing death and destruction to themselves and others, and so on, the rehearsal now includes this further feature that requires some comment before moving along this survey of central ciphers. This feature is found in the statement that 'With great power the apostles gave their testimony to the resurrection of the Lord Jesus, and great grace was upon them all.' It is necessary to try to decipher this added story and symbolism of resurrection before moving on, if only in order to understand better the continuity of the eucharistic meal through the death of Jesus and into the era beyond. That is to say, in order to understand the status of Jesus before, during and after his passion and death, and the nature of what has been called his real presence, particularly at the sacramental meal, throughout all of that continuity. His real presence as the one *par excellence* through whom the reign of God, the power and the kingdom, God's own self as Holy Spirit moulding Jesus's whole person and life, moulded also and in like fashion the lives of his disciples down all the ages. For through these disciples, it will be claimed, the real presence of Jesus transformed anew what had never really ceased to be the same eternal God's good world, at least to the extent that they kept faith with Jesus and the God he called Our Father.

To put quite bluntly this question that now inevitably suggests itself: what does this image of resurrection do to confirm, or lessen, or even leave unchanged what has so far seemed a complete continuity between what Jesus and the guests at his table were doing, achieving, promising and expecting, through the eucharistic meal that featured on either side of the passion and death of Jesus? For it does sometimes seem as if almost nothing of any great additional significance had intervened between the before and the after. Certainly in Luke's scenario of the symbolic forty days, Jesus is staying with the same group in the same upper room that he left to go to the Mount of Olives on a night that would bring him to his execution. The meals before and after have exactly the same symbolic structure and imagery. And as far as the actual death of Jesus for the cause of the kingdom of God is concerned, one could look on it like this. Just as the stock market discounts in advance for the effect of some expected disruptive event on the world economy, so that before, during and after the event the figures on the board remain more or less the same, so the symbolism of the eucharistic meal that commits its partakers to give of their lives for others, even to the point of giving life itself, if it is, and it certainly is, 'made real' in the death of Jesus, is made just as real in the execution of Stephen. For Stephen was elected to a leadership role in that first commune under the apostles, when the latter decided that there were more urgent things for them to do than 'to serve tables' (is this the beginning of the apostolic drift away from the radical servant image of lordship?). And Stephen sheds his blood for the same covenant of the same reign of God, having been found guilty by the same council of the High Priest of the temple as Jesus was, and on precisely the same charges. (Acts 6:8–7:60)

The clue that best deciphers this image of resurrection in this particular part of the biblical story is found in a characteristic turn of phrase in Peter's speeches: 'This Jesus God raised up, and of that we are witnesses. Being therefore exalted at the right hand of God, and having received from the Father the promise of the Holy Spirit, he has poured out this which you see and hear … Let all the house of Israel therefore know assuredly that God has made both Lord and Christ, this Jesus whom you crucified.' (Acts 2:32-36) This grand finale to Peter's first speech on Pentecost Day shows a symbolic structure almost identical with that which Paul uses at the opening to his Letter to the Romans, when he is describing the good news he brings to the Romans as 'the gospel of God … the gospel concerning his son, who was descended from David according to the flesh and designated Son of God in power according to the Spirit of holiness at or by his resurrection from the dead, Jesus Christ our Lord' – the piece of Paul's letter noted already above when the question of the genealogy of Jesus and the succession of Jesus in the kingly line was the issue. The seat at God's right hand symbolises the con-veyer of God's power, the power of the vice-regent in God's kingdom. Son of God conveys the idea that he behaves as does God; and Son of God in power modifies that idea further to sym-bolise that he rules (as one who serves existence and life to all), as a lord or regent would rule who acts always in full accord-ance with God's own continuously creative reign. And so he can also be said to be raised, that is to say, elevated to God's right hand and to this status of Son of God in power by the Holy Spirit who breathes into him now such a life as, especially through him, the same God breathes into all – a life that can be hoped will be eternal, because God is eternal.

That is all very fine as far as it goes, but then one could say that Jesus was raised, was Son of God in power, and the one through whom the Holy Spirit breathed life into a dying world, before or even at his death (John's crucifixion scene is read, quite rightly, to have resurrection take place on Calvary), at his bap-tism, or even at his conception – all times and events at which the coming of the Spirit and the ensuing special sonship of Jesus was proclaimed in the Bible. True, but what then is the possible meaning of that little phrase, 'from the dead,' that so often ac-companies the proclamation of the resurrection of Jesus of Nazareth? The common Christian tradition from olden times has interpreted the phrase about raising Jesus from the dead by regarding the resurrection of Jesus as a one-off event that oc-curred on the third day after his certain death by crucifixion.

CHAPTER FOUR

And on this interpretation of the raising of Jesus from the dead the common Christian tradition based our only hope of being raised after our deaths, for some of us a long time after our deaths, 'on the Last Day' – a day which unfortunately for us has been pictured traditionally as a day of judgement on which a prospect of eternal death rather than eternal life might well await us. In that familiar and traditional scenario of church teaching, the image of resurrection evokes the restoration of life after that apparently definitive destruction of our present gross bodily form that we designate as our death. Resurrection, in short, refers to revivification of our bodies.

Is there not some confusion here in the texts already surveyed, even some kind of clash, between the image and story of the raising of Jesus to the status of son of God in power, which happened during his life, through his death, and simply continued in his life hereafter, on the one hand; and, on the other hand, the image and story of the resurrection of Jesus and of us that is thought to consist essentially in the revivification of all our earthly bodies after that final disintegration that we call death? The key to the origin, and therefore to the solution of this problematic question is well on the way as soon as one realises that the phrase, 'the resurrection of Jesus from the dead,' has traditionally run together into a kind of unity-through-combination the distinctive symbolism of two different stories of resurrection. And the confusion is caused by the fact that the same term, resurrection, is used for the distinctive, but different symbolism and story in each case. That sounds as complicated as an abstract analysis could be expected to sound. But it becomes crystal clear on a close and attentive reading of the famous chapter 15 of Paul's first letter in his Corinthian correspondence, on the question of resurrection.

Paul, exasperated as he seemed when dealing in chapter 11 of his letter with the Corinthians' utter de-meaning of the Lord's supper, is if anything even more exasperated now. Exasperated at the fact that these Corinthians deny the resurrection of human beings in general, despite the fact that the resurrection of Jesus has been the very centre-piece of Paul's preaching to them, a preaching presumably fortified by the list of witnesses to the resurrection of Jesus that Paul draws up again for them at the very opening of this chapter of his letter. He continues then: 'How can some of you say that there is no resurrection of the dead? … if there is no resurrection of the dead, then Christ has not been raised … If Christ has not been raised, your faith is futile and you are still in your sins. Then those also who have fallen asleep in Christ have perished. If for this life only we have hoped in Christ, we are of all men the most to be pitied.' End of rant; and then he goes ahead with the story that he believes will end in a risen humanity and world, in which God will be 'everything to everyone'.

You need to know a little about the popular Platonism of the more educated Corinthians in order to understand that Paul and they are, most likely unwittingly, talking at cross-purposes here. This mutual missing of minds and points is caused by the fact that Paul and the Corinthians actually have two different stories about resurrection, and each side hears the other side's story in the terms of their own, thereby causing the confusion the origin and clearing-up of which is now necessary. But halt! Just a moment, some reader might interject at this point, foreseeing and fearing an excursion into an ancient philosophy, with the sole aim of clearing up some ancient cross-purpose talk and its ensuing confusion about resurrection, so as to arrive at the true biblical perspective on the matter. That is surely unnecessary, the anxious reader might well add, since few of us today are likely to be living anywhere near to a colony of popular Platonists, who might confuse us as to the true biblical story of resurrection. I am sorry, the response must be, but you see, we ourselves *are* the popular Platonists in the matter of the understanding of resurrection. Because from the moment that our early forebears borrowed the Platonic philosophy of the time in order to furnish their faith with a theology that would convert the cultural elite of the empire, Christianity took on board with that Platonic theology the Platonic view of resurrection, and to this day that prevents us from seeing the true biblical view of that pivotal image in the story of our Christian faith.

Briefly, very briefly, and with the least possible intrusion of the philosophical mode in which the Platonists cast their beliefs about death and resurrection, the story of resurrection that is characteristic of Corinth can be said to be based on another story characteristic of popular Platonism. This other story is a story of the make-up of the human being, and it is a story of a strong dualist make-up and, as a consequence, a story of a split destiny for each human being. This dualism means that one imagines the human body and the human soul as two (*duo*) quite distinct kinds of stuff or substance. The body is a physical substance, like Descartes's *res extensa*, (to throw a sop to the philosophically erudite). The soul, to the contrary, is a spiritual substance. So the story of the make-up of the human being for Greek-educated Corinthians, together with their story of life and death, is as follows. The human body, being made of physical matter, of the kind that is everywhere around us in the physical world from which this body originates, and which nourishes it, disintegrates finally in death. And nothing is left of it thereafter except, as we say, the remains – a scattering of the dust from which it came. The human soul, on the other hand, is made of spirit, not gross matter, and so it can neither be nourished by such matter nor can it disintegrate and die for the want of it. The human soul is immortal.

The dreadful difference between these two substances, and as a consequence between their respective destinies, is captured perfectly in the Greek metaphor, *soma sema*, the body is a tomb. Death, which consists in the final disintegration of the body, and of the body only, is a blessed release for the soul from this body-tomb in which in this world it has been, quite literally, incarcerated. For it is in the soul that the very essence and substance of the human person consists, together with all that is of value in human life and destiny. Then the soul, not being subject to the disintegration that affects body as opposed to spirit, and thereby not subject to all the ills to which human flesh is heir, is immortal. And if it does not die, there can be no possible need to resurrect it. Indeed, to resurrect the body and attach it once again to the soul would surely prove to be, not only unnecessary for a happy and fulfilled life with God in eternity, which is what Platonism promised to those who lived their lives on this earth on the principle of the '*omoiosis theou*,' the likeness of God, the Spirit and their Father (Zeus); it would be downright perverse.

So, no resurrection of the body, please. Let those of us who have become followers of what we have accepted as the new and truer way preached by Jesus and his apostles, we who shun the works of the flesh, look forward to a happy eternity of our very souls with Jesus and God. No more bodies and so not even the remote possibility of getting and spending and laying waste our powers, as some poet put it, and getting ill and growing old and bits sagging and falling off – in short, no more of the ills to which the flesh is the natural heir. No more of *any* of that kind of thing, *please. No resurrection.* It is easy to imagine the placards outside the synagogue in Corinth, or wherever it was that Paul was preaching. But it is also possible to inspect a biblical scene drawn by Luke in which the two different mind-sets, shall we say the popular Platonist and the Hebrew, simply fail to make contact. Acts (17:16-32) describes Paul's arrival during one of his missionary journeys at Athens, the home of Greek philosophy at its zenith. He meets there some Epicurean and Stoic philosophers (Stoicism by this time had become heavily Platonised), who 'took hold of him and brought him to the Areopagus (either the council chamber or the hill itself), saying, "May we know what this new teaching is which you present: For you bring some strange things (foreign divinities, Jesus, resurrection are instanced) to our ears; we wish to know therefore what these things mean".'

It does sound somewhat menacing, more like an arrest than an invitation. But Paul went with them quite voluntarily and proceeded to make his case for his preaching. He preached, he said, the Creator God they too believed in, the God who did not live in shrines made by man, but who gives life and breath and everything, and of whom therefore, as he reminds them one of their own poets had said, 'we are indeed his offspring,' (sons and daughters of God). And he appeared to be doing quite well for himself before this distinguished audience. Until without ever mentioning Jesus by name – perhaps because his listeners seemed to have the impression that he preached a questionable foreign god called Jesus – he declared that this Creator 'will judge the world in righteousness by a man whom he has appointed, and of this he has given assurance to all men by raising him from the dead.' And there, in the words of the poet, the matter ended it. For 'when they heard of the resurrection of the dead, some mocked; but others said, "We will hear you again about this".' Which, when translated from the Greek in this context means: 'Don't call us; we'll call you.' A rather polite form of dismissal, but dismissal it was for all that.

The truth of the matter is that what Paul understands by resurrection is something quite different from those who now dismiss it and him; and different also from the common understanding of resurrection amongst so many Christians down to the present day. For the Christian church has long taken over the position of the popular Platonists, as evidenced by the habit of talking of the resurrection of the body, where Paul and the creeds talk of the resurrection of the dead. For we still picture our human souls as being naturally immortal, as the Platonists of long ago insisted. And what is immortal does not die, and so cannot possibly need any raising from the dead, by God or by anyone else. So the same confusion reigns today as it did between these early Corinthians and the Pauline and general biblical understanding of resurrection. In fact, we are even more astray today than the Corinthians were, because we then add on a resurrection of the body only, and not of the person, which neither Paul nor the Corinthians would dream of envisaging. In short, we have managed over the centuries to preserve in aspic the worst of both these ancient cultures, and as a consequence we have lumbered ourselves with the inevitably impossible task of making resurrection sound in the least reasonable to our quite rightly cultured interrogators.

But in the case of Paul and his fellow Israelites who gave us most of the Bible, although most of the images of body and spirit and so on are the same – they are after all universal – the ensuing story of the make-up of the human being and of its destiny is very different from that promoted by Greek Platonic theology. That Hebrew story of human make-up and human destiny begins as part of the story of creation that opens the first book of the Bible, Genesis, when it describes the creation of Adam as follows: God, like a potter, took some of the dust of the ground and moulded it into human shape and then breathed into its nostrils so that it became a living self, *nephesh*. The breath here is the ancient and universal symbol of God acting as Creator Spirit and making the human being we know into a living, embodied self. So the make-up of the human being is described as a self that is breathed into the material of the earth by the Holy Spirit who, it must then be assumed, works permanently within living human beings, as within the whole of creation. For whenever God withdraws his Creative Breath, life ceases entirely for the creature in question.

Then Paul supplies more detail to that story, precisely in the context of his famous chapter on resurrection in which he is answering for the Corinthians the question, with what bodies do we rise? (1 Corinthians 15) You can be sure that question was asked with at least a hint of taunt or hostility in the voice, for Paul was bullying them into believing, as they saw it, in the raising of a body only, and they would want to know where the bodies were to come from. Paul first reads Genesis in Greek to have said that 'the Adam', the man, was made into a living psyche, *eis psuchen zosan*, or an embodied psyche, *soma psuchikon*. And he never afterwards dismisses the bodily element from that story of the make-up of human beings, not even when he comes to describe its risen status. There is then no question of a soul, or a psyche for that matter, surviving the death of a body, needing no resurrection for itself, but for some doubtful reason requiring either the revival of a corpse or the construction of an alternative body in order to make it once more an embodied soul or psyche.

Embodied psyche, that is what we are, and that is what we will remain, here on earth and in whatever life or state or place we may find ourselves hereafter. So Paul, after a slightly exasperated bit of a rant at the Corinthians, reminding them of just how many different types and kinds of bodies they already know to exist – this particular apostle was easily exasperated – finally informs them that we are raised in 'a spiritual body,' *soma pneumatikon*. In view of Paul's next statement that Jesus, the last Adam, was raised to the status of life-giving spirit, that phrase must then mean an increasingly creative and effective power of the Holy Spirit operating as always within the psychical body, so as to transform its life into a life more and more like the life of God, into a life eternal and as perfect as the life of a creature can be, *shalom*. Jesus is then called a life-giving spirit, because so powerfully did the Holy Spirit come upon and remain in Jesus even during his earthly life, that he himself became the source of that Spirit's fuller and fullest power in the lives of those who were inspired by Jesus to live and die like him.

This reading of this Israelite story of human make-up and destiny is corroborated by rehearsing, very briefly and crudely, the story of that story as much as it can be recovered from Israel's history. For at first, it seems, some at least of the Israelites imagined that death was the end of us. The Creative Spirit-Breath was simply withdrawn, and there was no more life, or even existence. But then, perhaps during their Babylonian exile when the Israelites came in contact with the religion of the prophet, Zoroaster, with its strong emphasis on a grand resurrection and a definitive end-time cosmic conflict between good and evil, some of them began to revise the view of death as the stark and simple end. They now thought of the self, *nephesh*, radically altered by death, yes, but still surviving, if only now in a much more tenuous version of material body. Material still, but like an empty intangible entity only barely and occasionally visible, like a spirit, a ghost. A seemingly empty and insubstantial form of matter, to use the twin Hebrew images (*tohu w' bohu*) that appear in the Genesis creation story in order to characterise the material reality of the deep, the watery chaos, before the great bird, the Spirit of God, came to brood upon it and by doing so enabled it to source substantial forms. But then, some thought, if there is a form of human existence that survives death, no matter how insubstantial its form and how unwelcome its future may be in the dark and dismal place of shadows they now called *She'ol*, there must also be some presence and activity of the Creator Spirit. For without the power of that Spirit nothing at all can survive, not even in the utterly attenuated, intangible form of material existence called *She'ol*. So the Creator Spirit must be there, even in *She'ol*, although perhaps only in the Holy Spirit's conservative rather than creative mode.

And yet, some people like the Pharisees of Jesus's time, and like Paul who was of that party, refused to believe that the Creator Spirit's power could ever be restricted, even in *She'ol*, to the bare task of preserving human life through and beyond the death of this very tangible and grossly material earthly body. If the Spirit's power is by nature creative, that is to say, if it goes beyond pure preservation of life in mere existence – if in our experience of this world the Spirit always and everywhere advances life creatively, enabling all life to evolve to ever higher forms, and with no end in sight of the final perfection of life, *shalom*, that we can then try to envisage – it must be possible, it cannot be denied us, that we should be able to entertain the blessed hope that somehow and sometime that same eternal divine Creator should bring us and all that exists to that ultimate perfection of life to which divine creativity must for all eternity aim.

So Paul's Hebrew story of the make-up and destiny of the human person and of all of its natural universe is poles apart from the popular Platonic story. There is resurrection of the body for Paul, but not resurrection of the gross material body from which death separates out a soul, a purely material self that is constitutionally immortal and so needs no resurrection. There is instead a divine conservation of the existence of a *soma psychikon*, an embodied self, throughout this earthly life, through death and into the hereafter. And that conservation is forever inseparable from the creative activity of the Holy Spirit by which life is not merely sustained but advanced, raised up to higher and higher levels in this life, through death, and onward and upward to the ultimate *shalom*. That story of make-up and destiny, which Paul inherited from his own Hebrew tradition, explains why he says to the Corinthians that if there is no resurrection from the dead then Jesus has not been raised. Rather than base his belief in resurrection on the resurrection of Jesus, Paul if anything sees the resurrection of Jesus as part of a general belief in resurrection from the dead. Only so can one explain why he talks of being raised from the dead during this life, and why he talks of the body in which we continue to be raised through death and in the hereafter as a (more) spiritual body.

Of course, at this point of this clear alternative to the popular Platonist story of make-up and destiny, the question does become acute: with what bodies will we rise, after the death of this earthly body? Or, more to the present point, what can be meant by this more spiritual body in which we are to be raised hereafter? For we can scarcely imagine after the disintegration of the only earthly body we ever knew, an existence that could be called in any sense bodily. Eye has not seen, nor ear heard, and that is what has Paul blustering about all over the place concerning this kind of body or that. Yet strange as it might seem contemporary physics, so often seen as the enemy of all religious belief in divine creators, does offer us a metaphor, if not a strict analogy for the prospect of a more spiritual body. The clear image of matter as hard lumps of stuff that can be broken down into smaller and smaller particles gave way, in the course of that very down-breaking, to the scientific discovery of deeper levels of the stuff that physics studies and calls matter. Levels that still counted as matter presumably, but that carried few if any of the characteristics of the gross touchy-feely thing made up of distinguishable particles that science up to recently has imagined in the main as the make-up of bodily matter, as distinct from soul or spirit.

'Two centuries ago,' as one recent science-writer, Patricia Williams, put it, 'our concept of matter was of small, indivisible, hard, inert entities that interacted deterministically ... In contrast, spirit was ineffable, uncatchable, hazy, active and responsible for life. Today, we know that matter is a form of energy and that it is ineffable, uncatchable, hazy and active, creating life.' Worse still, Richard Feynman tells us, 'We have no knowledge of what energy is,' to which Paul Davis adds, 'You cannot see or touch energy.' In such a climate of the apparent meltdown of a hard, dichoromous dualism of matter and spirit by modern physicists, there can be little remaining difficulty in talking about our psyches or spirits being embodied by the ever-transforming Creator Spirit in a more spiritual form of matter than that grosser form of matter in which we exist during our earthly sojourn. For that same Spirit is ever also operating in (or as?) that created energy that continually creatively evolves life on earth. So contemporary science does indeed offer us the possibility of envisaging, even if we cannot visualise how, that the final disintegration of our current physical bodies that we call death, amounts in the event to a transformation of the existence of the human self into a more spirit-like body, Paul's spiritual body. And we can then envisage the disintegration of the gross material body as a transformation rather than an annihilation, and with that we can see a continuous role for the Creator Spirit through our deaths, doing what the eternal Creator Spirit does eternally, namely, sustaining and constantly transforming or evolving existence and life.

However that may be, in this second story of the make-up and destiny of the human being, the Hebrew rather than the popular Platonic one, there are no souls that are of their essence and nature immortal. There are only human beings that exist and live by the continuously creative power of God during their lives on earth. Humans who by that same power live through their deaths and into whatever state or place they will then find themselves, as their earthly bodies are utterly deformed in the process of having them changed into what Paul calls spiritual bodies. And then live on into whatever ultimate state or place the eternal God who rules the world by creating everything ever anew has destined for them. Therefore, and as a consequence of placing it in the context of this Hebrew story, the image of resurrection, the image of being raised up, acquires a range of reference and level upon level of meaning in one coherent story that differs radically from its range of reference in the Greek-Platonist story.

For in its Platonic context the image and story of resurrection finally and strictly amounts to little if anything more than recovering corpses out of graves and/or somehow reconstructing living bodies and uniting them again with souls at some apparently quite variable interval after their death. But the biblical image and story of resurrection allows it to be applied to every stage and range of human life, in advance and decline, from its origin and through its evolution and all the way to the endgame in eternity that it must most likely share with some equally unimaginable version of the wonderful physical world of which it is such an integral part. Further still, that image and story allows us to see the creative act of the Creator Spirit, not as a one-off act of putting the world there in the first place, but as a continuously creative activity, ever operative through the things that are made, and especially through that most creative human creature that the Creator Spirit made in its own image and likeness, in order to continuously make the world, and make it ever-new, through all setbacks, whether natural or maliciously incurred, until the final *shalom* is reached for all. This is a vision of Creator and creation that actually complies completely with the current scientific view of an evolving universe. And it is found in the Bible, whenever there is talk of healing the damaging results of set-backs, mostly of human derivation, and these are then described as a new creation. Or it is found in single portraits of creation reaching its end and perfection, portraits such as Paul also paints, for instance, in his Letter to the Romans. (8:18-25)

Therefore it is never legitimate to limit the range of reference of the imagery of resurrection to that of reviving a corpse, as was naturally done by the Platonists in the very course of rejecting resurrection; and as has been done by Christians ever since they adopted Platonism as a suitable theology for their particular faith. Nor does the fact that Christians have long used this Platonic idea of the resurrection of the body alone as a proof miracle in order to prove something about Jesus – for instance, that he was what he claimed to be, the Son of God – justify their adoption of the Platonist view of the make-up and immortality of humanity. For this flies in the face of Jesus telling his followers that only an adulterous (i.e. an idolatrous) generation would clamour for such a miraculous sign from God, and Paul in his turn condemning the Jews for seeking such signs. (Matthew 12:39; 1 Corinthians 1:22) It is the death of Jesus, as it happens, that does most to prove that he was the Son of God, in the biblical sense. For his dying for a rule of life by which he lived, a rule that is the exact replica of the reign of God the Creator and that is so dramatically symbolised in eucharist, shows him to have been the very paradigm of sonship of God. And further, so fully did the Creator Spirit form and fashion his very being and life, and so final was the witness of his death to this Spirit, that it is his death that John picks out in particular as the consummate moment in which he breathed that Spirit into his disciples, and then through them into all others who would join their eucharistic community. In other words it is the death of Jesus that John picks out as the point *par excellence* of the raising of Jesus to the status of sonship of God in the fullness of its power.

And so it is for all who in the course of history have aimed at the ideal of discipleship of Jesus. All are, each one in his or her own degree, being raised to the status of offspring of God, as Jesus was son. And if any of them, like Jesus, die for the rule of life by which they thus lived, their deaths also will prove to be the point of the Spirit that breathed through Jesus raising them also to the highest degree of sonship or daughtership that they could achieve. As their lives, like those of all human beings, are by the same Creator Spirit transformed through death to the life of the end of the ages. Yet of course, since Jesus is for them the prime earthly source of the Spirit that still breathes through him into them, he is son of God in a pre-eminent degree, a degree characterised by his relative source-ship. That gives him an original part in the very source-ship of the Creator Spirit. His true followers are sons of God as he is son of God, but he is also thereby their Lord.

The Bible has different ways of picturing the fulfilment of the promise sensed by his disciples, that their incipient raising to the status of the sonship of God must include in its range of reference the continuity of that raising to ever more blessed life through the very gates of their respective deaths. Paul, for instance, believes that this particular point of the divine raising to life, the raising at or from our earthly death, must have a communal dimension. It must consist in a general event, rather than a series of individual events. He also believed that that general resurrection must come soon. For the full and definitive raising of people to the status of sonship of God had just come into the world through Jesus. That, Paul seems to have thought, surely ushered in 'the last days' of which the prophets spoke, and the last days surely meant the end of the present cosmic age. Yet in the story of the execution of Jesus and its immediate aftermath, Matthew introduces us to this Jerusalem scene: 'The tombs also were opened, and many bodies of the saints who had fallen asleep were raised, and coming out of the tombs after his resurrection they went into the holy city and appeared to many.' (Matthew 27:52-53) Now that story seems like a summary replica of the resurrection of Jesus himself, and it loosens any bonds that might tie us exclusively to a picture of a still postponed but general raising by God from (or through) death.

The story of the raising of Lazarus, set during the lifetime and mission of Jesus, points also in that same direction. For as soon as people can be dissuaded from abusing this story also as a miracle story meant to prove what they understand to constitute the divinity of Jesus, the true point of the story will come through. And that point is found in Jesus's response to Martha when she misunderstands his statement, 'Your brother will rise again,' by saying 'I know that he will rise again in the resurrection at the last day.' Jesus corrects her: 'I am the resurrection and the life; he who believes in me, though he die, yet shall he live, and whoever lives and believes in me shall never die.' (John 11:21-26) That more or less confirms the view that our Spirit-resourced resurrection to ever more blessed life that operates in face of all the death-dealing experiences of life, continues for all of us to transform our lives from their beginning and through the natural death of our present material form. So that we do not need to wait for any 'general resurrection'. And certainly not for a general resurrection 'of the body' only, a wholly un-biblical image and story of earthly life and its ending that is borrowed, it does no harm to repeat once more, from a Platonic-type theology.

This extended range of reference of the imagery of resurrection that includes but is not confined to the survival of the death we all must as material creatures die, is corroborated by the Bible in an indirect but impressive manner by a corresponding extension of the normal range of reference of the imagery of death. This correspondence is characteristic of the imagery of the gospel of John, as the Lazarus scene itself might lead one to expect. The extended range of reference of the imagery of death is mainly contrived by taking back into the on-going life of a person the contrast between life and death and the overcoming of one by the other that usually is confined to the point of the person's natural death itself. This contrivance John achieves by picturing the followers of Jesus enjoying eternal life already during their earthly sojourn. And then painting the opposite picture of a diptych when he portrays these same ones during the same life as being dead in sin, when they follow the rule of some other spirit, besides that of the eternal Creator Spirit. This diptych is further clarified by John's image and story of divine judgement on human kind. For this divine judgement is now portrayed as the very coming of Jesus into the world. (John 5:24, 9:39, 13:31, 16:11)

By that very coming of Jesus the world, according to John, is already judged. Because by the standards of the covenant with the one true reigning Creator, lived out so perfectly by Jesus, all can see that they are either condemned to continuing death or already enjoying eternal life. It is all simply a way of saying that the service of any god (the Bible often suggests Mammon) other than the infinitely good and benevolent Creator Spirit will result inevitably in death-dealing by each against all, and an existence that is as a consequence more like daily dying than daily living. Whereas following the rule of the true Creator Spirit to the point of being the Creator Father's human image, as the followers of Jesus are daily inspired to do, raises the whole human species to life and more life, both here and through death itself into the hereafter. Confirmation, if any more were needed, of the continuity of the resurrection imagery in the life of Jesus and of all people up to, through and after the natural deaths of each and all. And a consequent extension of the image and story of dying in order to live; an extension of that story backwards from the point of the natural and final disintegration of our current material bodies that we normally describe as our death, back over all the years of our lives and to our very conception. For shortly, all too shortly after our conception we must learn the lesson of having to die to one condition of existence in order to live more abundantly, as our mothers quite literally push us to tear ourselves away from the uroboric unity of the womb, in order to face the dangerous and painful journey out into an unknown and utterly uncertain world.

It is of some historical interest to note that it was in the context of baptism that Paul made that crucial observation about the extension of the imagery of dying and raising to all the time that passes between conception and natural death. It is not at all clear that Jesus himself baptised, or told his disciples to baptise. He had, after all, started out as a convert to John the Baptist's movement for a change of heart and the restoration of the true reign of God in Israel. And so, when he realised that he was called to a similar mission, but with an even more radical understanding of the reign of God than John could envisage, he possibly thought it inappropriate simply to repeat John's initiation rite. Telling his followers instead that they would be baptised by the creative fire that is the Holy Spirit, as described in the 'tongues of fire' scene in the story of Pentecost Day in Acts, rather than being baptised simply in the cleansing drama of the application of water. Yet Paul is our witness to the fact that the water-drama is also quite naturally capable of carrying the full and entire creative symbolism that fire-dramas, which are in any case much more dangerous, can carry. So after the death of Jesus his earliest followers began to baptise their converts in water, and said that this was in accordance with the will and indeed the command of Jesus to them to spread the reign of God. In their way they were right, and so the baptism-drama joins the eucharistic drama of the meal, as the two sacraments that can be traced back to Jesus himself, according to both Protestant and Catholic churches.

'Do you not know that all of us who have been baptised into Christ Jesus were baptised into his death? We were buried therefore with him by baptism into death, so that as Christ was raised from the dead by the glory of the Father, we too might walk in newness of life.' 'But if we have died with Christ, we believe that we shall also live with him. For we know that Christ being raised from the dead will never die again; death no longer has dominion over him. The death he died he died to sin, once for all, but the life he lives he lives to God. So you also must consider yourselves dead to sin and alive to God in Christ Jesus.' (Romans 6:3-11) The dramatic participative symbolism here, the sacrament so described, seems to have in mind baptism by immersion. The water in which one is immersed evokes the watery chaos in the opening creation story of Genesis, the dark abyss in which no formed or fashioned thing could survive, and certainly no life could long exist. Until the Holy Spirit like a bird (the dove that brings the promise of *shalom*) comes upon the abyss and empowers the water with that original sourcing of life that evolution theory confirms.

So that water then offers us a participatory symbolism of that limitless divine creativity of life that raises human beings in particular to the status of sons of God, and heralds and heirs to God's kingdom on earth and in all the ages to come. No matter what the cost extracted by the powers that wage war and spread chaos over the earth, even if that be the cost of life itself. No matter how difficult the endurance then required of those who would remain faithful to the God who will do nothing other than continue to create life and life more abundant for all. In such contexts Paul also extends the imagery of both death and resurrection all through life on earth, and through the death of current bodily form, and into the currently unimaginable forms of life beyond that death. For so many of our fellow humans daily life is more like dying than living. As for some heroic human spirits who would die for justice for others, rather than live in complicity with injustice or kill for others, their very deaths are the highest and most intense forms of all their living. And so it is that, particularly in its Hebrew versions, the imagery and story of the deaths of the sons and daughters of God, and their simultaneous raising to the status of heirs to the eternal kingdom, finds its continuous application from conception, through the death of current bodily forms, and beyond.

Resurrection Meals
Finally, then, what does all of this yield, in the line of hard information, about Jesus of Nazareth and his disciples on this earth, after the passion and death of Jesus himself?

In order to answer this question it is first and foremost necessary to observe that all of these appearances of Jesus to his disciples after his death, gathered together by Luke through the conceit of having him *stay* with them for forty days, are then said by Luke to have had the objective of 'speaking of the kingdom of God', the very thing he had spent all of his public life doing. But Luke does also gloss his remark about Jesus's forty-day stay, with the words, 'He presented himself alive after his passion by many proofs.' (Acts 1:3) What proofs are these, and what are they meant to prove? Looking back for answers first to the end of Luke's gospel where he gives some detail for some of these appearances, the first story we meet is of an appearance of Jesus to some disillusioned disciples on their way to Emmaus – running away really, like virtually all of the others. Their leader has been executed; some women had been going on about not finding his body in his tomb, and about a vision of angels who said he was alive. The kind of silly prattle, the tone of this biblical story suggests, that you'd expect from women emotionally overcome by grief and anxiety.

But now Jesus, whom these disillusioned disciples did not recognise for some reason as he joined them on their journey, tried to show from the scriptures that the Christ was prophesied to be a suffering servant. With no result, until they invited him to 'stay with us' and he did. And during the meal 'he took the bread and blessed, and broke it, and gave it to them.' And then, and only then, 'he was known to them in the breaking of bread.' Then, and only then, in this eucharistic meal – for that is undeniably what this is – Jesus had really and truly appeared to them; he was really and truly present with them. And only then did they really see and know what they, like so many others of his followers had failed to see or refused to acknowledge, namely, that their true messiah was of course the crucified one who reigned as God's vice-regent on earth from his throne on the cross. The cross was the victory for his cause and theirs, and not, as their despair painted it, a defeat.

Then, as Luke continues the story, these disciples, eyes now wide open, turned back to Jerusalem from Emmaus. Going up to Jerusalem and facing the music there always was and always would be for these first followers of Jesus an unavoidable part of the preaching of the true reign of the true God. On arrival in the guesthouse they began to tell their Emmaus story to 'the eleven', only to be interrupted by a further appearance of Jesus. This time Jesus tries to allay the fears of the eleven that they are seeing someone's ghost, by inviting them to 'handle me, and see.' They handled him, 'and while they still disbelieved for joy, and wondered, he said to them, "Have you anything here to eat?" They gave him a piece of broiled fish, and he took it and ate.' The same strategy for ending the same stubborn disbelief? Recognition in the sharing of food? The camber of the story would certainly suggest so. And a trawl through the other gospel endings reveals that only John has some appearances stories that do not yield much more than this. (Luke 24)

John, the last of the gospel-writers, begins by re-telling the story of the women at the tomb; well really, of the woman at the tomb, for Mary Magdalene plays one of the two speaking parts in the scene. The other speaking part is played by Jesus himself, for it is he rather than an angel who accosts her, although again in some unrecognisable form. And she does take the story to his disciples, though it is not now the story of his being risen, but rather the story that he is about to ascend to 'my Father and your Father, to my God and your God'. A hint here perhaps of some twilight zone between the death of Jesus and his final raising to the right hand of God, reminiscent of the conceit of Luke's forty days? Then John has Jesus himself appear in the room where the disciples were gathered 'for fear of the Jews', the supper room no doubt. He appeared 'on the evening of that day, the first day of the week', the day already identified in Acts as the day on which eucharist was celebrated. And he offered them the *shalom* of God, and sent them on their way as heralds of the reign of God, as he himself had been sent, by breathing on them and saying 'Receive the Holy Spirit.'

There follows in John's story two handling scenes that are much more elaborate than the one painted by Luke. The first of these scenes is set at a time when Thomas was absent and Jesus showed the rest 'his hands and his side', and 'The disciples were glad when they saw the Lord.' The second handling scene took place just when the redoubtable 'doubting Thomas', as he has ever since been called, returned and informed his fellows that he did not believe a word of what they were reporting about the appearance of Jesus they said he had missed. So Thomas is explicitly invited to poke Jesus's hands and side, and then he confesses, 'My Lord and my God.' (John 20)

And finally, in what is regarded as an epilogue to John's (original?) gospel, there comes a story of an appearance of Jesus to a group of his disciples now back in Galilee on which occasion he invites them to share a meal of bread and fish. (John 21) The story in fact specifies the very spot in Galilee at which this encounter with Jesus took place: 'by the sea of Tiberias', the very place at which, as John's gospel had earlier recorded, Jesus had broken bread and distributed fish to five thousand. And it may be worth recalling the very words of John as he describes this earlier and much, much larger meal of bread and fish. If only because of the clear echoes it contains of what must now be familiar to any reader of the Bible, namely, the eucharistic formula: 'So the men sat down, in number about five thousand. Jesus then took the loaves, and when he had given thanks, he distributed them to those who were seated; so also the fish, as much as they wanted.' (John 6:10-11)

So having located this group of disciples 'by the sea of Tiberias' John goes on to describe how Jesus, as usual unrecognised, re-directs towards a fine shoal of fish the disciples who were fishing just offshore where the fish were few and far between. This resulted in a catch so great that it dawned on 'the disciple whom Jesus loved' that the figure on shore was 'the Lord'. When they came ashore 'they saw a charcoal fire, with fish lying on it, and bread', the very food on offer at that earlier feeding of the five thousand by the sea of Tiberias. 'Jesus said to them, "Come and have breakfast." Now none of the disciples dared ask him, "Who are you?" They knew it was the Lord. Jesus came and took the bread and gave it to them, and so with the fish.' Another meal of bread and fish then by the sea of Tiberias. A eucharistic meal on one or both of these occasions? This matter will arise again; but for the moment it is necessary only to recognise the fact that the terms of the eucharistic formula are represented in differing degrees between these two sea of Tiberias meals. After the meal, the talk then turned to certain matters concerning the roles of Peter and 'the disciple whom Jesus loved, who had lain close to his breast at the supper'. The talk, in short, had to do with the furthering of the reign of God, just what Luke in Acts had said the post-passion appearances of Jesus were all about. More specifically in this case, the matter seems to concern the relative roles of certain leaders, in particular Peter and John 'the beloved disciple,' in the company of those sent by Jesus to promote the true reign of God.

What, finally then, do all of these more detailed stories about appearances of Jesus after his passion and death tell us? A clear and full answer to that question can occur only upon the realisation that these stories belong to vision literature. They are therefore not stories about the normal kind of encounters people could have with Jesus while he was still in the bodily form that began to disintegrate already with his death on the cross, and was then buried. The stories themselves have their own ways of implying as much. Mark gives no detail of an appearance of the risen Christ, and Matthew in his account of an appearance in Galilee seems to be interested only in the transfer of Jesus's own authority to baptise and make disciples, mainly by teaching people what Jesus commanded. But Luke and John do give full details of a number of appearances, and chief amongst these details, for present purposes, is the failure of those who encounter Jesus to recognise him at first, at the tomb, on the road and in the hostelry, or in an upper room in Jerusalem, or at a lakeside in Galilee. One would instantly recognise the familiar body of some acquaintance that one had seen quite recently 'in the flesh'. So these are not just encounters with the Jesus as he was when they walked the dust tracks of Galilee with him, or the streets of Jerusalem.

Luke's description of Paul's first encounter with the risen Christ corroborates that conclusion. This is a description of Paul's encounter with the risen Christ to which Paul points, and which makes him a witness to the risen sonship or lordship of Jesus. Furthermore, this privilege of having been in this way a witness to the resurrection of Jesus Paul then claims as his qualification for apostleship, just as being a witness to the resurrection of Jesus was one of the qualifications for filling the place in The Twelve vacated by Judas, a qualification that Matthias, the successful candidate for that position, possessed. (1 Corinthians 15:7-9; Acts 1:21-26) The appearance of Jesus to Paul took place on the road to Damascus, after 'Saul (a previous version of his name), still breathing threats and murder against disciples of the Lord (we met Saul previously in Acts 8:1, revealing his part in the execution of Stephen), went to the high priest and asked him for letters to the synagogues at Damascus. So that if he found any belonging to the Way (Jesus once said, I am the Way), men or women, he might bring them bound to Jerusalem.' When suddenly, on his way to carrying out his grisly mission, 'a light from heaven flashed about him. And he fell to the ground (no horse) and heard a voice saying to him, "Saul, Saul, why do you persecute me?" And he said, "Who are you, Lord?" And he said, "I am Jesus, whom you are persecuting".' (Acts 9:1-5)

The vision imagery of this story is very familiar in the Bible. The light is the blinding light of the glory of God, itself a metaphor for the active presence of God in the world. That glory shines first in the Bible in the opening of the creation story, 'Let there be light'; it shone from the face of Moses when he came down from Mount Sinai where, face to face with God, he had been given the definitive Torah, the way of God and to God; it shone round the shepherds near Bethlehem in Luke's nativity story, lighting up the birth of Jesus; just as it shone, according to John, when the Spirit breathed most powerfully into this world at the death of Jesus, and glorified Jesus in the process. And now it shines through the risen Jesus, as the Spirit breathes now through him, and it flattens Paul. In fact the light from heaven blinds Paul, as we learn a few sentences later. That is to say, it shows him that he has been blind to the true reality of things on which he is beginning now to be enlightened.

And the other metaphor, the voice from heaven that Paul is said to have heard? This also is a traditional motif of Jewish vision literature, very familiar from scenes like the baptism of Jesus, when God declares him son of God. In the case of this voice-mail metaphor the message is often delivered by an angel rather than come directly from God. But since 'angel' means 'messenger', this amounts to nothing more or less than is conveyed in the phrase 'message received'. Just as in the case of the metaphor of the light of glory, all it really means to convey is that the truth dawned with the clarity and brilliance of the first light of every day. What truth then, and how exactly does it dawn? In general, the biblical answer must be as John's prologue, crafted after the Genesis creation story, suggests. God's glory and God's way with the world and the way of the world back to God's paradise shines in the creation as such. So the Creator Spirit (a metaphor cognate with fire and light), or as in John's prologue, the Creator Word (a metaphor cognate with voice) enlightens everyone in the world. In the more specific case of this truth shining, dawning or sounding for Paul, it was through his experience of persecuting the followers of Jesus that this larger truth concerning God's ways with the world, perfectly manifest in Jesus, flooded into his mind like a blinding light, stopped him in his tracks, knocked him off his feet; so he had to get up again and set out on an altogether different way than the one he had so far walked.

So it is that this metaphor of *son et lumiere* conveys to us an unexpected and overwhelming dawning on Paul of the fact that his true Lord also should be the crucified Jesus whose disciples he is prepared to imprison and kill, with all due legal process of course – this Saul is not a lawless bandit. Paul's blindness was lifted, the light dawned, and he recognised the fact that in persecuting these who took Jesus as the Lord of their lives, he was opposing the one whom God had raised to lordship, the one who was the way, the truth and the life.

But what about these handling, not to say wound-poking incidents that are also part of the stories of appearances in both Luke and John? These surely suggest the same kind of meeting, seeing, hearing, touching, eating with Jesus in the body that were so familiar to his followers before his death. They surely cannot be absorbed without remainder into the category of visions, or vision literature. For are they not specifically designed to prove that Jesus is encountered after his death in the self-same body that his closest disciples knew so well during his earthly life? So that what is rather dismissively called the revival of a corpse is indeed a crucial part of resurrection for Jesus and for the rest of us, no matter what Paul himself may have thought he meant when he said we would rise in 'a spiritual body'? No, it is perfectly clear to anyone who can decipher this vision imagery, especially in John's version of poking the wounds in Jesus's hands and side, the very emblems of his passion and death, that what is being said, and said so graphically through the imagery of poking, is that they now saw that the crucified one is by that very fact the one raised to the pinnacle of the power of a son of God. And that is something that could not be seen, much less proved by any amount of physical, factual poking of a revivified corpse. Any more than the Jesus who met the disgruntled disciples on the road to Emmaus was able to make them see, through that very encounter, much less prove to them even with the help of the scriptures, that the one raised to sonship of God in power was and had to be the crucified one.

All that the handling of hands and side could possibly prove to these disciples was, once again, that the corpse of Jesus had been revived. And that would be more likely to make them believe that Jesus would now go about restoring the kingdom of Israel according to their glorious expectations, with all the invincible power that a man who had walked away from death itself could command, than enable them to believe at long last that his triumph in bringing God's reign was through suffering. Remember Luke's remark to the effect that some of these disciples did in fact take some of these appearances of the crucified and now risen Jesus as the very basis for their preferred answer to their question, 'Lord, will you at this time restore the kingdom of Israel?' (Acts 1:6) – the kind of answer they never could get from him during his earthly sojourn with him. So how then did these disciples come to see, what they then expressed so graphically in terms of having touched his very wounds, that it was the crucified one as such that was raised to sonship at the right hand of God? The very thing that even these closest disciples of Jesus refused to see, blinded during the earthly mission of Jesus by their vision of him as a victorious and glorious King Messiah, and blinded at the death into final betrayal and flight by the sheer panic and fear at the cost he was having to pay in fidelity to his cause as he saw it, and would pass on to his followers.

Only the imagination can answer a question like that, focused as only imagination can be on the imagery of which vision literature is constructed. So tell the story of the days after the execution again, and enter it with imagination. Something like this. After his execution the inner core of the company of the followers of Jesus huddled together in the last lodgings they had shared with him, still in fear of the Jews, because there seemed to be nothing else they could do, for the moment anyway. And there in sad memoriam they saw his familiar face again, and heard his words again. Even those words of his about dying for the cause, words that previously they had no intention of heeding. They rehearsed once again the high and awesome demands of the reign of God – love your enemies, do good to them that hate you – with such vividness that they could hear him still, and even see the puzzled look on his face as he realised that the highest of these demands was simply not getting through to them. This was the requirement that they should give their very lives when those who took leadership to mean lording it over others and living magnificently at their expense came to kill them for threatening that self-centred lifestyle and the god it served.

But it was when they sat at table and conducted their meals as eucharist, as he had done, taking in gladness the food and drink, the staff and symbol of life itself, and thanking God who gives all of it to all, and breaking it out and pouring it out to others, that they saw the fearful relevance of the broken bread to the breaking of their bodies, if occasion demanded, and the pouring of the wine to the pouring of their own blood. And as the frames of the motion picture of that last harrowing night and day of his life on earth flowed together in their imaginations at the meal, they saw and heard the one speaking these words about body-bread breaking and wine-blood pouring. They saw and heard him now, the self-same one at that last meal and at every later meal, as the wounded and dying one. And with such vividness that they could feel the wounds.

And slowly but surely they began to sense the Spirit that shaped his person, his very life and his destiny; the Spirit of steadfast love that brought their servant-master to this state and end, and through it to a real presence in their very hearts and souls that no previous word or act of Jesus himself had or could have achieved. They felt this Spirit flow into them from this crucified figure now so persistently part of their *paysage interieur*, as the presence of that familiar figure continued, especially at their distinctive eucharistic meals, to talk in his familiar and characteristic phrases, to enlighten, to heal, to help. And as this was the self-same Spirit of the Most High God that had formed Jesus from his mother's womb and empowered him to live and die as he did, they now felt that power come to them through him, and seep slowly into their bleak hearts. And they unlocked the doors of the upper room and they walked fearlessly out into the city, and into the very temple to face the men who had condemned him to death, retracing the path of their retreat, and out into the wide world. A world that to one view looked as dark and threatening and fear-full as it ever was, mainly due to man's inhumanity to man and beast. But through that deathly vision of it they now could see its deep and wonderful goodness, and the glorious and eternal promise it held out to those who would at last keep faith with their Lord, and with the Creator God he always addressed as their common Father.

And that explains how Saul saw the risen Lord, and saw Jesus in just the manner in which he named himself explicitly in the course of that vision, as the persecuted, the crucified one. For Paul never saw Jesus in the flesh, and so neither at his table nor on the cross. But as the disciples did with Jesus in the familiar surroundings of their supper room, so Paul in the now familiar course of another journey in search of these Christ-freaks (an intentionally insulting nick-name at the origin of the name,

Christians), found himself calling them to mind, the now familiar features of the way they lived, and above all the way, like Stephen, that they died. For Stephen, 'full of the Holy Spirit,' just as he was about to be dragged to his death, saw the man, Jesus, standing at the right hand of God; that is, he saw the crucified one as risen Lord. (Acts 7:55-8:1) And suddenly the blindness of the exclusivism that had come to characterise Paul's own religion disappeared and it came to him like a flash of light, and metaphorically flattened him: they were right; they followed the true way; they were never more like their master than in their deaths; theirs was the true messiah and lord.

Paul saw the risen crucified one through the features and life-form of the ones he was out to imprison and kill. He felt the breath of the same Spirit that transformed their lives and their deaths. He was baptised in the same baptism of fire that he later wrote of so powerfully in his Letter to the Romans. And he carried the good news fearlessly out beyond the national limits at which some of the leaders of the Jesus community wanted to stop, out into the great world. He lashed out at the Corinthians for ruining the Lord's supper, as angry as if that same supper were the principal locus for the encounter with the risen Jesus, and the correspondingly central focal point of the Spirit that breathed life through Jesus into a dying world.

For that perhaps is what the eucharistic meal undoubtedly was in those earliest days, and what it should still remain to this day. Nothing else explains its presence and prominence wherever the Bible gives fuller details of appearances of the risen Lord, particularly in the writings of Luke and John. Apart perhaps from Luke's general statement to the effect that Jesus ate with his closest disciples during the forty days before the final ascension scene, the period of their persisting failure to recognise their true Lord, the desert period during which their lust for a different kind of Lord saw them face the fear and deprivation that must always accompany such infidelity. Apart also from the lovely picture painted in Revelation, of the risen Jesus coming round our doors to knock on them and invite himself in to dine, and the frequency with which 'the breaking of bread,' the sacrament in which the 'real presence' of Jesus is recognised to the present day, is mentioned in the very briefest accounts of the characteristic lives of the communities of Jesus-followers.

All in all, an impressive array of persistent references to table-fellowship with the Lord, to eating and feeding, drinking and sharing that symbolises something that they simultaneously participate in, the forming and transforming power of the Creator Spirit that for them has stamped all over it the *persona* and *curriculum vitae* of Jesus, who in fact channelled the Spirit to them. The euchatristic meal then that gives his followers the experience of Jesus eternally alive and with them, and with that the promise and hope that their lives also are eternal and destined to be transformed in some unimaginable way through their own deaths. That's the only 'proof' they have, or could ever need, of the raising of Jesus to the status of son of God in power through the power of the Creator Spirit, and of their own eternal hope of a sonship like his.

Vision literature then? All of these stories of encountering, recognising and knowing Jesus in rooms, but principally at meals in Jerusalem and Galilee, or in the process of facing execution oneself, as in Stephen's case, or in the course of killing expeditions to Damascus? Yes, vision literature. That is made clear both by the language chosen, and by the subtle yet clear suggestions in the stories that what was seen, what was known, was not that familiar pre-Calvary body that walked the dust roads of Galilee. And yet many people would not be in the least satisfied by such apparently abrupt answers to an obvious question concerning visions. They would certainly want to ask a supplementary question, such as: are these visions to be classified as genuine divine in-formations or as merely human image-inations? If we are to leave behind the possibility of the earthly body of Jesus re-appearing, were these experiences of the continuing presence of Jesus produced by God forming images of Jesus, and with these images in-forming the imaginations of those who were then the recipients of the resulting visions? Perhaps that is how most people think of religious visions. But then, of course, the scene-settings of the meals, mostly, and of other divinely produced visions would be superfluous to the needs of the stories.

The in-formation-vision might just as well have taken place when each recipient was asleep. As in the case of the in-formation-vision vouchsafed to Joseph in order to inform him that the son to be born of his betrothed was 'of the Holy Spirit'. (Matthew 2:20) So why would there be the need for such elaborate and persistent detail of persons, places, times and activities? And why, if God were informing apostolic and other imaginations with the forms of Jesus speaking and acting in specific ways, would the form of Jesus be one that was at first unrecognisable to those who knew his earthly form so well? On the other hand, if one decided to ignore the sentences that highlighted the failure to recognise Jesus, in favour of the sentences that spoke eventually of recognition, one could all too easily fall back on the interpretation of these appearances stories as proofs of the revitalising of Jesus's corpse. With all of the failure to understand the true and full biblical connotation of resurrection imagery that is thereby entailed. Not to mention the forbidden reduction of the resurrection of Jesus to the status of a proof miracle for something or other.

So human image-inations it is then? Yes, but without any 'merely,' please. The vision literature of encounters with the risen Lord Jesus records genuine in-sights into the risen Lord that apostles and others had after his execution and burial. No specific miraculous or supernatural in-formations in-coming? No. Such things may happen, of course, but they are not necessary. Rather, then, something of the order and nature of an experience of the presence to us still of our dearest departed loved ones, talking to us, re-assuring us, guiding us perhaps? Experiences that any and all of us may have, provided only that we be not victims of the dogmatic and gross materialism that has until quite recently come to dominate the imagination of a so-called scientific age? Yes, something like that. So that the settings in which the insight emerges, the details of persons, places, times, activities and other mundane circumstances can then be quite crucial to the very possibility of the insight itself? Certainly so. As is so clearly the case when we become aware of the continuing presence of departed loved ones, the places and times and happenings of their earthly sojourn with us incorporate always the experience of their continuing presence, especially when that experience is at its most powerful.

Take the details of the meal-setting first, since the meal-setting is far and away the most frequent and prominent occasion of encounter-insight with Jesus after his death. Taking and thanking, breaking and pouring out, giving and receiving to and from each other – a sign and earnest of human preparedness at all times to serve life to others at whatever cost to oneself. Even if the enmity of others to that very lifestyle, and their consequent wish to eradicate it, means that one has to die for it, rather than kill those who are prepared to kill one for requiring it as part and parcel of the new, yet oldest, covenant with the Creator God. The God who gives life with all of its necessities and enhancements equally and eternally to all. And who endows human beings in particular with the creative powers that especially enable that species to co-operate fully in bringing all to final *shalom*.

So the setting in the upper room, doing the meal as Jesus had always done it with them, doing eucharist, is all of it crucial for the dawning at long last of the blinding insight that the permanent sharing of life with others was of the very essence of the covenant with God the Creator. Even to the point of giving life itself, if that is what keeping faith with the Creator Spirit required in some particular circumstance, and thereby inspiring others to live by the same faith. For it was this insight at this depth that Jesus was still trying to convey to them at their very last supper together, before he went to his cruel but consummate death. And now at last they saw what Jesus had tried so often to convey to them, but failed to do so because their little hearts were so set on a very different reign of God. Now, just doing eucharist in memory of him, they saw it all, lit by a kindly light that shone from his cross, in the suddenness and surprise of an insight that carries the force of the revelation that was always and will always be lurking in the depths of that profound yet commonplace drama.

They saw Jesus literally giving his life as part of the covenant with God, just for the spread of the reign of God that would bring life and life eternal to others. They saw that the true son of God, the one who was so truly possessed by the Creator Spirit from his very conception that he became himself a life-breathing spirit, was none other than their crucified leader. They saw all of this at these memorial eucharists with such graphic force that they could almost feel the wounds in his hands and side. They suddenly and unforgettably saw how consummate was his dying witness to the Creator's utterly altruistic love. So much so that they would immediately understand if they were amongst those who later heard Paul say that he wanted to know nothing amongst them except Jesus Christ, and him crucified. And in the dark but now gentle light of that death, all that he had tried to tell them during his earthly life, but largely in vain, they now remembered. That is what Luke suggests in summary form when he describes the purpose of the 'forty days' that Jesus 'stayed' with them as 'talking of the reign of God' – the very thing he had spent years doing with them and that, especially when he walked the walk as well as talking the talk, led to his death.

Of course things are somewhat different with us latter day participants in the eucharistic drama, though that need not at all mean that we have any the less access today to the real presence amongst us of the life-breathing Spirit that these earlier ones named their risen Lord. The apostles and others gathered in fear in the upper room saw, eventually, the known features of the crucified man as the one who breathed into them the very spirit of the Creator Spirit. Whereas what we can come to encounter and to feel more directly at each eucharistic meal is the Spirit that shaped the whole life, death and destiny of Jesus. Furthermore, we are likely to see as the human embodiment of that Creator Spirit, not the features distorted by crucifixion of a man we know from history as Jesus of Nazareth, but rather the features of those around us who are true to eucharist in giving of their lives for others, as they receive life from others. And most particularly the features of those truest sons and daughters of the prophet, Jesus, and then of his Father, who give life itself so that the rule of the Father's covenant and kingdom be preserved and promoted. The rule that commits us to advance life always, and never to set it back under the law of evil and death.

Yet that very feature of our latter-day eucharistic access to the reign of God does link us right back to that earliest community of the followers of Jesus in the years immediately after his death. It links us to others who had not known Jesus in the flesh, and who had other circumstances in addition to eucharist in which they could see Jesus raised to the status of son of God in power. It links us to Paul, for instance, who never met Jesus in

this life, and who certainly first saw the risen Lord Jesus in a setting other than eucharist. Paul, as already observed, saw the
risen Lord Jesus in the very process of hounding the followers of
Jesus to prison and death. As Luke put the matter so succinctly:
the voice asking Paul, 'Why do you persecute me?' is asked in
turn, 'Who are you, Lord?' and answers 'I am Jesus whom you
persecute' – the Lord is the crucified Jesus. (Acts 9:4-5) No more
graphic a way of saying that Jesus is seen in the persons and
deeds of his true followers, and never more so than when these
die like Jesus did for the rule of God's steadfast love in the
world. In fact the picture that Luke paints in Acts, of Paul watch-
ing and consenting to the execution of Stephen, might well serve
for all time as a cameo of the kind of dramatic scene in which
anyone else, like Paul, can see Jesus in his followers, and most
especially in his followers-unto-death. The picture painted in
Acts is a kind of double take: Stephen sees Jesus as son of God in
power in the very process of imitating Jesus's death; so Paul sees
Stephen seeing in this way that the crucified one is Lord.

Distance in time then causes no crippling difficulty in encountering the one who was raised to the status of son of God in
power from the moment of his conception, but most definitively
as he breathed his spirit into a dying world at the moment of his
death. Any more, apparently, than nearness in time and space
conferred any particular advantage on those who walked with
him on his public mission, and ran away when his would-be
killers came calling. And people now and in the future would
not know Jesus for what he was and is, if he did appear in some
visionary event in some materialised body that resembled the
one he brought to Calvary. But then neither did his very first disciples when they met him on the road or at the lake, or even
when the scriptures were quoted to prove that the true Christ
had to die as a criminal rather than reign as an earthly king. No,
they knew him in the breaking of bread, in the courage at last to
follow him to death, and in the admiration of those who followed him as wholeheartedly as that. Just as people today and
in the future have the access to his presence through eucharist,
through the life-witness of discipleship, and more generally still
through the on-going activity of the Creator in creation by the
daily experience of which he lived and died, and whose true son

he was. The Creator Spirit who makes the sun and the rainwa-
ter, the twin created and creative sources of life on earth, to serve
equally, limitlessly and quite indiscriminately, the good and the
evil, the just and the unjust.

In summary then, the nature of resurrection in both dimensions of its meaning – the transformation through death of our
present bodily forms to more spiritual forms, and the raising to
the status of sons and daughters of God and the ensuing eternal
shalom – is meant to be the same for all human kind as it is for
Jesus. And both dimensions of resurrection are equally verified
for all, the man Jesus and us, in freeing us from the curse of
death – in the two corresponding dimensions of death: the daily
dying that displaces daily living in a sin-infested history of humanity, and the death that consists in the disintegration of our current material bodies. Where Jesus of Nazareth differs from his
followers is that for his followers Jesus is the unobstructed channel of the Creator Spirit incarnate in him, and as such the earthly
source of their raising to the full status of sons and daughters of
God in eternal *shalom*, 'eternal rest'. So that his followers rightly
revere him, not as an accomplished equal but, in addition to his
being son of God, and the one sent, or Messiah in that sense, as
being also their Lord.

Correspondingly, the stories of the appearances of the risen
Lord are stories of visions, seeings-at-last of what he really was
in life, from cradle to crucifixion, but not in the material body he
then wore. So as the paradigmatic case of Luke's description of
the appearance of the Lord Jesus to Paul on the road to
Damascus so clearly illustrates, these appearances stories are in
fact fictional means of depicting a real dawning of a hitherto unseen truth, and the reception at last of a long resisted message:
light of truth at last dawning, message finally received. From
what concrete empirical and verifiable media did such light
come? From waht was such a message as that of Jesus as God's
true Lord received? For Paul on the road to Damascus it came
from the very people he was hounding to prison and death, as
he walked along the road browsing through his memories of
how they lived and how they carried themselves in the very face
of death; how Stephen for instance died. Without warning, in a
flash Paul found himself thinking the unthinkable: the true way

is the way of these Jesus-freaks? Never! Still he was stopped in his tracks by what his mind now seemed to see. What to do? Something told him he should go and look again at these people, now in more neutral mode: 'I am Jesus whom you persecute.' Blinded to his previous certainties, but with no ready alternative, he went to see some of them. His eyes were opened and he saw that the crucified Jew was after all the truth of his own Jewish faith, the life inspired by that faith, the way to go. And so powerful was this seeing that Paul went from persecutor to apostle.

Luke's other conceit in Acts, the fiction of the forty days that Jesus shared bed and board with an inner circle of close disciples, and most particularly with The Twelve reduced temporarily to eleven, offers yet another answer to the question concerning the concrete experiential circumstances in which the true Lord of the true Way was seen regularly, in a kind of seeing that is as available today as it was back then. Celebrating eucharistic meals as they had done with him during his earthly life, would-be followers were able to see him, with characteristic conduct and demeanour as clear and distinctive as ever, still presiding as the one who served. They heard his voice, as so often before, patiently explaining the critical commitment required if ever their meals were to part-prophesy, part-realise the fullness of the life that God has in store for all. And this real presence of his in the very perceptive centre of their spirits fired their hearts and lighted their paths to paradise, through all intervening trials and through death itself. But it is the strange contrivance that is the original ending of Mark's gospel that provides the most general answer to the question about ordinary, concrete empirical affordances, experiences and events that can facilitate and inspire a true seeing of, and hearing from Jesus of Nazareth, after he is dead and long gone from this lean earth.

Remember the scene: an angel at the empty tomb tells some women that 'Jesus of Nazareth ... has risen, he is not here ... go tell his disciples and Peter that he goes before you to Galilee; there you will see him as he told you.' (Mark 16:6-7) Then let that last phrase to the women trigger a memory of another scene, now from John's gospel – the gospel that sees deeper and explains in more detail all that Mark had written – the scene in which Thomas and Philip ask respectively to be shown the way to the Father, and to be shown the Father. Only for both of them to be told in different words that they were looking all along at what they were still asking to see. (John 14:5-10) In the life and flesh of this Galilean, the uniquely beloved son of God, right now heading for his execution, there was to be seen, as nowhere else in the world, the Father and the Way. There in the life and death of this poor, mortal man was the most complete revelation, in terms most intelligible to all other persons in that peculiar species, of God and of the way back to the paradise that God daily created for them. There would be no matinee, no repeat performance. So the gist of the angel's message is; that is to say, the message is: send the inner eye of your minds back to the life of the Galilean. But this time, listen to what he says, watch what he does, let it dawn on your blinded eyes, let it breach your blocked ears.

Mark then hints that the message never even reached the disciples, because the women were afraid. And on this deadening note the gospel suddenly ends – the nearest thing in ancient literature to the characteristically meaningless ending of a modern existentialist tale or drama. But yet as perfect a rounding-up ending as one could find in the more classical mode, in view of the fact that the whole gospel of Mark seems designed to argue against those who expected and would settle only for glorious, powerful sons of God. For then Mark's refusal to countenance any return appearance of Jesus, which would of course be expected to manifest itself in suitable power and glory, is perhaps due to his gloomy experience of the fact that after the death of Jesus the party still calling for glorious, regal, enforcer messiahs was still well in the majority, as it has remained to this day. And it would depend on gospels like Mark's to call this sad, straying race back to our senses, to the ever-new dawning of the real truth, and the welcoming reception of the true message.

So it is, in any case, that Mark extends the sources of the empirical occasions for the dawning of the truth of God through Jesus of Nazareth, from the true eucharistic meal and the encounter with true followers of Jesus, to the public mission of Jesus that began in Galilee and ended in apparent tragedy in Jerusalem. For in effect what he is saying to his readers through the literary strategy of the strange, abrupt ending of the story of the women is: 'do not look forward from the last sentence of my gospel for some account of a second coming of Jesus who, this time around, will really reveal the reign of God in its true nature to you; for nothing of this nature is ever going to happen; so look rather again at the account I have given you of the life and death of Jesus, his preaching and practice of the true reign of the one true God, together with the persistent and deliberate misconstructions of this matter in which even his closest disciples engaged, because of what I have identified as their lusting after glorious and all-conquering sons of God: and, this time, *see* it.' If Mark had known of the other gospels, he would no doubt have had to put this point more explicitly and more polemically, at the very least in the case of Matthew, as we must later see. But for the moment it suffices to take his point that we have to this day another. and very necessary access to experiences of Jesus in his promotion of the reign of God, and these are captured in the gospel histories of the life and death of Jesus.

Apart altogether from Mark, the indications are that the quester after the historical Jesus should turn back at this point, back from the endings of the gospels to their beginnings, and then back to the rest of the Bible. It was right to seek the first opening onto the meaning of the reign of God as Jesus understood it in the meal imagery, but then the opening metaphor of the meal quickly ran on to join other apparently assorted metaphors, like the metaphor of a divine creator spirit, the metaphor of a son of same, and yet other metaphors of reigns and covenants, of death and resurrection, and swathes of vision literature that provides such fertile soil for metaphors of seeing, hearing, touching, falling, changing direction, and so on, and so on. Like the man who jumped on his horse and proceeded to ride off in all directions. Admittedly, it does seem as if it all hangs together, like an increasing number of ciphers in a code that do mutually confirm and illuminate each other's significance. But it could be that guesses are at work here, some inspired perhaps, but others more forced than inspired. And, to revert now to the metaphor of images out of which the (hi)story of Jesus is woven as ciphers in a great code, what has happened to the first rule of the would-be code cracker, namely, that each cipher must be patiently followed through the whole of the relevant literature that is available, in order to make the decoding of

any one cipher as certain as in the nature of things it can be? Yes;
it is of course necessary to leave this section of the Great Code,
the Bible, the section that begins with the ends of the four
gospels and takes in Acts and the letters, and to go back towards
the beginning of the Bible in order to pick up on these metaphors
and more, and to fill out the connotation of each cipher, or at
least to confirm the connotations that have been suggested from
the section of the Bible investigated so far.

However, as soon as one turns for this backward look, a dis-
turbing question must already arise concerning this picture of
the eucharistic meal as a central means by which the wholly
beneficent reign of the one, true God in this essentially good and
endlessly promising world is both honoured, celebrated, experienced and promoted. And the question is this: this picture of
persistent centrality of the eucharistic meal from the beginnings
of the Jesus movement down to the present day is drawn, after
all, from a short survey of the continuance of the table-compan-
ionship of the Lord from the Last Supper, through the death of
Jesus and into the communities of his followers from then on.
However, the impression that most people have is that the Last
Supper was the first eucharistic meal. It was in fact the meal at
which Jesus instituted the sacrament of the Eucharist, the first
table-fellowship designed by Jesus to introduce prospective followers to the covenant that formalised and instituted the true
reign of God. And if that is the case it must seem odd, to say the
least, that such a means of inculcating and spreading that reign
should only have occurred to Jesus at the very last minute, and
that eucharistic meals should be found not at all over the whole
course of his earthly mission, during which he did what he sig-
nalled he would do, with his opening call to his contemporaries
in Galilee to 'change your hearts, for the reign of God is come
amongst you'. The only way to resolve this conundrum is to go
back once again, first quickly one more time to the Last Supper,
and then more slowly and searchingly back over the gospels and
over the place and time of the public mission of Jesus. Before
going and surveying further back still, in order to trace the cipher of eating and drinking, and in particular its relationship to
the metaphor of the reign of the Creator that is already present
in the Bible's opening pages.

III: *The Public Mission of Jesus: Meals, Healings and the Message*

As you turn the pages of the Bible backwards from the beginning of The Acts of the Apostles, you meet first the end of the gospel of John. And there on that backward journey you meet first, as in the case of the gospel of Luke, those accounts of meals-cum-visionary-appearances that the evangelists locate after the passion and death of Jesus, and the meanings and implications of which have been discussed at some length. So leaf back further again, back before the judgement and execution scene in John. Begin there the backwards quest for meal symbolism acted out in the course of the public mission of Jesus. And you may well find yourself suddenly hesitant. Why? Simply because the last supper as described by John does not appear to contain the characteristics that would qualify it as a eucharistic meal. And it is after all eucharistic meals, with their distinctive formulae of both word and action, and their distinctive meanings and implications for the following of Jesus, and for the nature of sonship and the reign of God, and so on, that provide the primary and proper focus of the search for meal symbolism as a dominant cipher and symbol in the Great Code that is the Bible.

John, it must be remembered, in addition to letting his readers know that the last meal of Jesus with his closest followers is not the Passover meal, quite simply omits the definitive eucharistic formula of taking, blessing, breaking, pouring out and sharing – a formula that the other evangelists and Paul repeat in almost set terms. So, you might conclude at this point, if John does not offer us a clearly recognisable eucharistic meal at the same juncture in the destiny of Jesus at which all the others offer it, it must surely be a waste of time to leaf back through that long gospel in the hope of finding a eucharistic meal somewhere else on its pages.

Better to skip John then. Leaf back instead to the end of Luke, and start this new backwards search for this distinctive meal symbolism from the beginning of Luke's account of the passion and death of Jesus. Then do the same for the remaining two gospels of Mark and Matthew. Stop wasting time on John and get on with it.

It would be a very bad mistake indeed to do so. For in doing so, and especially if you are one of the vast majority of Christians who assume that the Last Supper was the first eucharist ever, you would miss one of the rarest events in the whole quaternity of gospels in the Bible. This rarest of events is what is described in a note to the *Revised Standard Version of The Oxford Annotated Bible* as 'the only miracle recorded in all four gospels'. Some further reflection on the idea of miracle may be required shortly, but for the moment it suffices to name this candidate for the rarest instance of evangelical recording as the feeding of the five thousand with 'five barley loaves and two fish'. (It is recorded in John 6:1-14, Matthew 14:13-21, Mark 6:32-44, Luke 9:10-17.) According to John this meal for guests in the unexpected number of five thousand was served up by Jesus with the help of his disciples 'at the other side of the Sea of Galilee, which is the Sea of Tiberias'. The very place at which what has already been identified above as one of the resurrection eucharistic meals was served, consisting of the same humble fare of barley loaves and fish, the staple diet of the poor. Except that here and now any doubt that might remain as to the eucharistic status of the resurrection meal at the Sea of Tiberias is removed. For the formula used at the resurrection meal might fall a little short of being fully convincing: 'Jesus came and took the bread and gave it to them; and so with the fish.' But in the earlier scene from the public mission of Jesus the eucharistic terminology itself is clearly used: 'Jesus then took the loaves, and when he had given thanks, he distributed them to those who were seated; so also the fish, as much as they wanted.' There can be no remaining doubt about the fact that it is eucharist that the reader must now know is on show in these scenes, all four of them in all four gospels. And if there did remain any residual doubt on this matter, it would certainly be dispersed by the long discussion between Jesus and his disciples about the meaning and implications of this meal of bread and fish served to the five thousand, a discussion that fills the rest of the sixth chapter of John's gospel.

But before coming to that extremely instructive discussion it is worth observing this: that if the feeding of the five thousand in John presents us with eucharist as part of the public mission of Jesus, the same must be said of the feeding of the five thousand in the other three gospels. And then also the stories of the feeding of four thousand from seven loaves that are to be found in Mark and Matthew are also stories of eucharist as part of the public mission of Jesus. For all clearly contain the eucharistic formula. (Mark 8:1-10, Matthew 15:32-39) Furthermore, it is worth observing the immediate responses of the crowd to this meal service, as recorded by John. They said: 'This is indeed the prophet who is to come into the world.' This shows that Jesus was seen as a prophet, a prophet like Moses who brought mana-bread from heaven, and of whom it was said that a prophet like him would come in the last days. This is a view of Jesus that Matthew also held, when he had Jesus bring down the renewed law of God from the mountain, as Moses had done before him (Matthew 5-7) and when, in the little *contretemps* that occurred in Matthew's account of the aftermath of the feeding of the four thousand, Jesus deciphered the symbolism of the bread as a reference to the true teaching he gave about the way to live under the true reign of the one, true God; this in contrast to the 'bread,' the false way and the untruth, that the Pharisees were offering them.

That certainly seems to have been a view of himself as prophet that Jesus himself endorsed as the correct view of his role and status. But John's text on the feeding of the five thousand also alerts us to the fact that fully paid-up members of the kingly messiah movement were there in numbers. And these were interpreting the feeding of the five thousand as a heaven-sent sign that just such a kingly messiah was now amongst them at long last. As Jesus himself put it to them: 'You seek me, not because you saw signs, but because you ate your fill of the loaves.' In other words they were there for the actual bread (and circuses) in a land of plenty, freed from Roman oppression and taxes. And this time Jesus could avert their mistaken ambition for him only by fleeing into the neighbouring hills. 'Perceiving then that they were about to come and take him by force to make him king, Jesus withdrew again to the hills by himself.'

But it is in the ensuing posing and counter-posing of view-point and argument as to what Jesus really and fully meant in his references to 'the bread of life' that a full account and explanation of the eucharistic practice of Jesus emerges from this chapter 6 of John's gospel that began with the tale of the 'sign' of the feeding of the five thousand with five barley loaves and two fishes. And with that there emerges also the best reason for believing that this, together with all other gospel stories of feedings of four or five thousand, is indeed a story of eucharist as Jesus practised it, set now in the context of the public mission of Jesus. As this final development begins to emerge, the interlocutors of Jesus are still in their 'more bread' mood. But this is no longer the 'more bread' mood of those who wanted a land of milk and honey governed by their own king for their very own selves. Rather does it now represent the mood of those who want a sign from Jesus to enable them to believe that he is the Moses-like prophet who was to come. So the 'more bread' theme here means more miraculous feeding. After all, Moses did not produce merely one substantial meal of manna. So if Jesus is to be seen and accepted as the promised prophet like Moses, he should at least be able to keep the food coming, and perhaps with a little more variety and class.

Jesus did not on this occasion respond with his usual rebuff, to the effect that only an evil and adulterous generation would seek a sign, and they would not be given one. Perhaps he had grown tired of doing that, for the peremptory form in which Mark produces that rebuff to sign-seekers was having no effect. (Mark 8:12) And the other form of the rebuff that Matthew records, one which appears to contain an exception clause, 'except the sign of Jonah,' (Matthew 16:4; 12:40-41) might possibly mislead some into thinking of Jonah's three days in the belly of the whale, and linking this with Jesus's resurrection on 'the third day', thereby reducing the raising of Jesus at one and the same time to the reviving of a corpse, and with that to the status of a proof miracle. As a matter of fact, it is plain from the gospel records that Jesus himself would never have condoned, much less initiated, such a use of the Jonah reference. That is obvious to all who know how Jesus himself did regard the raising of our kind from the dead, even in the minimal sense of our being held alive by God through or after the death of our current bodily persons.

The view that Jesus himself held as to the resurrection of all people is implicit in the course of answering a question put to him by a group of Sadducees, who did not believe in resurrection. The case concerned the marital status in the afterlife of a woman who had according to Mosaic law been married to all of seven brothers one after another as each one of them died: to which of the seven would she be wife after resurrection? Jesus responded by pointing out that the kinds of bodily arrangements envisaged in matrimony would not obtain in the resurrection life. 'For when they rise from the dead, they neither marry nor are given in marriage, but are like the angels in heaven.' (Paul's spiritual bodies?)

But then Jesus went further than answering the immediate question. And in doing so he offered his would-be clever questioners a reason for believing in the resurrection of all by God that was no miracle, and certainly not an event for which we could only hope on the grounds of his own resurrection from the dead. He simply said to the Sadducees: 'And as for the dead being raised, have you not read in the book of Moses, in the passage about the bush, how God said to him, "I am the God of Abraham, and the God of Isaac, and the God of Jacob"? He is not the God of the dead, but of the living. You are quite wrong.' (Mark 12:18-27) Resurrection is a normal matter of course, for Jesus as well as for the rest of us, in a world in which the creative source of all existence and life is the eternal God. As Luke's version adds, 'all live to him.' (Luke 20:38)

Indeed, in one of the parables attributed to him in the gospels, Jesus offers another indication to the effect that raising someone from the dead, especially in the reduced format of bringing them back into this life, would not succeed as a proof miracle in any case. In the parable of Dives and Lazarus, the rich man and the poor man, (Luke 16:19-31) the poor man's only hope of staying alive is the scraps that fall from the rich man's overflowing table. But when they die the rich man goes to Hades, and the poor man 'was carried by the angels to Abraham's bosom'. From Hades the rich man makes certain pleas to Abraham, finally asking him to send the poor man back to earth to warn his kin not to behave as he did, lest they too end up in Hades. To which Abraham replied, 'If they do not hear Moses and the prophets, neither will they be convinced if some one should rise from the dead.' And that finally copper-fastens the true meaning and force of the reference to the sign of Jonah, when Matthew concludes the passage on the sign of Jonah by pointing out that the Ninevites changed their hearts as a result of the mission of Jonah the prophet; so that the only sign of the kingdom of God in these more recent times would be the success of the mission of the prophet, Jesus of Nazareth, and a change of heart that brought with it into or amongst the people the true reign of the one true God.

Here, however, Jesus does not respond to these sign-seekers in John 6, spurred on by the recent feeding frenzy, with any form of his usual rebuff. Instead, he takes occasion to extend the metaphor of bread, already a natural metaphor for life because it is such a basic necessity of life, our daily bread. And he extends it gradually to a depth and breadth of revelatory power that is truly breath-taking. He certainly knocked the wind out of those who were listening to him, according to John's story. He reminds them that those who ate the manna in the desert all died. That manna was just food that kept them alive in desert places, and it did nothing more than keep their ancestors alive in these extremities. But then he carries the bread metaphor well beyond Matthew's metaphorical reference to a true teaching for the truest and the best living. He talks of the true bread from heaven that only God can give, and he makes the metaphorical reference more precise again by saying: 'The bread of God is that which comes down from heaven, and gives life to the world.' And a little later Jesus adds the final precision to the truth conveyed by this metaphor: he describes this life that God hands down from heaven as 'eternal life'.

His listeners would already be running rather fast in order to keep up with all of this. But when they say to him, 'Lord give us this bread always,' and he responds rather blithely, 'I am the bread of life,' then the breath of his interlocutors is really taken away and some, when they regain it, can only turn a little caustic under their barely regained breath, so that a certain amount of muttering could be heard. 'The Jews then murmured at him, because he said, "I am the bread which came down from heaven."

They said, "Is this not Jesus, the son of Joseph, whose father and mother we know? How does he now say, 'I have come down from heaven'?"' (So Jesus is the natural son of Joseph then; for this evangelist will have no truck with the strange manoeuvrings of Luke and especially Matthew in their mixum-gatherums of genealogies and virginal conception stories.)

You might expect that the evangelist would have Jesus slow down a bit at this point, if only to allow his listeners to draw breath and catch up. Or maybe at least offer them a little preliminary explanation of a rapidly deepening and broadening range of metaphorical fire-power. Not at all; quite to the contrary. John has Jesus plunge on, extending the metaphorical range of bread by specific reference to the eating of it. And since Jesus has already said, 'I am the bread of life,' he now extends the range of the metaphor to the imagery of the eating of himself. 'I am the living bread which came down from heaven; if anyone eats of this bread, he will live forever; and the bread which I shall give for the life of the world is my flesh.' Needless to say, at this point the muttering escalates into a full-scale dispute: 'How can this man give us his flesh to eat?' To which Jesus, according to John, responds not with an explanation of the truth of the metaphorical expression, but with a more graphic and, to those who do not understand it or do not understand that it is a metaphor, a more offensive version of what is and remains in essence the same metaphor.

'So Jesus said to them, "Truly, truly, I say to you, unless you eat the flesh of the Son of Man and drink his blood, you have no life in you; he who eats my flesh and drinks my blood has eternal life, and I will raise him up at the last day. For my flesh is food indeed, and my blood is drink indeed. He who eats my flesh and drinks my blood abides in me, and I in him. As the living Father sent me, and I live by the Father, so he who eats me will live because of me. This is the bread that came down from heaven, not such as the fathers ate and died; he who eats this bread will live for ever".' And John concludes this purple passage of the preaching of Jesus, as a man would who had just recorded something that he felt would later prove so much more significant than the Gettysburg Address: he concludes with an indication of the time and the place of its first delivery. 'This he said in the synagogue, as he taught at Caper'na-um.'

What then can one make of all of that? What can one say? A number of things. First, that John is using the self-same strong imagery of eating and drinking body and blood that is used in the last supper scenes as painted by the other evangelists: the imagery of the words spoken to those invited to take and eat the bread, 'This is my body', and the imagery of the words spoken to those given the wine to drink, 'This is my blood.' Only John is using this strongest imagery of bread-eating and wine-drinking of a eucharistic meal set in the context of the public mission of Jesus well before his last supper with his disciples, a eucharistic scene that John omits entirely from his account of their last supper together. Therefore, we should be able to apply to this strongest metaphorical imagery used in John's chapter 6, on that symbolic meal, whatever we have already made of the same imagery as found in the last supper accounts by the other evangelists.

Second, that although Jesus, on John's account of the matter, lifts not a single finger, metaphorically speaking, in order to help his general audience in the synagogue at Caper'na-um to see the true and full sense of his awesome, and to some object-ionable imagery, he does in fact later on do something to help his own disciples to avoid and reject a meaning of his metaphor and hence of the symbolism of the meal that anybody at all could well find objectionable. For John observes also of this im-agery of eating flesh and drinking blood that 'many of his disci-ples, when they heard it, said, "This is a hard saying; who can listen to it?" But Jesus, knowing in himself that his disciples murmured at it, said to them, "Do you take offence at this? Then what if you were to see the Son of Man ascending where he was before?"' Now that, if it means anything at all, surely means this: that neither the meal metaphor that Jesus is using, nor the sym-bolism of the eucharistic meal itself which that metaphorical language seeks to express, has anything whatever to do with an actual consumption of an actual human body in any manner, shape or form, with or without soul and 'divinity'. Not even in the form of a body-blood human being who is concealed from ordinary view under the outward appearances of bread and wine by a mysterious process called transubstantiation, and who is then consumed by placing these 'outward appearances' of bread and wine into one's mouth – the 'substance' of the bread and wine having disappeared – and swallowing them. Jesus is clearly telling his own disciples that nothing at all like this is or ever was intended even by the very strongest version of his eating metaphor – else it would not be a metaphor, would it? The full-blooded body, he is saying, that some people seem to think he means to be eaten and its blood to be drunk will one day soon disappear entirely, as he goes back to God. There will then be in this world no more body-blood Jesus of Nazareth, but there will be eucharist, and where even two or three of them are gathered round that eucharistic table, he will be with them. Not any longer 'in the flesh' of this earthly existence, for as Jesus finally puts this misunderstanding to rest: 'It is the spirit that gives life; the flesh is of no avail.'

So that is what the metaphor of the bread of life, with its transposition into the metaphor of eating the flesh and drinking the blood of Jesus, does not mean – what many of his disciples feared it must mean, so much so that they 'drew back and no longer went about with him'. But what then is the metaphor of Jesus as the bread of life truly meant to convey, especially when it is transposed on the same page into the strongest and most graphic images of the 'eat me' category?

Many theologically erudite Christians today, and many to whom the very spelling of the term, transubstantiation, is uncertain would still insist that the earthly and revivified body of Jesus is indeed consumed. They rebut the rebuttal above with the observations that the latter applies only to a gross imagery of chewing flesh and slugging down blood, and that transubstantiation refers to a body (blood, soul and divinity) replacing the substance of bread and the substance of wine by an action that only God can perform, a mystery therefore and no mere magic, and with the addendum that this trans-substance-ing is only ever produced by God, if through the actions and words of a priest, in the case of Jesus of Nazareth and none other.

It may be conceded that the few who are *au fait* with the extremely abstruse and long obsolete medieval metaphysics could use its conceptual structures of substance and accident, essence and species, and so on, to give some meaning to what is meant by these biblical metaphors. But extreme caution would need to be exercised here, and for a number of reasons. First, most people who have transubstantiation explained to them in generally understandable terms, do end up with the crude impression of a human-body-substance concealed under the whiteness, roughness, and so on of bread, and under the redness, liquidity and bouquet of wine. And they believe that the living body of Jesus is therefore really present (miniaturised?) *in* the little white circle from which the essence of bread has disappeared, or *in* the wine that is no longer wine *in* the chalice, *in* the tabernacle, *in* these small spaces thus delineated, while the same body is also *in* heaven. And all of this seems highly improbable, to say the least.

Second, this kind of claim that can be made in the strong, distinctive 'eat me' form of the meal metaphor, is believed to be unique to the case of Jesus. Hence also, in the case of Jesus and only in the case of Jesus can one take the meal metaphor to mean that the body and blood of Jesus really is received in the eucharistic meal of the Christian religion. And transubstantiation theology is then justified as an admittedly poor human attempt to express that result of the eating and drinking in purely logical-conceptual form. However, a sneak preview of the range of meal metaphor in what is often called Old Testament times would be sufficient to show that in fact such uniqueness in the case of Jesus of the strongest and most graphic form of the 'eat me' metaphor cannot be upheld. To take but one example: in a book entitled The Wisdom of Jesus the Son of Sirach we read: 'Those who eat me will hunger for more (of me), and those who drink me will thirst for more.' (Sirach 24:21) Now whoever we may later discover the 'me' in this quote may be, it is certainly not Jesus of Nazareth. So that this strongest and most graphic form of the meal symbolism then is not used uniquely of Jesus. And therefore the transubstantiation explanation, even where it succeeds and is correctly understood, is not an abstruse conceptual account of a one-off mystery accomplished by God for Jesus and his followers only.

How then are we to cash the intended meaning of the metaphor of eating and drinking the flesh and blood of Jesus of Nazareth in terms that will convey the real metaphorical meaning of the matter, but without simply repeating the metaphorical images as such? Jesus, according to John's story, offers a little help towards the answer to this question about this metaphor. He does this immediately after he has mentioned the disappearance of his flesh-and-blood body after his death, in order to prevent his listeners from taking a non-metaphorical meaning from his strong form of the meal metaphor, and then having to swallow the belief that they are actually to consume a live body. He says, 'It is the spirit that gives life, the flesh is of no avail; the words that I have spoken to you are spirit and life.' And that's it. He says no more on the subject, but straightaway goes on to speak of betrayal and especially of Judas the son of Simon Iscariot, another central and characteristic incident that John has imported into this public mission banquet and its aftermath, from its common place in the accounts of a last supper by the other three evangelists. And the best that can be said at this point is that Jesus, according to John, leaves us guessing a bit as to what precisely is conveyed by these few additional, cautionary-explanatory, but still very cryptic phrases.

In other words, if we are to understand this matter as fully as we can, John has Jesus leave us with no option except to carry on with our quest for the dramatic symbolism of the meal and the ensuing forms of the metaphor, in the hope that we will finally understand as much as we are ever likely to know, from this central and constant cipher from the Great Code. But we do not have to await the final harvest of meaning in order to gain some additional light on the cryptic explanatory phrases that Jesus offers here and now. For this can be gained simply by taking these cryptic phrases back into the rest of the admittedly frequently cryptic material of this great eucharistic chapter as a whole, and then aligning them further with memories of similar phrases that we retain from as much of the Bible as we have so far surveyed. The phrase, 'the spirit of life', surely must echo 'the life-giving spirit'. 'The flesh is of no avail' must call up the memory of the story of the composition of the human being in its Hebrew form: a piece of tangible matter into which God, the Creator Spirit, breathes a life of psychic dimensions or a self, *nephesh*; without whose breathing this piece of tangible matter would disintegrate definitively, although the breath (*ruach*, spirit) of God could and would keep the living self alive in some other form. And finally, 'the words that I have spoken to you are spirit and life,' surely recalls the use of the metaphor of bread for the true teaching of the true way, the sense in which Matthew a short while ago used the metaphor.

With all of this in mind then, look back towards the beginning of the discourse which has Jesus use the imagery of eating and drinking human flesh and blood, and the cryptic cautionary phrases with which he ended that same discourse are easily and quickly fleshed out. The key is contained in the saying of Jesus: 'The bread of God is that which comes down from heaven, and gives life to the world.' That which comes down from heaven to give life to the world is the spirit of God, God in the *persona* of Creator Spirit. The Creator Spirit gives existence and life equally to all, and enables all to co-create existence and life and to advance it equally for all, to degrees at present unimaginable. The conscious human creature can breathe in, or drink in that Spirit by eating up or drinking in the words of wisdom of someone who knows the Creator Spirit and the way of co-creative responsibility for all that must be followed by those who would be sons and daughters of that Spirit, for the best outcome for all. That Spirit will then be *in* them and working effectively *through* them.

But there is a more powerful way in which this can happen, more powerful and effective than preaching and taking in and drinking in and being inspired by the wisdom in the teaching. There is the way of a participative, symbolic drama, a drama that begins to realise what it symbolises. The drama consists – no harm to repeat it – in taking bread and wine, or bread and fish, or fish with white wine, or beef with red wine, or a dead dog found on a rubbish dump that a starving group of Koreans once were desperate enough to eat and graced enough to share, or canapés and champagne, or any and every kind of food or drink; taking these as gift from God to all, and in thanksgiving (*eucharein*), receiving them as God's own pledge of life into eternity, eternal life. Then it is not simply the bread, the single cipher now for all food and drink and for all the supports and enhancements of human life, but rather the manner in which the bread is taken, blessed for, broken and shared, that is the true symbol of the Holy Spirit ever creating and advancing the world through the creatures. It is the always shared partaking of the bread that

is the symbol that effects and inspires the ever-renewed beginning of the realisation of that divine project in the lives of every
generation. For by that shared eating, each generation can truly
be said to have taken into their own spirits and into their own
very bodies that will then be given up for it, to have taken in and
to have consciously made into the real presence in their lives
that it always is in any case, the Creator Spirit. 'For the bread of
God is that which comes down from heaven, and gives life to the
world.' That which comes down from heaven and gives life to
the world is the Most High, the Holy Spirit. And those who eat
their daily bread in eucharistic mode are taking into the stomach
and soul of their earthy lives that same Spirit. That is the
metaphor; that is the dramatic symbol, the sacrament; that is
how it works; and that is what it all means.

Ah, yes! the residual sceptic in all of us responds to anything
that sounds like a grand finale, that may be all very well when
the bread and its special breaking stands for God the source and
guarantor of life eternal for all. But is it to be forgotten so soon
that it was a rather handsome five-foot-two-inch, swarthy-
skinned, slightly hook-nosed Israeli who is said by John to have
claimed: 'I am the bread of life ... I have come down from heaven
... For this is the will of my Father, that everyone who sees the
son and believes in him should have eternal life; and I will raise
him up on the last day'? And he did rather keep on about this: 'I
am the living bread which came down from heaven (previously
'the bread of God' was what he said comes down from heaven);
if anyone eats of this bread, he will live forever; and the bread
which I will give for the life of the world is my flesh.' Yet, no.
Nothing untoward is going on here.

In order to realise what is going on, it is necessary only to recall once more something of what the Bible has to say in the
course of the virginal conception stories and the baptism of Jesus
stories and so on, about the Most High, the Holy Spirit coming
on and into Jesus from the very moment of his conception in
Mary's womb, and breathing through or from him, from the
moment of his conception and through his very death. Or indeed the totally similar thing that was said of Jesus at the opening of John's own gospel, except that the Most High is now personified as Divine Word rather than Holy Spirit, and the coming

of this Divine Word into the man, Jesus, is not specified to any event or time in the life and death of Jesus. In these texts the same general truth concerning Jesus is conveyed by two slightly different image-schemes or metaphors. And this is the general truth of the matter: that the Most High through its Divine Word was so 'incarnate' in Jesus, or that Jesus was so fully possessed of the Most High's Holy Spirit, that the whole of the existence and life of Jesus, his very humanity from conception and through death itself, was so moulded by the Most High God operative within him, and with his full human consent, that he was, as far as any human being could be, the perfect human image of his Divine Father as Enlightening Word and Empowering Spirit – the incomparable son of God.

John is merely reflecting this truth of the matter of Jesus in his storytelling technique. And he simultaneously provides his readers, it might be added, with a paradigmatic example of the manner in which a story, a fiction in the metaphorical mould, can convey a truth that would otherwise be dependent for its expression upon the most abstruse of metaphysical concepts and logic. In order to grasp this point, one need only ask this question: in statements such as, 'I am the living bread which came down from heaven; if anyone eats of this bread, he will live forever; and the bread which I shall give for the life of the world is my flesh,' who precisely is speaking here? The answer cannot be simply: the Most High, through its Word and/or Spirit, for that would reduce the human existence of Jesus to the status of a megaphone. But neither can the answer be just: Jesus of Nazareth. For, as his puzzled and alienated listeners in John 6 quite reasonably observe, they know very well where he came from – from the very earthly seed of Joseph and the womb of Mary.

Who then has the principal speaking part in this pivotal chapter of John's gospel? Who could this speaker possibly be, who claims to be the one symbolised by the cipher of bread, who came down from heaven and conveys to eternal life those who would put their faith in him? The answer is obvious: the speaker is the Spirit-possessed, Divine-Word-enfleshed historical human being known as Jesus of Nazareth. But all that this human being is and did, achieved and represents is, first and foremost, due to the presence and action within him, body and soul, of God as Spirit/Word, God as Empowerer/ Enlightener. It is not primarily due to the flesh-and blood human being that emerged from Joseph's seed and Mary's womb, a human being who could be spoken about without reference to the Creator Spirit ever breathing life and life ever more abundant into the world. (This distinction is not new, not introduced at this point of the quest for deciphered meaning now being conducted, in order to get through a particularly difficult part of this quest. On the contrary, it is the same distinction that Paul, for instance, drew between Jesus as son of David according to the flesh, and Jesus as Son of God in power according to the Spirit of holiness by his resurrection from the dead.)

So the 'I,' the first person singular, the speaker, is named primarily from the primary source and instigator of all that Jesus was and is, for that power and source is from eternity, and can be so represented in the metaphorical language of coming down from heaven. But it is yet the one agent, in a unity that is caught by the phrase, Spirit-enfleshed, that speaks and acts, that enlightens and saves those who have faith in that historical phenomenon. (This is not to say that only those who chose to follow, or otherwise find themselves amongst the followers of Jesus of Nazareth, are saved. John himself is anxious to point out, in the very oft-quoted passage of his that introduces the image of the 'Word incarnate,' that the same God in its *persona* as Word is also everywhere and at all times active in creation, and thereby enlightens every one who comes into that creation. John 1:1-14) In what remains perhaps the best, though by no means a perfect orthodox answer to the question, 'Who speaks in John 6 in the metaphorical terms of being the bread of life that comes down from heaven and conveys to eternal life those who eat it?', the Council of Chalcedon forged the language of the one person constituted in the historical individual, Jesus of Nazareth, by that perfect historical union of the divine and the human.

Then the rest of the meaning of that long-tailed metaphor of bread in John's eucharistic discourse is easily accounted for. To eat in eucharistic mode is to eat shared bread or fish and to share drink, and that makes the metaphor a metaphor for swallowing or imbibing the Creator Spirit as source of life equally for all.

Swallowing and imbibing being further extension metaphors for our consenting to have the Spirit that shaped the very being of Jesus, possess us and shape our lives also in the perfect if always finite and creaturely image of the Father Creator who shares out life equally to all. The strong form of the eating metaphor, the imagery of eating Jesus, simply follows on. First, from the former extension metaphor for consenting to have the Holy Spirit possess us and, second and simultaneously, from the experience of those of us who would follow Jesus – the experience that it is in Jesus, one of our own flesh-and-blood, that we most nearly encounter and are possessed and inspired by the Holy Spirit that the first extension of the bread-eating metaphor imagined us swallowing.

Finally, the furthest extension of the metaphor of the bread so that it now stands for the flesh that Jesus (and his followers) may have to give up to death for the life of the world, is also easily deciphered in this context. To eat and drink in the spirit of the God whose sole aim and act it is to pour out life eternally to all, may bring upon us the sometimes fatal hostility of those who bet their lives on accumulating as much assets and corresponding power as they can for themselves, at whatever the expense to others. And if they come to kill us, as they did Jesus and Stephen and so many others, we may never kill instead of helping them to live. We must die, rather, in final fidelity and most powerful witness to the Spirit that moulds our lives in the well-founded hope of eternity. There are further images, of saving for instance, that already seem to want to join the growing cluster of images that extend the core image of bread-eating. But these will emerge more clearly and insistently soon, together with questions such as, saving from what? But for the moment enough has been said about the metaphor and symbolic drama of eucharistic meals set in the context of the public mission of Jesus.

Or has it?

What part in the Public Mission did Eucharistic Meals really play?

All of that deciphering of the feeding of four thousand at one sitting, or of the strikingly unanimous witness of the four gospel writers to the feeding of five thousand at one sitting, and all of the repetitive evidence to the effect that these mass fish suppers were indeed eucharistic meals, all of that is all very well and good as far as it goes. But the conclusion that then seems to be sought from these large scale feedings of four and five thousand men, namely, that eucharistic meals did indeed feature as a crucial part of the public earthly mission of Jesus, and that it is not then the case that a eucharistic meal did not feature at all until the night before his execution, this conclusion is as yet simply 'not proven,' as a Scottish court of law might put it, not acceptable without further ado. For, someone might well argue, these feeding stories are surely to be read as miracle stories, whatever anyone might say about the dismissal from his programme of miracle-signs by Jesus himself. And if that is all the evidence there is for a crucial, and therefore presumably a continuous occurrence of eucharistic meals in the course of the public mission of Jesus, then the case is not only not proven, it is not yet even on the way to being well made.

Two points may be made in answer to this complaint: first, a brief recall of something already said about miracles in the life of Jesus and, second, it must be conceded that a larger search of the gospels is of course necessary in order to establish the status of eucharistic meals in the course of the public mission of Jesus. First, then, as was said in the case of the virginal conception stories, miracles may well have taken place about and by Jesus. But if so they were and are largely if not entirely irrelevant to the extension of the reign of God on earth by the same prophet and Son of God, Jesus of Nazareth. And in addition, they were unnecessary, if not downright harmful to the prospect of people seeing and keeping faith with the true Creator Spirit, through their encounter in life and death with the man named and entitled Jesus the Christ. To tell the story of the conception of a human being, or of a great feeding of thousands, as a miracle story – as a story, that is to say, which is so set up as to suggest that God and only God could do this thing – is a mythic way of telling a deeper truth that lies behind and within every emergence of a daughter or son of God into this world. It is a way of telling the truth that God and only God could bring it about that all of us humans on earth could feed all of us, and feed all other creatures that need food and drink to stay alive, and become increasingly enriched and enhanced by it, and blessed with hope of life unlimited. For only the unlimited and unstinting Source of this whole universe could equip it to support all existence and especially all the life that has evolved within it. By doing this, God also inspires those who have sufficient levels of consciousness to be inspired, to share all with all for the advancement of life for all. Miracle stories, no matter whether they be fact or fiction, are simply a very good way of stating this otherwise obvious truth, a truth that is equally and always available without them in all of creation. For miracles, should they occur as discrete incidents, really consist in bringing into existence and life what at first does not exist or what no longer lives. And that is what divine creation does for the whole of creation in any case. The universe is itself the universal miracle.

But, second, all of that may be all very well and good, yet the question must be asked, does it bring us any closer to the conclusion that the Bible does actually set any eucharistic meals in the actual concrete context of the earthly mission of Jesus, apart from the very last supper? For if the suggestion now is that the feedings of the four and the five thousands were not actual historical miracles produced by Jesus and recorded by the evangelists, when that is what they appear to be on the pages concerned, what else is it about all of these stories of mass-feeding that 'sets them in the concrete context of the public mission of Jesus'? Could these stories not be fitted into the category of 'post-resurrection stories,' as some perceptive readers and exegetes of the Bible call them? By post-resurrection stories is meant stories of features or facets of Jesus the Saviour and his mission of restoring the reign of God that his disciples just did not notice or could not accept until he was raised from the dead and appeared to them. They then saw and accepted what they could not see or accept during his earthly mission, and certainly not at his execution. And then they wrote it up as (if) it was an obvious part of his teaching and practice during that public mission that his inner circle of disciples so intimately shared with him.

True, all very true. And yet it would be a very strange thing indeed if what appears to be a central sacrament for the acknowledgment of Jesus, and a consequent dramatic participation in his promotion of the true reign of the true God, did not play any significant part in his public mission. It would be odd then if the stories of the mass feedings were not mythic ways of portraying a symbolic, sacramental manner of participating in and celebrating this reign of God throughout the public mission of Jesus, and not just at its very earthly end. It would be odd indeed if our evangelical chroniclers of the life of Jesus did not leave us any evidence of a eucharistic meal celebrated by or with Jesus well before that end. But as a matter of fact such evidence does exist, with a story of a meal that is almost as close to the beginning of the public mission of Jesus as the Last Supper is to its end.

The opening Eucharistic Meal of the Public Mission and others celebrated during that Mission

Leaf back then to the beginning of Mark's gospel, reputedly the first of the gospels to be written and with much borrowing later by Matthew and Luke, the other two of the so-called synoptics. John the Baptiser appears first, 'preaching a baptism of repentance for the forgiveness of sins.' (Matthew has John preach, 'Repent, for the kingdom of heaven is at hand.') Jesus arrives at the river Jordan and is baptised by John, and the Spirit descends upon him 'like a dove; and a voice came from heaven, "Thou art my beloved son, with thee I am well pleased".' (Spirit comes, son of God results.) Then after forty days in the wilderness 'tempted by Satan,' and after John was arrested, Jesus appeared in Galilee 'preaching the gospel of God, and saying, "The time is fulfilled, and the kingdom of God is at hand; repent and believe in the gospel".' Then 'passing along by the Sea of Galilee,' part of which was known also as the Sea of Tiberias, he called to his cause four – Simon (later called Peter), Andrew, and the brothers James and John – and went with these to Caper'na-um, where he 'entered the synagogue and taught. All were astonished with the newness and sheer authority of his teaching.' An unclean spirit cried out from a possessed man, 'Have you come to destroy us?' yet was forced to confess, 'I know who you are, the Holy One of God' – an unclean spirit recognising the Holy Spirit that had come upon and remained in Jesus. Jesus exorcised this unclean spirit, and his fame immediately began to spread. In the house of Simon, Jesus healed the latter's mother-in-law of a fever, 'and she served them.' Eucharist already? Not possible to say. The story continues: 'At sundown, they brought to him all who were sick or possessed with demons. And the whole city (it seemed) was gathered about the door. And he healed many who were sick with various diseases.' He tried to get away to 'a lonely place,' but his newly appointed disciples 'found him and said to him, "Every one is searching for you".' So he went public again, 'to the next towns,' and indeed 'throughout all Galilee, preaching in their synagogues and casting out demons,' and healing lepers and all who were in need of healing.

It is at this point of the story of the very earliest stage of the public mission of Jesus that there occur twinned accounts: one an account of yet another healing, and the other an account of a meal. And the reason that these can be called twinned accounts is that, first, both of the events recounted are set in Jesus's own home in Caper'na-um. For the account of the first event, the healing of the paralytic, explains that 'It was reported that he was at home' – the kind of fast spreading report that, as usual, brought out the crowds in such numbers as to quickly take up all the room in the house of Jesus, 'even about the door'. A circumstance that, in turn, drove four men who were carrying a paralytic into the presence of Jesus with the hope of a healing, to the ingenuity of climbing onto the flat roof, hoisting their friend aloft, removing the part of the roof that was immediately above the spot where Jesus was sitting, lowering their friend through the hole, and thereby giving him by far the best chance in that crowded house and quite possibly clamouring crowd, of having his paralysis healed. And then, second, the ensuing account of the meal also has Jesus at home. 'And as he sat at his table in his house, many tax collectors and sinners were sitting with Jesus and his disciples, for there were many who followed him.' A simple and spare picture of the common table-fellowship of Jesus and his disciples that is reminiscent surely of his last supper with them, itself just an ordinary meal as John paints it. And reminiscent therefore also of the resurrection meals at which these same disciples felt his presence as vividly as when he was alive amongst them on this earth. But here, at the beginning of his public mission rather than at its end, the picture painted features the additional factor of having tax collectors, always likely candidates in the popular imagination at least for the category of crooks, together with (other) unspecified sinners.

But the most substantial and almost Siamese-type twinning of these two events, a healing and a meal, derives from their common ownership of one further most striking, if at first sight most puzzling feature: the inextricable intertwining of healing with forgiveness of sins. In the first account, the account of the adventure of the paralytic and his friends, the first response, 'when Jesus saw their faith,' was his word to the paralytic, 'My son, your sins are forgiven.' A point in the narrative at which the reader would half-expect at least one of the hard-pressed but triumphant four friends to say, most respectfully of course, 'Excuse me, sir, but we came about his legs.' Instead the story records the reaction of 'some of the scribes who were sitting there'. Were these the same scribes who, just before the scene of the mother and brothers of Jesus wanting a worried word with him, are recorded as having come 'down from Jerusalem,' here hounding him into his own home? Whether or not, these scribes here accuse Jesus of blasphemy, where on the other occasion they accused him of being possessed by the devil – two accusations that amount to the same thing. And in the present instance the accusation is based on his conceit of being able to forgive sin, something only God can do. In his response, Jesus draws the bonds that combine healing and forgiveness even tighter. 'Which is easier,' Jesus returns their questioning, 'to say to the paralytic, "Your sins are forgiven," or to say, "Rise, take up your pallet and walk?" But that you may know that the son of man has authority on earth to forgive sins' – he said to the paralytic (much to the relief of the latter, no doubt, who must have begun to feel at this stage that his legs were off the agenda, replaced by some obstruse theological debate) – "I say to you, rise, take up your pallet and go home".'

In the account of the second event, the meal, the combination of healing with forgiveness is just as unified and solid, even if it is conveyed much more subtly and indirectly. It is constituted and conveyed by the combination of the image of sinning for those who are here at the meal in need of remedy, with the image of the physician as the one who will supply the remedy required. When the scribes witnessed the composition of the table-fellowship of Jesus (did these people not have the manners to leave the house even when dinner was being served?), and objected to his eating with tax collectors and sinners, Jesus answered, 'Those who are well have no need of a physician, but those who are sick. I came not to call the righteous, but sinners.' And that is why the sinners are guests at the table of Jesus as honoured as the closest of his disciples. But the main point here is that the meal heals sinners, so that healing, or making well again, and forgiveness of sin are here again so closely interwoven in the narrative as to seem interchangeable. And there is one more feature that binds healing and forgiveness of sin, although it occurs only in the healing story here and not in the meal story, namely, Jesus linking forgiveness with the faith of the supplicants: 'and when Jesus saw their faith, he said to the paralytic, "My son, your sins are forgiven".' Whereas, in other stories in the gospels, stories of healings, Jesus links the healing of the sick with their *faith*: 'Your faith has made you whole.'

Now this particular combination of imagery – of meals, healing, forgiving, and of course faith – can be somewhat puzzling, at least on first encountering it. So it would be well for the prospective code-cracker to ask if this kind of table-fellowship of Jesus with disciples and sinners alike, and with some or all of this imagery attached, features any further in the evangelists' account of the public mission of Jesus. Or if it is something of a one-off here, for in that case we may be looking at an accidental combination of images that is due only to the fact that here at the beginning of Mark's account of the public mission of Jesus a particular healing and a particular meal just happened to come, one immediately after the other, as required by the narrative. And so images that otherwise have their separate connotations in different contexts, just got a little mixed up, due to the brevity of the narrative.

If one were reading Luke instead of Mark, the answer to the question would be found no later than the seventh chapter. There one finds a generalisation, followed by an account of a meal that reveals striking similarities with the one just seen in Mark. The generalisation echoes the scribes' complaint about the invitees to a meal with Jesus at the beginning of Mark. Jesus himself is the speaker in Luke and he is complaining about the constant complaints he hears from certain people: 'The son of man came eating and drinking, and you say, "Behold, a glutton and a drunkard, a friend of tax collectors and sinners".' So his table-fellowship with the sinners, or presumed sinners, was a regular and noticeable feature of the public mission of Jesus, and as regularly regretted by members of the Jewish faith? It certainly seems so. In fact an account of a particular meal that follows this complaint against the complainers in this passage from Luke's gospel secures this conclusion.

This meal takes place, according to Luke, not at the home of Jesus or at his table, but at the table of a Pharisee, a member of the party of strict observance of the Mosaic Law. The meal is dramatically interrupted by the uninvited entry of a woman who is a sinner. (Were these sinners now turning up to table with Jesus, even when the table concerned was not presided over by Jesus? No wonder people complained. Social etiquette was gone to the devil, religious and moral sensitivities trampled on, and who knew which of these outcomes was the worse?) She proceeded then apparently to serve the needs of Jesus with some of the forms of hospitality that a guest at any table could expect, over and above the food and drink that was shared. She replaced with her tears the water customarily provided in order to wash before meals, and dried him off with her hair. She gave him the formal kiss of love that all guests could expect to receive, and she anointed him with the oils that were offered as a matter of course for the personal grooming of the diners. But she watered, dried, kissed and anointed only the feet of Jesus – remember the last supper according to John, and Jesus himself washing feet – for she did not feel worthy to touch any other part of his person.

The Pharisee took umbrage immediately, as scribes and others had done before: Jesus must surely not know that a sinner had blustered so rudely into their table-fellowship, for otherwise he should surely have rebuffed her and her effort at offering him those precious tokens of hospitality, even though the Pharisee had not himself offered any of them to Jesus on this occasion. But Jesus reacted in precisely the same way as he had in Mark's story, and with the same combination of imagery: 'He said to the woman, "Your sins are forgiven".' And when those at the table interjected with a query as to who this fellow thought he was – forgiving sins, indeed! – Jesus simply added, speaking always to the woman, "Your faith has saved you; go in peace (*shalom*)." For she had shared the good things of God's creation, the water and the oil and the love with which God had blessed her heart, and made eucharist of the meal for the man whose meals were all of them eucharists. (Luke 7:34-50) The host, the Pharisee, by contrast, seemed to have done all he could to botch the natural eucharistic sacramentality of the meal, short of refusing food and drink to the one he had invited to his table.

There are other generalisations in the gospels, and other stories of individual meals, and between them they amply confirm the impression that meals as Jesus understood and participated in them, either as host or guest, were indeed a regular and quite noticeable feature of his public mission. One of these generalisations could be seen when Jesus defends what people commented rather adversely upon, his apparent enthusiasm for table-fellowship while on his mission: 'Can the wedding guests fast while the bridegroom is with them?' he asks, hinting at the Creator Spirit within him and the metaphor of that Holy Spirit taking Israel as bride, until she was seduced into adultery with other gods. (Mark 2:19) Or in Luke again: 'Now the tax collectors and sinners were all drawing near to him. And the Pharisees and the scribes murmured, saying, "This man receives sinners and eats with them".' (Luke 15:1-2). Or, again in Luke, 'The son of man has come eating and drinking, and you say, "Behold, a glutton and a drunkard, a friend of tax collectors and sinners".' (Luke 7:34)

And then there is a parable that Luke inserts in a section of his gospel that reads like a less complete version of Matthew's ethos of the reign of God as handed down from the mythical mountain. The parable appears to have been a favourite vehicle for Jesus to communicate the nature and features of the kingdom of God that with him was coming once more amongst them: how it would grow from small and apparently insignificant beginnings (the parable of the mustard seed), how it would fare with different types of people (the parable of the seed-sower), how nevertheless it would benefit all equally (the parable of the labourers in the vinyard), how it is therefore a treasure so great that it is worth sacrificing everything for it (the parable of the treasure in a field), how God will let no sin stand in the way of bestowing its beneficence on all, sinner and righteous alike (the parable of the prodigal son), but how it does require of us at least an opening of our doors to it, a waiting upon it, that in itself represents the *metanoia*, the change of heart that Jesus asked for specifically when he first announced his public mission of bringing the reign of God amongst them again, and now in its perfect form. This last is the parable that Luke tells (12:35-40) and it goes like this: The master of a house is away at a marriage feast (the prime symbol of the reign of God in full effect), and when he comes to the house he does indeed find his faithful servants waiting for him, to open the door to him.

Then in the extension to the parable itself, Jesus expands on the duty of the steward in particular to give the other servants of the household their portions of food and drink at the proper times. And if that managing servant, when his master comes home, is found instead to have been gorging himself and getting drunk, depriving the other servants and beating them, he will reap the penal consequences of his actions. As Luke has Jesus generalising in conclusion: the one who comes to bring on the kingdom of God appears at times to be bringing, not *shalom*, but the sword of hostility and mutual destruction to set the most intimately related of human beings against each other. But this is all really due to the lack of waiting upon and being prepared for a change of heart, insisting instead on a violent opposition to the reign of God. For if the preparatory change of heart were forthcoming – and here is the relevance of this parable at this point to the investigation of the presentation of the reign of God during the public mission of Jesus – then, as the parable puts it, the master on coming and finding the faithful servants waiting to open the door to him 'will tie on his apron and have them sit at table, and he will come and serve them'. The very scene painted by Luke at the last supper of Jesus with his disciples, so that a clearer generalisation of the centrality of the table-fellowship of the Lord, as at once dramatised and operative symbol of the reign of God coming through the public mission of Jesus, could scarcely be imagined.

For one other example of an individual story of a mission meal, take the example of little Zacchae'us, a tax collector and so, presumably, a sinner. A nosey parker who seemed to want no more than a gawk at Jesus, the man that so many were talking about. But because of his diminutive stature Zacchae'us had to climb up a sycamore tree in order to see Jesus over the heads of the crowds that habitually surrounded him. To his surprise Jesus noticed him and called to him: 'Zacchae'us, come down, for I must stay at your house today.' The crowd, at this stage almost like a Greek chorus in the familiar caste of characters in these stories, all murmured: 'He has gone in to be the guest of a man who is a sinner.' But then Zacchae'us interrupted the hospitality he was offering Jesus to announce: 'Behold, Lord, the half of my goods I give to the poor; and if I have defrauded any one of anything, I restore it fourfold.' And Jesus said to him, 'Today salvation (*soteria, salus*) has come to this house ... for the son of man came to seek and save (*sosai, salvum facere*) the lost.' (Luke 19:1-10) Ignore for a moment the Greek and Latin terms inserted here – they will be helpful shortly to the on-going task of cracking this biblical code. Simply notice that Zacchae'us, while sharing hospitality with Jesus in his house and at his table, felt the effects of the eucharistic meaning and spirit of that hospitality, as evidenced by the fact that he resolved immediately to share the supports of life with those who needed them most, the poor, and in particular with any whose livelihoods he may have stolen.

That is surely more than enough to show that the institution of the eucharistic meal by Jesus did not await his last supper on this earth. Quite to the contrary, the prominence of table-fellowship as part of his public mission is constantly acknowledged, even by those who either misunderstand it as a penchant for the sybaritic life, or who see perfectly well what it is meant to achieve, and deeply resent this, this time on properly religious and moral, rather than lifestyle grounds. And now one can see also that the stories of feeding the multitudes, already clearly seen to be eucharistic stories, are cast in the form of multitude-feeding precisely in order to serve as generalisations of the kind of sacramental meals that were, are and will be central to the mission of Jesus and his followers in their efforts to spread the reign of God. In these stories of the four thousand and the five thousand, this eating, the feeding, in the spirit and style of simultaneous gratitude and sharing, is itself a dramatic, symbolic and at the same time an active participation in the reign of God, a sacrament, in short, a symbol or sign that participates in and thereby advertises and promotes the reality that it symbolises.

This becomes even clearer if one considers John's story of the wedding feast at Cana, for that also is a eucharistic story, every bit as much as the stories of the feeding of the four and the five thousand. As Jesus had produced the bread for the multitude-feeding stories, so he produced the wine for the wedding guests at Cana, and it was the best wine they had ever known. And John's comment is: 'This, the first of his signs, Jesus did at Cana in Galilee, and manifested his glory; and his disciples believed in him.' 'His glory' is biblical imagery for the active presence of the Most High, the Holy Spirit, the Glory of the Lord, in him. And the second sign, according to John, also occurred at Cana, when an official came from Caper'na-um to see Jesus and to ask him to heal his son who was at the point of death. The official believed, and his son was saved from death. A meal and a miracle, both in themselves signs that already make real part of what they signify, namely, the God who reigns purely by creating life, healing it when it is diminished, and furthering it eternally, and who does this also through those creatures that can act in this respect as God does. (John 2:1-11; 4:46-54)

So John could as easily have added to the bare description of the wine-making at the wedding feast the kind of explanation of eucharist that he later added to the feeding of the five thousand. He could have explained that it was not the wine as such, but rather the gift-nature and the sharing of it as part of the feast that made it a sacrament of the reign of God in their midst. He could have gone further and, following the imagery of the bread, said that he was the living wine that came down from heaven. Like he said to the Samaritan woman he met at a well that 'he would have given you living water,' and that 'the water that I shall give will become a spring of water welling up to eternal life.' (John 4:1-41) But he didn't; he simply told us it was the first sign that Jesus offered, and left us to deduce the rest. To deduce that here at the wedding feast, as in all of the other meal sacraments, it is the style of provision and consumption of those necessary supports and then symbols of life, that becomes the symbol of the eternal presence of the life-giving Spirit reigning in the world principally through the changed hearts and minds of women and men.

'The kingdom of God is not coming with signs to be observed,' so Jesus told some Pharisees who asked when it would come, 'nor will they say, "Lo, here it is!" or "There!" for behold the kingdom of God is in the midst of you (or within you).' (Luke 17:20-21) The same thing that Jesus said in his reference to the sign of Jonah: the coming of the true prophet of the end time, Jesus himself, and his success in bringing people under the true reign of the true God, was the only sign that would be given. As Nietzsche, a better reader of the Bible than most of his Christian critics, put it: '(the good news or gospel of Jesus) does not prove itself by miracles or rewards and promises ... it is every moment its own miracle, its own reward, its own proof, its own kingdom of God.' It was Christianity, the religion as it had developed up to his time, that Nietzsche criticised so relentlessly, not Jesus. And in that he may have been in part a prophet. He certainly would not have been the first flawed prophet, or the last, to contrast the cult and the alleged divine rules by which a people lived, with the faith of a founder they professed to follow.

The scattered stories and comments about signs in the gospels show that sign-talk takes on different meanings for different groups. When John calls the wedding feast at Cana a sign that revealed the active presence of the Glory in Jesus, his description is true and fully accurate in two senses. First, the feast, and in particular the wedding feast, was a traditional metaphor for life lived to the fullest under God's gracious rule, often pictured as the life of the end-time or the new age that was to come. And the fact that the eschatological feast, as theologians in need of big words often call it, is also pictured as a wedding feast adds a further layer of significance to the imagery. For the wedding feast sign affords the added significance of Israel at last committed to fidelity as the bride of the true God, instead of whoring after false gods as she had so often done, and ending up in adultery – an adulterous generation. And second, a feast celebrated in gratitude and in the grace to all that gratitude inspires, is a natural sacrament, a drama-type sign (the play's the thing) that enables participants to experience the *shalom* it signifies. It enables them simultaneously to experience through Jesus the Spirit that inspires them to make every meal a eucharist: taking, blessing for, breaking-pouring out, sharing; an experience that then requires the strongest form of meal-imagery, the imagery of Jesus as the living bread and wine from heaven that they consume and share.

But the same sign-talk that some understood in this correct sense, others insisted in understanding in quite a different sense. These did not understand whatever was going on, either in these eucharistic meals or in the healings, as natural things, albeit as natural things done by human beings under the everyday inspiration and power of the eternal life-giving Spirit. No, what these others wanted to see, what they expected to see and therefore saw, in both the meals and in the healings of prophets like Moses and Jesus, was an imperious irruption into the natural course of events of the raw omnipotence of a god whose actions could not be curtailed by anything other than his power. The actions, in short, of a god made in the very image and likeness of the greedy, self-securing power mongers that so many of us human beings so often want to be; a god that coerced belief in himself by such arbitrary acts of power, the first of which was pictured as an original act of creation that simply put the whole thing there in the first instance, like it or lump it. A god who favoured certain people and not others with such displays of raw power, and a god, correspondingly, who dictated what his people, favoured in such ways, should do to acknowledge him, by laying down laws that were to be obeyed simply because he said so. A god who would then give them victory when they made war to occupy other people's lands, but would equally demand blood sacrifice of them, either for purposes of being assured of their loyalty and sense of utter dependence on him, or for purposes of paying the penalty that his justice demanded for any offences against him of which they might occasionally, even inadvertently, be found guilty.

It was the signs of such a god that these critics of Jesus sought and saw, despite anything Jesus could say or do to persuade them otherwise – to persuade them of the eternal coming of the reign of God with the signs only of the true God's continuous creation of the natural world. An act of creation conceived, not in the form of shouting it into existence, but in the manner of ever creatively forming and fashioning it in such a way as to advance always and into eternity all of existence and life. And to persuade them also that the corresponding and co-operative signs of the coming of the reign of the true God amongst them, consisted further in the lives of those who acted naturally and creatively with that God's powerful, loving and ever-beneficent Spirit in them, to the common and universal end of perfect *shalom*. Jesus did all he could, in short, to persuade those who sought the coercive signs of a coercive idol, that all of this natural and true coming of the true reign of the one, true God, the natural, human word and deed, life and death of Jesus, and of all who would follow him, wittingly or unwittingly, was its own miracle – and no other kind of miracle was either necessary or welcome.

A more attentive reading of the multitude-feeding stories, and indeed of the Cana wedding feast story, would secure that conclusion concerning different kinds of miracles. For such a reading should cleanse the perception of those of us whose eyes have been habitually blinded by prattle about 'the miracles of the multiplication of the loaves and fishes' featuring, with many, many other such miracles, as apodictic proofs that God exists, that Jesus was divine, that his claims were all true, and so on, and so on. For the one thing that these stories do not say is that Jesus multiplied loaves or fishes, or anything else for that matter. What he did instead was to ask his disciples to find out just how much food the people had, as you would, when it is getting late and they might go hungry home to their beds. And when the answer came back that five thousand men appeared to have only five loaves and two fishes between the lot of them, Jesus did not roll up his sleeves and perform a miracle of divine power of creation out of nothing to multiply the miserable amount of food on offer. What did he do, then? He took the food that was on offer and made a eucharistic meal out of it: 'taking the five loaves and the two fishes – these and only these – he looked up to heaven (to the throne of his Father who to this day supplies this lean earth with more than enough food for everyone), and blessed, and broke the loaves, and gave them to the disciples to set before the people.' And the experience and inspiration of that natural sacrament, the experience of the Creator Spirit coursing through the persons who make eucharist of any or all of their meals, this in itself saw to it that no one went hungry, much less starved to death, as would happen over all of this earth – for this is an exemplary story – if only the reign of God were spread.

And in the case of the wedding feast at Cana? A comparison with the story of the sinner-woman who crashed the Pharisee's dinner party can be instructive here. She had nothing to do eucharist with except some materials for anointing, but she used her tears to offer to Jesus the water to cleanse himself for the meal that he would then be offered. So, even if only water is offered in the eucharistic spirit – a cup of cold water, Jesus said elsewhere, given in my name (as son of the Creator Spirit) – then the spirit of eucharist will see to it that no one will ever again go short of anything, and every wedding will have the best of wine. And people may notice in this story also that the one thing the reader is never specifically told is that Jesus changed the water into wine. He simply tells the servants to fill jars with water and take it to the steward of the feast, and the steward tasted the water 'now become wine'. How a eucharistic gesture with water metamorphoses into a eucharistic sharing of the best of wine is not spelt out. But does it need to be?

It is depressingly obvious then that sign-talk, from the time of Jesus to the present day, takes on two different and indeed conflicting meanings, despite anything that Jesus could do about it, by telling those who had frankly idolatrous ideas on the matter that none of the signs they lusted after would ever be forthcoming. As he tried to persuade them instead to see and believe that the only sign of the coming of the reign of the true God would be their experience of that reign in the ordinary human lives of Jesus and his followers, together with the ultimate fruits of that reign in final *shalom*. The signs of the kingdom of God would be the preaching of it, like Jonah; the ordinary meals dramatised as eucharistic meals; the consequent living for others, particularly as we must shortly see in the healing of their ills; and above all the willingness to die for this rule of God when its opponents, driven by their idolatrous lust for possessions and power, put those who did try to live by it to the ultimate test. It is depressingly obvious that by far the predominant part of the people that Jesus preached to and ate with and healed, from the farthest edges of the crowds who came to hear and be healed, to the innermost group of his closest and constant disciples, whenever there was talk of signs of the reign of God that Jesus said he came to promote, heard and understood that talk in terms of conquest and reign like David's, accompanied by coercive signs that shared in the nature of that kind of overpowering conquest and reign.

Even as Jesus at last entered Jerusalem for his own ultimate testing and certain death, the great crowds who met and accompanied him were still crying out, 'Hosanna! Blessed is he who comes in the name of the Lord! Blessed is the kingdom of our father David that is coming! Hosanna in the highest!' (Mark 11: 9-10) Those who composed that enthusiastic if deluded crowd must never have heard anything like the dismissal of the title, son of David, that Jesus himself uttered as a piece of exegesis: 'How can the scribes say that the Christ is the son of David? David himself, inspired by the Holy Spirit, declared, "The Lord said to my Lord, sit at my right hand, till I put thy enemies under thy feet." David himself calls him (the Christ) Lord; so how is he his son?' (Mark 12:35-37) Or if some had heard this exegetical undermining by Jesus himself of his sonship of David, they either failed to heed it, or conveniently forgot it again. All the more reason why exegetes of the Bible ever since should not similarly mistake the manner in which meals, and healings, and other significant events in the life, death and destiny of Jesus, are signs of the kingdom, by the age-old and deadly mistake of reading them through the lenses of the idolatry of power.

The Mission Table-Fellowship and the Healing Stories

At this point a suspicion may well raise its awkward head: could it be that the reading and deciphering so far has begun to run too far and too fast ahead of itself? For before making some attempt to decipher the stories of healings so abundantly represented in the gospels, we seem to have already decided on the kind of power that is connected with the signs that Jesus offered and, therefore, on the kind of power that was exercised by Jesus himself as son of God. This despite the fact that the healing ministry of Jesus, at first blush, seems to offer evidence of a much greater and more consistent instance of the miraculous than might ever be detected in the meal-ministry, with the resultant suspicion that the kind of coercive power so righteously rejected in the former ministry, may prove much more difficult to remove from the scenes of the latter, the healing ministry. That suspicion is increased when the matter of forgiveness of sin, as already noted, seems to attach itself to meal ministry and healing ministry alike. For the forgiveness of sin does seem to be quintessentially a power-process, in which the Creator as King of the universe lays down the laws for the behaviour of human creatures; the same Creator as Judge tries these same creatures on charges of offences committed, and punishes them severely if they are found guilty and unrepentant – surely a paradigmatic instance of coercive power.

The best way to respond to all of these suspicions is, of course, to bring the healing stories into the prominence in reading and deciphering that the gospels as well as the Acts of the Apostles and other Bible accounts require by reason of their very abundance. And the best and briefest way to begin to do this is to look for a moment more at that initially puzzling feature, already mentioned, that these mission eucharists when combined with mission healings exhibit. This feature consists in the double binding together, first, of healing stories with meal stories, and then, within each of these sets of stories in turn, binding together the images of healing with the images of forgiving sin or saving from sin. That double binding, it has already been noticed, is found in the twin stories at the beginning of Mark's gospel when a paralytic who comes to be healed is told that his sins are forgiven, followed by a remark that seems to confer some kind of equivalence of forgiveness and healing ('Which is easier? So I will heal him in front of your very eyes, and thereby show that I can forgive him'). And in the meal story that follows immediately after this healing story in Mark, Jesus through a meaning and efficacy of the meal that does not in the least escape his enemies, deals with sinners as a physician, a healer.

Now it might seem, from a comparison of two stories from the stock of meal and healing stories in the gospels, that one writer at least noticed a possibility for confusion in these double bindings, and decided to do something about it. Luke, for he is the one writer, according to the translation in the *Revised Standard Version of the Oxford Annotated Bible*, has the sinner woman who crashed the Pharisee's dinner party and turned the meal into eucharist, told by Jesus: 'Your faith has saved you; go in peace.' An educated Christian reader, even moderately versed in the theology of her church, would see that reference to being saved as a cipher for receiving God's forgiveness for sin as a result of Jesus dying on Calvary to save the sinners of the world. Whereas in healing stories generally what Jesus is reported as saying is: 'Your faith has made you well; go in peace.' Precisely the formula one would expect to end a healing story. And this is then like a set formula placed on the lips of Jesus after various healings. (Mark 5:34; 10:52; Matthew 9:22) But the problem of accepting that distinction between 'made you well' (for healings) and 'saved you' (for sinners) as a clarification of what might otherwise seem a confusing biblical manner of speaking that Luke tried to clear up is this. The distinction exists only in the English translations. In the original Greek and in the Latin versions of the gospels, both in Luke's texts and in the other two synoptics, the terminology is precisely the same for the treatment by Jesus of the sinners and the unwell alike. And this is where a little dictionary work is necessary in order to decipher the full and precise meaning and significance of this common and crucial imagery.

The phrase that is used by Jesus in saying his farewell to sinners and sick alike, in Luke as in the other gospels, and in Latin first, is always the same: *fides tua te salvam fecit*, your faith has made you well. The key phrase here is *salvam facere*. From the verb, *salveo*, which means 'I am well,' 'I am in good health,' or the parting phrase, *salve*, which means 'fare well', the precise counterpart of 'go in peace,' a phrase that often follows 'your faith has made you well.' For as peace, *shalom*, means more than the absence of strife and violence, since it means life prospering and advancing towards limitless prospects, so 'fare well' also means 'I wish for you that you go on your life's journey in such a way that it takes you forward to well-being unthreatened and without limit.' *Salvus* means 'well, safe and sound'; *salus* means 'health, welfare, safety'. Jesus, according to John, is the one through whom the whole world is made well or whole (*salvetur*); so he is the saviour of the world (*salvator mundi*). (John 3:17) Of course, since *salvus* can mean 'safe,' the verb can mean 'to make safe,' 'to save,' or 'to be saved'. But this in turn will refer to such service to well-being as consists in freeing one from some condition, such as slavery for example, that is in itself life-diminishing, life-threatening, so that well-being is still the dominant significance of the word-set that is represented in English by the term, salvation. The same results would be achieved by dictionary work on the corresponding gospel phrases in Greek, *soter* and *soteria*, saviour and salvation. Salvation, from *salus/salveo*, refers then primarily to well-being, restored or promoted.

So when the 'making well' meaning of the salvation terminology is applied to the sinner and to her sin, as well as to the sick and the suffering, and even when that 'making well' meaning is expressed by the word 'save' in English, it must not be taken to convey some forensic content of meaning, as in the case of someone who has had a penalty paid for their offences and can then be forgiven as a declaration of pardon by a judge. A perfect example of this forensic understanding of the forgiving of sin is found in the Roman Catholic practice of the sacrament of penance. You appear before a priest in what is referred to as a tribunal of penance, confess your evil-doing, profess your sorrow and contrition, declare as your purpose the amendment of your sinful ways, receive your penitential sentence and then, and only then hear the sentence of absolution from the legal bond that binds you to the status of evil-doer with all of the painful and potentially eternal consequences that is thought to be entailed.

Nothing even vaguely like that, however, is intended by this gospel language that applies to the sin and the sinner the same 'making well', the same salvation language that is also applied to straightforward making well by healing whatever makes people ill in any of the multitudinous manners, whether natural or malicious, in which their lives may be ill-experienced, when they should be enjoying a life-long 'faring well'. Again a little dictionary work would be enough to persuade readers of the gospels of this fact. The Latin word which lies behind the word 'forgiven,' as in 'your sins are forgiven' is *remittuntur*. *Remissio* means remission, as in abatement; *remitto* means to send back, to abate, to relieve, as in sending sin into remission, like cancer can be sent into or kept in remission by the proper healing or making-well process. A cognate image is used by John the Baptiser when he says that Jesus takes away, *tollit*, the sins of the world. Once again just like cancer, for example, instead of being sent into remission by radiation treatment or chemotherapy, can be surgically cut out, taken away completely, one always hopes, so as to leave the person well again. (John 1:19)

Correspondingly, when Jesus at the very opening of his mission asks people to repent, it is the original Greek text of the gospels in this case that makes clearest what he requires of them. And again it is not a forensic declaration of contrition for the sins we have committed that we are asked for as a condition, together with the penalty, or dues to society, upon which release from the condition of guilt or sin may follow. No; the Greek word here is *metanoia*, a change of heart that inspires a change of life. That is what is required when Jesus asks people to repent: a change from a life lived in destruction of self and others, to a life that, like the life of God, is spent in sharing with others all the supports and enhancements of life, and life itself, to the mutual enrichment of all, and the walking together to eternal *shalom*.

And that is precisely the experience of any meal that is partaken in truly eucharistic spirit. The taking and sharing of food and drink, the necessities of life and one of the most pleasurable enjoyments of life, and therefore the dramatic symbols of life fulfilled, in gratitude to the eternal God; that in itself at one and the same time sends into remission the selfish greed for all of the supports and enhancements of life and the ensuing self-inflicted illnesses and damages from which we suffer, and sets us positively on the road to *shalom*. For the illnesses from which we suffer take the form simultaneously of an evil spirit within us and the self-destruction and the destruction of the lives of others that this evil spirit can and does wreak. And both can begin to be cured or cut out by the inspirational spirit of the eucharistic meal, as participants in that sacramental drama begin already to feel the life-enhancing prospects of taking life and all of its supports and enhancements as gift and sharing them with all, instead of trying to appropriate as much as possible of life and its supports and enhancements for oneself, with the violence that, directly or indirectly, must then be visited on others. Just as the effects of an evil spirit, the destruction of self and others that it

entails could be cured or taken away by the healing ministry of
Jesus.

So then, to the healing ministry. And the first thing that must
surely strike the reader and would-be decipherer of this great
code is a certain contrast with the meal or, better put, the eucharistic ministry. The contrast consists essentially in this:
whereas in the case for the eucharistic ministry playing a substantial part in the public mission of Jesus one has to analyse and
argue quite a lot, in the case of the healing ministry there is not
the slightest need to do anything like that. Not only is there
evidence on practically every page of the gospels to prove that
Jesus did during his public mission engage in healing people,
there is so much evidence and it accumulates so steadily
throughout, that the question is bound to arise in the mind of the
reader, did he ever do anything else?

Flip through the pages of Mark once more, and notice this
time around the number of healing stories that pile up from the
coming out of Jesus at John's baptism until his arrival in
Jerusalem for the final, and for him fatal showdown. And then
notice something even more significant still in this respect.
Notice the number of generalisations about the overwhelming
demands made on the ministry of Jesus by the people's calls for
healing and his response. The best example of such generalisation is found in Mark: 'And when they had crossed over (from
the scene of the eucharist of the five thousand), they came to
land at Gennes'aret, and moored on the shore. And when they
got out of the boat, immediately the people recognised him, and
ran about the whole neighbourhood and began to bring sick
people on their pallets to any place where they heard he was.
And wherever he came, in villages, cities or country, they laid
the sick in the market places, and besought him that they might
touch even the fringe of his garment; and as many as touched it
were made well (*salvi fiebant*, salvation).' (Mark 6: 53-56)

There is another kind of generalisation with respect to this
matter of healing. It takes the form of the more precise complaint that Jesus was so pressed upon by constant crowds seeking salving, that he had indeed no time for anything else. And it
is quite intriguing for the amateur cracker of codes to notice how
the 'anything else he had no time for' is more than once specified.

You would think it would be preaching he would complain that he lacked the time to pursue. But apparently not; he seemed to get through quite a bit of preaching. After all, the word of the reign of God qualified also for the metaphor of living, that is to say, life-giving bread. No, it was lack of time for eating that formed a repeated cause for complaint. At the scene outside his home, when his mother and brothers came to take him away, 'The crowd came together again, so that they could not even eat.' And again, when the twelve returned from the mission on which Jesus had sent them with authority over the unclean spirits, and told Jesus how they had 'cast out many demons, and anointed with oil many who were sick and healed them,' the remark is repeated, 'Many were coming and going, and they had no leisure even to eat.' And that remark is in this instance followed by the story of the feeding of the five thousand. (Mark 3:20; 6:7-13, 30-44) So that it almost seems as if the thing they particularly regretted not having time for was eating together, that is to say, eucharist. What should be co-operative processes in the salving of the people, were in fact in the unhappy state that one was blocking the opportunities for the other.

However that may be, it is necessary to note that casting out demons or unclean spirits and healing are not to be thought of as two separate categories of the deeds that characterised the public mission of Jesus – one a category of healing, and the other a category of, well, casting out demons. These are, rather, two separable kinds or classes that exist within the one category of healing. For the image of demon or unclean spirit in ancient myth was meant to indicate a certain spirit within a person that had taken over that person's life in such a way as to make her destructive of herself or of others, or of both self and others. The RSV Bible glosses 'unclean spirits' as 'malign, destructive forces'. So there really is no point in asking: do demons really exist? Much less in castigating these writers of earlier times for superstitious belief in malicious but invisible entities that modern science could never condone. It is the actual spirit that is within every person, and that in these cases is palpably malign to self and others, and therefore deemed to have been turned demonic (the *yeser 'a ra*, in the Hebrew story of the make-up of the human being), and that must be 'taken out,' like a surgeon takes out a life-threatening cancerous growth.

It is a real spirit within a human being. It does exist. It is the kind of spirit in any human being that Jesus implies in his answer to some Pharisees who had complained that his disciples broke the law by eating with unwashed hands. It is not what enters a man through his fleshly body that defiles a man, Jesus explains, for whatever is unclean in that way is evacuated through similar bodily channels. It is what comes from within a man, from the inner man, from the heart or spirit of a man, it is this that makes a man unclean: covetousness of the possessions or wives of others, envy, licentiousness, theft of other people's necessities and enhancements of life or their livelihoods, or killing people for this or for other purposes, or prideful lusting after such power as would entail such theft and killing. A spirit grown demonic can take over a person's life, to the destruction of that person's life as much as of the lives of those others unlucky enough to come within its range. (Mark 7:1-23) And when that ancient powerful and subtle symbolism talks in terms, not now of demons or unclean spirits in the plural, but rather of a single demon adversarial to life, called Satan, the reference then is to the same process by which the spirits of human beings turn communally destructive instead of creative of God's good world for all. For as some perceptive sociologists have noticed, there does exist such a thing as a crowd spirit or a national spirit and so on. And these always prove to be much more than the sum of their individual parts, whatever the metaphysical explanation for this common level of human consciousness might be.

A tolerable metaphysical explanation of the phenomenon might well begin from the point of view of the Jewish imagery of the composition of the human being, and the subsequent story of the Creator Spirit ever breathing life into the human spirit from within, and through that human spirit ever breathing life into the whole world. That self-same Creator Spirit can now be seen as having its constant power and inspiration for existence and life ever more abundant turned satanic by the wilful human spirit it formed for better things. In this way: in the freedom it enjoys as the greatest gift of its Creator, the human spirit can turn satanic or adversarial the power and inspiration of the Creator Spirit ever creating life and *shalom* within itself, by using

144

that power and inspiration to destroy rather than create. It is in this sense that Jesus called Peter 'Satan' when he saw, on the occasion of Peter's confession that he was the Christ, that Peter expected from him the inspiration of a cosmic Power that would gain its ends by coercion and violence. It is in this sense that Jesus called the Jewish religious leaders that opposed his version of the reign of God to the point of plotting to kill him, sons of their father, 'the devil', in response to their charge that he 'had a demon'. And precisely the same meaning and message is conveyed when Jesus calls these leaders fornicators, as when he called that generation of Jews 'an adulterous generation': namely, that it was this Creator Spirit turned satanic, his God now turned by them into an idol that these people lusted after and worshipped, rather than the true Creator Spirit of steadfast love. (John 8:31-48) For they turned the image of God, which human beings are and should be, into the image of a god that is the very adversary of the true Creator Spirit that breathes in them and in all the world.

This is nothing more nor less than the theme that is so commonly found in the folklores of the world, the Faust theme, or in Irish the *Séadna* theme, the stories of the one who sells his very soul, who barters his spirit with the devil for earthly possessions and the power they promise, and in the event gains nothing but despair and destruction. It is the same theme that appears in the gospel story about Jesus when, just before he sets out to promote the reign of the true God, he is pictured being 'led by the Spirit into the wilderness to be tempted by the devil. And he fasted for forty days and forty nights, and afterwards he was hungry.' (Matthew 4:1-11) A clear reference to the Israelites being led to the *shalom* the true God would give them in a land flowing with milk and honey, but having first to spend forty years going through the wilderness where, as that story continues, their fears for their lives, their lack of faith in God, tempted them constantly to try other gods who might secure their lives by demonstrations of power exclusively in their favour. So Jesus felt the temptation that must affect all who doubt or cannot see in this wilderness world of mixed good and evil the daily presence of the benign Creator Spirit.

He felt the force of the temptation to have all the 'bread' his

heart could desire at his instant command. He felt the temptation to see on his side a god who would make him immune to
defeat or death no matter what risk he took. He felt the temptation to see placed under his will and rule all the kingdoms of
this world. In sum, he felt the strongest temptation to worship a
satanic power, to sell his spirit into the service of a satanic god,
like Mammon. The gospels tell us, and all the rest of what they
tell us shows, that Jesus resisted the temptation. And we must
not lose the point of that ancient and universal myth by thinking
that Jesus just swatted the temptation away with ease, in the
knowledge that he simply was the son of God in anything other
than the common biblical sense of that term, or that that status
could be established by him after a mere moment's thought. No,
the temptation was as real, and its overcoming as difficult, for
him as it is for any of the rest of us, if only because he was a man
of natural authority and influence over people. His rhetoric was
that of a man who had an inner authority unlike that of the
scribes, who were always quoting someone else, and often differed among themselves and confused people in their interpret-
ations of what they were quoting. Jesus was the kind of person
whose powers of rhetoric alone would see him far in politics,
apart from any other kinds of power, perhaps that of the faith-
healer, that he could also display in return for public allegiance.

So the healing ministry involves exorcism as much as the actual healing, the sending into remission or taking out, of whatever life-threatening conditions there are, from which people
suffer so much. If only because most of these life-threatening
conditions are in fact brought upon them by themselves. Or at
the very least these ills of body and mind that are inseparable
from our current material, bodily composition, and that lead by
the nature of things to that final disintegration of our current
bodily form that we call death, even these are greatly exacerbated
because of those who go about the business of destroying life for
others in a vain attempt to secure their own lives against death
by accumulating as much possessions and consequent power as
they can. These people who, in Kierkegaard's famous phrase,
vainly 'grasp at finiteness to sustain themselves', inevitably suffer the fatal despair of life that such a project naturally breeds,
and that despair spreads rapidly and to younger and younger

members of the race that these can so easily influence to emulate them. And the suffering and death these inflict upon others, by depriving the others of the very necessities of life, or killing these others in the process of doing so, make the sufferings that lead to death seem so meaningless, so unacceptable, so unbearable.

The natural suffering that attends naturally on our present life-forms could otherwise be lessened or at least mollified by our medical creativity equally shared with all. And death itself could be better borne, its sting drawn, by the natural hope engendered in our experience, transmitted also by our human efforts at co-creation, of a Creator Spirit sensed within ourselves and our world, a Creator Spirit that works incessantly as an eternal source of existence and life for all. That Spirit causes only such suffering and death as are required under the cosmic law of the transformation of older forms of existence and life into higher forms, in our case, the transformation of our current bodily form of life into what Paul called more spiritual bodies.

However that matter is analysed and argued, it is fairly clear that the full healing of the majority of our ills requires equally the exorcism of the evil spirits that by will or emulation can come to characterise and control each one of us, so as to turn into an adversarial power of destruction the power and inspiration of the Creator Spirit that of itself would always work *shalom* within and about us; so that the Creator Spirit itself is made to look like Satan. As Matthew's account of the sending of the twelve on their first mission has Jesus put it: 'heal the sick ... cast out demons ... as you enter the house, let your peace, *shalom*, come upon it; but if it is not worthy, let your peace return to you.' (Matthew 10:5-15) Or to put the matter in words more commonly used, the healing requires a change of heart, *metanoia*, a phrase that could as easily be rendered as a change of spirit. And it is also clear from all that has been said of eucharistic meals that the manner in which these exorcisms, these changes of spirit are brought about, is by offering to any who are demoniacally possessed in any degree a dramatic demonstration of the Creator Spirit in action through our spirits, creatively sharing life and all the necessities and enhancements of life equally with all.

It might seem a bit much to expect that the dramatic eucharistic symbolism of one meal, or even a number of meals, could change people from serving whatever malign, destructive forces might be thought to promise such ownership and power over the necessities and enhancements of life as would support their denial of death. A few curries, even a few chateaubriand steaks served with Chateau Lafitte, could scarcely achieve as much. But it is not the quantity or even the quality of the necessities and enhancements of life that is on offer, that saves human kind from the mutual destruction they inflict on each other in their search for control of all the world has to give. In fact, piling quantity on quantity in the course of grace and giving might only encourage the guests to take more than they were offered. Like Moctezuma who sent most generous gifts of gold to stout Cortez, in the hope of seeing him as a polite and therefore temporary guest, instead of the rapacious brigand that he (and his god) was and duly proved to be. But no; it is the spirit that can be detected in the manner in which the food and drink, or any other gift is given, the spirit of taking it as a gift intended by the original source as gift equally for all; it is the experience of this spirit in the giving and receiving of the food, or the gold, or the medicine or other service, no matter how small the quantity, maybe only five rough barley loaves and two fishes, or some oil and a woman's tears; it is this experience with these small things that can bring about a change of spirit that will in turn see that all have all they need in order to fare well, and in addition to that a hope for life that need fall nothing short of eternity.

This aspect of the reign of God Jesus explained in an unforgettable manner, as he explained so much, in parables. (Mark 4) In this case the parable of the tiny seed, so tiny it might be expected to produce no great plant, yet proves in the event to produce a mighty tree. Just so can one small gift or one small gesture, offered in the proper spirit, expose the receiver to the presence of the eternal Spirit who gifts life to all and who then through human giver and receiver alike can increase exponentially the gifting of life from all to all, together with all of life's needs and affordances. Jesus used the seed imagery also, however, in order to illustrate how such attempted planting of the seed of the reign of God might fail to have its natural and intended effect, for nothing is automatic when one is dealing with the free spirits of the human race. In this parable, Jesus pictures the 'seed' being snatched by a satanic spirit, by a spirit that is ruled still and always by 'the cares of the world, and the delight in riches, and the desire for other things.' (Mark 4:19) The change of spirit never follows automatically on any witness in any form, meal or healing or service of any kind. Change of heart and spirit, rejection of one's old heart in favour of the new yet oldest spirit of all, the move translated as 'repentance' in the Bible, that is something that can neither be imperiously ordered, nor forced, not even by threat or application of specific penalty designed to fit each crime committed by free spirits intent only on possessions and power.

This, according to Matthew in his literary strategy of having Jesus hand down the revised rules of God's covenant with humankind, from the mountain, the new Sinai, Jesus taught in his preaching also. Even if the ones we treated to eucharist remained in the service of their own spirits, and of the power of the Creator Spirit, both of which they had freely turned satanic; and even if they then continued to steal from us and injure us, we were never to punish them by depriving or injuring them in response. If a man steals your cloak, give him your coat; if he strikes you, turn the other cheek to show him how well you still are, and still as hopeful as ever of wholeness despite any more he could ever do to you. For, as Matthew continues the account that Jesus gives of this matter, you must be the sons of your Father, who steadfastly treats just people exactly the same as he treats the unjust, treating all alike to all of the supports and enhancements of life, symbolised by the rain and the sun, the twin creations that in this world exemplify the sources of life and the causes of its burgeoning. (Matthew 5: 38-48)

The lesson that Jesus taught is crystal clear. If we are to be sons and daughters of God, living and dying by the Holy Spirit, we would have to behave eucharistically in our meals, in our healings of the diseases and conditions that diminish and threaten life, and in every other form of service to our fellow human beings. Even and indeed especially all those who, despite any and all of the eucharistic love ever shown them, are found to be still in-service to a satanic spirit, still stealing from, injuring and killing the others. Like those imperial powers that still today pillage parts of our misfortunate world, under the guise of making them free for their free markets, or as they often prefer to put it, under the guise of exporting their values (so manifestly materialist) to peoples who then have to suffer in that process the most appalling deprivations and deaths of loved ones, either by the direct military actions of the new imperialists, or by their destroying and then failing to replace the security that every society must have as a natural right, or by drawing into the lands of these misfortunate people the violent enemies that such imperialists always attract. And when the leaders of these imperial and still-would-be imperial powers either brashly or shyly suggest that they do this under the guidance of God, then they blaspheme in the full and proper sense of that word. They turn the image of the Creator Spirit into the image of an idol, a god who gets his way by the shock and awe of indiscriminate, destructive, death-dealing and brute military power. Sons of Satan, Jesus would still call them today, for the same reason as he once called some Jewish leaders sons of Satan, namely, that they are killers, and with this difference only, that the more recent ones are killers in a massive managerial mode and on a scale such as those who were objects of the wrath of Jesus in his time could not even envisage. (John 6: 40, 44; Matthew 5: 21-22).

The healings then achieved what the meals achieved, and they are no more to be taken as miracles, in the sense of the powerful and wonderful overcoming of the natural, than are the meals to be taken to involve a miracle of changing human substance into the substance of bread, whatever that might be taken to mean. Indeed, if the healings were to be taken as miracles designed to prove something, to coerce us into believing something that Jesus was, namely, our Saviour, then the gospel stories would surely look very odd indeed. For these stories would then make it seem that Jesus spent most of his public ministry proving what he was and that he was doing something, and very, very little time was devoted to actually being and doing it, whatever it was. As remarked already, there is so much evidence in the Bible to show that he healed, that one begins to ask, did he do anything else? And if the preaching of the true word is deducted in terms of time, since talking the talk is not quite the equivalent of walking the walk, then the time for doing what he was to do and did, is even more curtailed. And the question becomes more anxious still: what precisely was his *metier*, his distinctive role in life, and when precisely did he (find the time) to do, to actually accomplish this distinctive work?

That particular and obvious line of questioning shows up the gospels in such an odd light that even if one paid not the slightest bit of attention to the severe strictures that Jesus put on appeals to proof miracles, one would have to conclude that the healings were no more miracles than were the meals. And then, eyes cleared of the blinkers that so many adulterous generations had placed over them, blinkers made of the material of millions of pages written about miracles, one can at last see that the healings like the meals are themselves the work of salvation proceeding apace, day after day of the public mission of Jesus. And right up to and through the last day of his life, when he consummated with his death the task to which he devoted his life, as he was now at the end quite literally giving his life for it. He was Saviour, as his Father had always been recognised in the history of his own Israelite religion as at once Creator and Saviour. And so Jesus was son of God also in the sense that he was Saviour. As could we too be, derivatively, sons and daughters of God and auxiliary saviours, if we dined and healed like he did. For the healings and the meals are both and equally saving processes, salvation activities. Just as both are equally activities that simultaneously induce repentance, as anyone can see who understands these terms, salvation and repentance, in the senses that the Latin reveals best, the senses, respectively, of making well and sending into remission.

Feeding to people the necessities and enhancements of life exemplified in food clearly makes them well, as does healing their life-diminishing ills, while simultaneously breathing into them, one hopes, the spirit in which the mutual feeding and the healing is done, and thereby inducing a change of heart or spirit, the *metanoia* that is too often translated as repentance. In fact it is that latter effect of the feedings and the healings that is by far the more salvific, and that makes the ones who engage in the dining and healing all the more effective as saviours who make all well and all manner of thing well. For the effect so frequently known

as the forgiveness of sins is an effect of sending the sinfulness of
the recipients of meals or healings into remission, and that is
done by meals and healings changing their spirits to spirits that
are now formed by the same Creator Spirit that inspired their
benefactors to feed and heal, changing these from being spirits
in the image of the satanic spirit that rules people who starve
and kill others in the effort to accumulate possessions and
power to secure their own lives all by themselves. So that it is the
change of spirit effect of both the meals and the healings that
promises far more well-being than the immediate feeding of the
hungry or curing of the ill can straightaway accomplish, if only
by ridding more of the world of the suffering and misery, destruction and death that people still possessed of a satanic spirit
continue to spread abroad in ever increasing circles. In other
words, sending sin into remission, that sin of serving a satanic
spirit to the detriment always of self and others, is by far the best
means of bring salvation to the whole world, so that all will be
well eventually, and all manner of thing will be well. And this is
what Jesus, according to the gospels, spent most of his life doing,
salving the world by meals and healings, when he was not an-
nouncing and preaching the reign of the one true God that redeems the world from the palpable effects of the sin of the
world.

The most comprehensive accompanying symbol that can direct the imagination to the fullest apprehension of the symbol of
salvation in the Bible is the symbol of *shalom*. For *shalom* encom-
passes both the overcoming of the negative, the ills of body and
spirit both naturally or maliciously induced, and the eternal
length and depth and height of life's positive élan, all under the
reign of the indomitable love of the Creator Spirit poured into
the hearts of all of humanity through the continuous creation of
a world that comes pure and fair with every dawn from the generous hands of God.

The Roles of Faith and of Judgement
in Salvation through Meals and Healings

Two other important pieces of deciphering need to be negotiated
if the full import of all of this talk of the simultaneous salvation
and remission of sin by the simultaneous means of meals and

healings is to be finally clear. The two ciphers of faith and of judgement are both scattered, albeit unevenly, around and within the texts devoted either to meals or to healings, or to remission and (other forms of) salvation, and so they too need to be deciphered correctly if the present part of the great biblical code is to be cracked quite open.

Take faith first. Remember the story of the paralytic and friends, how Jesus saw their faith, then declared their sins remitted and their friend healed. Add the story of Jesus in his home place, where the great majority of old friends and neighbours refused to accept him as a prophet. 'And he could do no mighty work there, except that he laid his hands upon a few sick people and healed them. And he marvelled at their unbelief.' (Mark 6:1-6) Throw in for good measure the stories that tell of how surprised Jesus was to find amongst foreigners the kind of faith so significantly lacking amongst his very own people. The most informative of these is the story told by both Mark and Matthew of the encounter of Jesus with a Canaanite or Syrophoenician woman. (Mark 7:24-30; Matthew 15:21-28) This woman, with many others, found Jesus in a house in which he had hoped to hide for a while from the insistent crowds, and asked him to exorcise an unclean spirit from her daughter. He informed her that he was 'sent only to the lost sheep of the house of Israel'. Making him consistent in any case with his own instruction to The Twelve when sending them on their first mission: 'Go nowhere among the Gentiles, and enter no town of the Samaritans, but go rather to the lost sheep of the house of Israel.' (Mathew 10: 5-6)

But the woman persisted: 'She came and knelt before him, saying, "Lord, help me".' A mother does not easily give up on her seriously sick daughter. And that makes the answer she then got all the more shocking: 'It is not fair to take the children's bread and give it to the dogs.' Now that truly is shocking. For apart altogether from showing a racist attitude to foreigners, by calling the decent woman and her decent daughter dogs, Jesus really is saying now that the 'bread' is for the children, for Israel as son of God, and not for outsiders. And the 'bread,' if one remembers how John deciphered that symbol, 'is that which comes down from heaven, and gives life to the world'. It symbolises the Creator Spirit who gives life eternally to the world, and who has now possessed Jesus to enable him to play his pivotal part in doing likewise. So is Jesus really saying here that the Holy Spirit comes exclusively through 'the house of Israel', that outside that *ecclesia*, that gathering, that 'church' there is no salvation? It would seem so. This exclusivism does not mean, of course, that there is then no salvation for the foreigner and the outsider. There is, but it comes through the 'house' that enjoys the exclusive franchise.

In another biblical scene, known as the cleansing of the temple, Jesus explains what he is doing by proclaiming that it was written in the Bible that 'my house shall be called a house of prayer for all the nations,' but that they, the entrepreneurs, had made it 'a den of robbers'. (Mark 12:17). That proclamation is made up of two quotations, one from Jeremiah and the other from Isaiah. The one from Jeremiah (7:8-15) is straightforward enough. Jeremiah has God ask: 'Will you steal, murder, commit adultery, swear falsely, burn incense to Ba'al, and go after other gods that you have not known, and then come and stand before me in this house, which is called in my name, and say, "We are delivered"?' For if they do, God will bring down their temple, and abandon them to evil doing. But in the other part of the quotation, the part about God's temple in Jerusalem being 'a house of prayer for all the nations,' the passage from Isaiah (56:6-7) reads: 'And the foreigners who join themselves to the Lord, to minister to him, to love the name of the Lord, and to be his servants, every one who keeps the Sabbath, and does not profane it, and holds fast to my covenant – these will I bring to my holy mountain, and make them joyful in my house of prayer.' So that it is on these clear and strict conditions, on the terms of the full Jewish Torah and on these only, that 'My house shall be called a house of prayer for all peoples.'

So is that the full story behind the insulting, racist rebuff with which Jesus responds to the poor Canaanite woman who asks nothing for herself but only that her daughter be healed? It would certainly seem so. But what is certain without any residue of seeming is this: that it is only when one adds this less than edifying story to the other stories about faith playing a pivotal part in the salvific effects of the eucharistic meals and the plain healings, that one can see clearly and fully what the faith in question means. And what it came to mean to Jesus and to those who approached him because of it, and were healed. For the woman persisted even after this quite humiliating rebuff; she even turned its metaphorical terms against itself. 'Yes, Lord,' she said, with a rhetorical skill that would rank with the best of them, 'but even the dogs eat the crumbs that fall from their master's table.' Upon which Matthew's version of the story continues: 'Then Jesus answered her, "O woman, great is your faith! Be it done for you as you desire." And her daughter was healed instantly.'

What was this faith of hers then? It was faith in the 'bread,' that is to say, as John explained the matter so succinctly, it was faith in that which comes down from heaven to give life to the world and, as part of that creative process, to restore life and livelihood to creatures who suffered diminishment or loss of either or both. It was faith in the sense of a keeping faith with the Spirit Creator of the cosmos who never does anything else except to pour out steadfastly salvation and life and life ever more abundant to all. And it was correspondingly faith in Jesus, a belief in him, a belief made real in the act of undeterred asking salvation from him, an acted-out belief that in all that Jesus was and did he was the very instrument of that same Creator Spirit that breathed through his very being. Yet more than this, and crucially, this faith of this Canaanite woman carried with it also the confidence that she could push her way with all the rest into the house where Jesus stayed, and go to his table, even if she was not an Israelite and had no intention of converting to his religion nor, unlike the foreigners of whom Isaiah spoke, of going up to his temple, and so on. Yet she could still receive from him, just as she was, the bread of life, the breath of life that would then heal her daughter.

Crucially? Yes, because it had to come to Jesus as it came to this Canaanite woman, that the creating, saving Spirit breathed life into the world through Jesus, but through Jesus the prophet as an otherwise ordinary man. And not as one of the officers or functionaries of the Israelite nation or the Israelite religion, the ones who ruled, who laid down the laws either from kingly palaces or from priestly temples or other forms of the religious establishment. It seems that Jesus had to learn this crucial aspect of the matter. That it did not come to him instantly or easily, even on his recognition of his vocation to be a prophet who, like Moses, both taught people about the true God, and brought them salvation from all worldly Egypts and all the other mostly self-inflected ills to which human flesh is heir. It seems indeed as if Jesus may have taken some time to learn that lesson, for otherwise there would not be so much evidence of a previously persistent 'only to and through Israel' policy. And when Jesus did learn that lesson, his sometimes somewhat forced recognition of the faith of the foreigners who came to him, as a true faith in all the respects outlined just now, and which he so well understood otherwise, played no small part in teaching that crucial lesson to him.

The stories and statements in the Bible about the satanic temptation of Jesus must be taken seriously as a real and true account of the state and experience of a fully human Jesus. They must not be interpreted as a hopeless attack of the devil that the divine presence in Jesus effortlessly swatted away. The satanic temptation of Jesus, so graphically described at the very outset of his public mission, must not be so interpreted as if in reality it constituted no real temptation at all to Jesus, the son of God. For only then can these temptation stories corroborate the account of the difficulty that Jesus had, like all of us have, in coming to live by a true faith in God's good world. For the primordial temptation that seems endemic to the human condition is the temptation to place one's faith in a power, any power, but most preferably one of possibly cosmic proportions, and at all events a power that will secure for us as much of the necessities and advancements of life as may prove a defence against the last enemy, death. A power that will act in us or for us, and act against any who would lessen or threaten our possession and complete control of the necessities of life. A power that will in fact kill off such challengers, if only as a precaution against some damage these might cause us in the future. (Will Saddam Hussein, and all members of Al Qaeda known or unknown, or known to be unknown, or unknown to be unknown, please stand up and be counted, and finger-printed, and point the printed fingers back at your accusers?) Powers that act in this way are always demonic, or are demonised by us in our demands that they act in such a way, irrespective of whether the 'us' in question refers to individuals, or groups, or peoples, or nation states, or empires, or races, or religions, or any combinations of these. So that the temptation that we can then see Jesus taking some time and effort to shake off, was the temptation to see as such a discriminatory power the almighty power of the Creator Spirit itself, exclusively exercised in its fullness in favour of Israel. And exercised in favour of others only on condition that these submitted to the law and the rulers of Israel. That is how Isaiah saw the matter when he talked about the Jerusalem temple as a house of prayer for all peoples, but only if they came under the rule and ritual of Jerusalem.

Jesus certainly went through the traditional programme of the prophets of Israel in warning people that the sacrifices offered in the temple and other such rituals would do nothing for them unless they kept faith with the steadfast love of the Creator, the eternal source of life for all. Further, Jesus took a principal ritual law, the law of sabbath observance, and reformulated it so that it revealed the God who ever and always served the life-needs of people, salving and promoting that life, rather than reveal a God who demanded a ritual kind of service from the people, at whatever expense to their lives and livelihoods. 'The Sabbath was made for man,' Jesus announced, 'not man for the Sabbath' – a quite extraordinarily radical principle that indicates as few other principles could do, how much the almighty Creator Spirit acts in the service of human kind, rather than lord it over them in a demonstration of his own power and glory of the kind that we are only too familiar with from those who govern us on earth. (Mark 2:27) Further still, Jesus reformulated laws that had formed the terms of the covenant revealed by God through Moses, for example, the commandment: 'Thou shalt not kill.' He reformulated this to forbid even humiliating other people, and to forbid injuring, much less killing, even those who did us harm.

And in issuing such reform of law, he appealed directly to the revelation in all of nature of the God who did nothing but creative and life-giving good to the virtuous and the evil alike, to the just and the unjust. Yet in spite of all of this, and of the conclusion it all pointed to, namely, the conviction that the

Creator Spirit directly graced with eternal goodness and life all creatures great and small, without distinction or discrimination, (a conviction that he beautifully illustrated with his parable of the hired daily workers in the master's vineyard: no matter how little work they did or, presumably, how bad it was, all got the same full wages in the end; every man a penny), Jesus did appear to have had his own difficulties in the matter. He appears to have taken time and trouble to let the Creator Spirit that came on and remained with him, exorcise the last vestiges of the idolatry to which we are all naturally tempted. That temptation to monopolise the sources and securities of life is so elementary, pluriform and ubiquitous that we seem to have been born with it. And of all the forms in which this temptation might affect Jesus, the religious form was always the most likely. For him the temptation was to continue to think of this God, whose Spirit taught Jesus that all of God's graces were intended equally for all, as being nevertheless a God who graced Israel first and principally, and the other peoples only secondarily and by the good graces of Israel. Until a poor illiterate Canaanite woman showed him that the Spirit and the grace of salvation that he was called upon to channel into this world had as little to do with his being an Israelite prophet as it had to do with her being a non-Israelite woman.

So when such strong hints are given in the gospels, hints of the length of time and the trouble it took Jesus to overcome that ancient temptation in religious form, it should come as no surprise to us that even the closest disciples of Jesus found it no less difficult to give up their expectations of a restored Davidic kingdom. Or indeed to give up the twinned expectation that any who would be saved by the Spirit that breathed through Jesus and now also through them, should keep the Torah, so as to make virtual Jews out of converts who were not Jews, and thereby make them servants of the God who was primarily the God of the Jews. Later, one could rewrite that last sentence with no alteration, except to write 'Christians' instead of 'Jews.'

Judgement

Finally then to the cipher of the judgement scenes so frequently painted in the Bible. It is best to begin here with a question and, if only for the sake of continuity, with this question: where in all of this material so far surveyed, concerning meals and healings, salvation and remission and faith, do we find the trappings and terms of judgement in its forensic form? That is to say, judgement in the form of the judge sitting in the court of law, the accused prosecuted, invited to confess or in any case found guilty of evil-doing, condemned and sentenced to a punishment proportionate to the crime? At first blush the answer to that question would seem to be: nowhere, not at all. When Jesus, in the course of a meal or a healing, either says or implies that the recipients' sins are forgiven, no effort is recorded to inquire after or to prove that certain evils have been done, or even to ask the sinners for a declaration of sorrow. There appears to be no more than the assumption by Jesus, born from his own experience no doubt, that all people are under the power of the same ancient and universal temptation, and need help from God to overcome it. The repentance that is so often talked about refers, not to a declaration of sorrow or remorse, though such may well be implicated, but to a change of heart. And the declaration of forgiveness in turn refers, neither to a forensic judgement of 'no longer guilty', nor to a sentence of limited penalty upon payment of which the evil-doer is deemed fit to return to the society of honest men and women. In fact there is no mention at all in all of this material of any sentence of guilt and penalty being handed down as a specific penalty for the gravity of a specific piece of evil-doing. Quite to the contrary, the declaration of forgiveness refers to a sending into remission, presumably of the felt and always somewhat efficacious power of the primordial temptation, the source of all the evil-doing so profligate in evidence in the history of the race. And even that sending into remission is either caused by the eucharistic nature of the meal itself, as a change of heart towards the sources and securities of life, or it is caused by the healings being offered in the same spirit as the meals are offered, either directly or through hearing about these. Provided, of course, that the hearers do not misinterpret these healings as power-signs of the coming of a messianic pretender in the mould of a Davidic king.

In short, the Spirit of the almighty Father, continuous Creator of heaven and earth, that breathes through the very human being of Jesus, so thoroughly as to make Jesus a prophet and son of God, never does anything in response to the evil-doing of the race made creator in the image of the same God, except to carry on pouring out existence and life, in the forms of healings and enhancements of life. For it is by that means alone that the Creator Spirit seeks to change the hearts of those who have entered upon idolatrous, satanic, and self-destructive ways, so to send that primordial sinfulness into remission, and to keep it in remission.

There will be many who will remain unconvinced of this deciphering of the cipher of judgement in the Bible, and rightly so. For they can point to the many, many instances of the cipher of judgement structured precisely along the lines of the judge sitting at his bench, surveying the record of evil-doing of those brought before him, declaring guilt and assessing its degrees, and condemning the guilty to punishments specifically applied, in addition to whatever these poor misfortunates might have suffered already from the hazards of life as we know it. A little more reading of the texts so far perused, or a little closer reading of these may then be necessary, but now in the frequently adduced biblical context of belief in God's application, both here and hereafter, of specific judgement and punishment of specific human sins.

People who believe that God does indeed deal with specific evil-doing by applying specific penalties are seldom satisfied with the view that God in all cases waits for an afterlife in order to do this. They expect rather, and quite reasonably so on their own terms, that God should allow in our own life and times examples of such judgement and its expected outcome for the condemned. And there are examples in the gospels of followers or occasional companions of Jesus giving expression to just such an expectation. But notice the reply that such people receive from Jesus. 'There were some present at that very time who told him of the Galileans whose blood Pilate had mingled with their sacrifices. And he answered them, "Do you think that these were worse sinners than all the other Galileans, because they suffered thus? I tell you, No; but unless you repent you will all likewise perish. Or those eighteen upon whom the tower of Siloam fell and killed them, do you think that these were worse offenders than all the others who dwelt in Jerusalem? I tell you, No; but unless you repent you will all likewise perish".' (Luke 13:1-5) Jesus is here as clear on the fact that these sufferings and deaths are not particular penalties to which God sentences particular sinners, as he is on the fact that unless we change our spirits from the satanic form in which we seek support and security of life at the expense of others, we will all suffer such sufferings and worse, at each other's hands.

'As he passed by, he saw a man blind from his birth. And his disciples asked him, "Rabbi, who sinned, this man or his parents, that he was born blind?" Jesus answered, "It was not that this man sinned, or his parents, but that the works of God might be manifest in him. We must work the works of him who sent me, while it is day; night comes when no one can work. As long as I am in the world, I am the light of the world." And Jesus then healed the man, on the sabbath day, which made the Pharisees conclude that 'this man is not from God', but the man whose eyes were healed retorted, 'He is a prophet.' (John 9:1-17) How much clearer could the matter now be? Neither this affliction of blindness nor anything else like it can be regarded as specifically devised divine punishment for human evil-doing. Rather must all such suffering and loss of life be regarded simply as occasions for the only work that God does, and does through Jesus and his followers for as long as they live. And this work that God does is not to condemn people and then punish them for their evil-doing, never that. These misfortunate people wreak quite enough punishment on themselves in the course of succumbing to the original temptation of the race. But the characteristic work of God, and of God's prophets and sons and daughters, is to heal the effects of such self-punishment. And that is what must be done also by all who would see their spirits changed by the grace of eucharist or other services to them, and who thereafter live by the rule of God. They must see such suffering as occasion only for co-operating in the work of God under the true reign of the one, true God.

This is the same lesson that Jesus hammers home in the famous sermon from the mount when, as Matthew sets up the scene, he reveals the terms of the renewed covenant that God makes through Jesus (the scene is modelled on that older story of God making covenant through the prophet, Moses, also from a mountain). The prophet Jesus, according to Matthew, preached that we must never return evil for those who do evil to us – and that presumably covers never bringing them to court and having them condemned and penalised for the evil or injury they perpetrated against us – but rather that we must always do good to such malevolent people. And Jesus then goes on to generalise that point as follows: 'You have heard that it was said, "You shall love your neighbour and hate your enemy." But I say to you, love your enemies and pray for those who persecute you, so that you may be the sons of your Father who is in heaven; for he makes his sun to rise on the evil and the good, and sends rain on the just and on the unjust ... You therefore must be perfect, as your heavenly Father is perfect.' (Matthew 5:38-48) Now how, in heaven's name, could anyone conclude that the prophet who preached such words, could still believe for a moment that the Father he asked us all to emulate, was in reality a god who would hammer the hell, quite literally, out of any who did evil to others and thereby could be deemed somehow to have offended himself, and do this for all eternity, and do it as soon as he got his heavenly hands on us in some other world in which he prefers to dwell? There is no acceptable answer to that question.

Yet there are further questions that can be put, always and on the basis of the biblical text. For the gospels, in common with other biblical texts, do contain references to judgement exercised in the common sense of our courts of law. There are full and detailed pictures of a final divine judgement of all humanity that is clearly cast in the mould of a judge examining the guilt or innocence of those before him, and sentencing all to either heaven or hellfire. Matthew paints the very paradigm of such a picture of final judgement. And in this picture he even has Jesus himself, now called 'the King,' doing what according to Matthew himself Jesus had in the name of his Father explicitly forbidden us to do in his sermon from the mount. Matthew has Jesus, now having come back 'in glory', discriminate between the just and the unjust (this is expressly forbidden by the same Jesus in Matthew's version of the sermon from the mount), invite the former 'into the kingdom prepared for you from the foundation of the world' (entirely contrary to the insistence of the earthly Jesus, that it is the sinners who should be invited to the eucharistic table from the head of which he and his disciples co-ruled the kingdom of God by serving the staff of life), and condemn, indeed curse, the unjust, saying to them, 'depart from me (that is, from the kingdom and reign of my Father, the Creator Spirit that is the bread of life) into the eternal fire prepared for the devil and his angels.'

But the most puzzling thing about the whole of this picture is that the terms on which the examining magistrate then pronounces his verdicts, and applies reward or penalty, are precisely the terms on which people, according to all of the earlier teaching and practice of Jesus, would remain under and enjoy the eternal *shalom* of the reign and kingdom of God. These terms are, that people should serve to each other the food and drink that are at one and the same time the supports and symbols of life, together with all other services that heal and enhance life. 'Then the King will say to those on his right hand, "Come, O blessed of my Father, inherit the kingdom prepared for you from the foundation of the world; for I was hungry and you gave me food, I was thirsty and you gave me drink, I was a stranger and you welcomed me, I was naked and you clothed me, I was sick and you visited me, I was in prison and you came to me." Then he will say to those on his left hand, "Depart from me, you cursed, into the eternal fire prepared for the devil and his angels; for I was hungry and you gave me no food, I was thirsty and you gave me no drink," and so on. It still seems to be all about food and drink and the salving of the ailing; or is it in the end really all about rules, whatever these may be, and an eternal roasting for those who broke them? (Matthew 25:31-46) The least that one can conclude at this point is that there is here a confusion of terms that, depending on how you read them, can characterise two very different pictures of the eternal reign of God.

Look at that famous judgement scene from Matthew as long as you like, as well known as it is graphic, amongst other biblical scenes and references of similar substance, and you will come sooner or later to that one conclusion. Two visions of the reign of God and, as a consequence, two very different images of the one, true God who reigns eternally over this good creation, are still jostling for supremacy in the minds and hearts of those who proclaim themselves followers of Jesus. And still jousting with each other – when was Matthew's gospel written? – thirty, forty, fifty years after the last supper and death of Jesus gave definitive witness to the true vision of the one, true reigning Deity he called Father. And then, just for interest's sake, look around you at any of the churches that call themselves Christian to this day. And ask yourselves if you can see two visions of God and of God's reign still jostling for the hearts and minds of ourselves and our contemporaries? Or if one of the visions has managed to win out over all the centuries between? And then ask if the right vision won? For, make no mistake about this, one of these visions is as blissfully true as the other is tragically and despairingly false.

These two visions of the reign of God are best distinguished and assessed by some further attention to the two key symbols of Matthew's judgement scene, the symbol of king and the symbol of fire. For this is the simplest way of seeing how these two visions are at one and the same time mixed up together and then jostling for our recognition. In the first vision, the false one, the picture painted of the king is that which is all too familiar to us from what one of our Irish poets, Cathal Ó Searcaigh, pictured when he complained of being plagued

by the brutal piety of the pulpit

threatening those who err with torment.

This is the vision of the God-King who reigns by raw and coercive omnipotence. He brings the world into existence by irresistible command, and by immutable command he controls the conduct of his creatures. And to those creatures on whom he has conferred the freedom to obey or to disobey, he applies the further coercion of the prospect of eternal punishment for any significant disobedience. Occasionally he even attempts to coerce belief in himself and in those who say they are especially chosen by him, by performing within the creation that always exhibits his awesome power further, quite extraordinary and often quite clearly preternatural acts of raw omnipotence. These are recorded as miraculous acts of God performed either to the benefit of those self-declared chosen ones, or to the manifest detriment of any who oppose them in any way. The laws that God then lays down by immutable command are mostly moral laws, designed for the welfare of free and responsible creatures. But there are also laws of a cultic and ritual nature that are also and immutably imposed for the purpose of ensuring that God's self-declared chosen ones, and those whom they successfully invite to confess and serve him, also feel suitably coerced into obeying. For both sets of laws are equally protected from the indifferent and the downright disobedient by the self-same overhanging threat of eternal punishment awaiting those who would ignore or disobey them. Except perhaps for the case of people who could claim never to have heard or known of this creator God and his chosen people, his laws and penalties, an eventuality that in this age of the omnipresence of the mass media must be increasingly difficult to envisage.

The second vision of the reign of God, the one that Jesus lived and preached and died for, is as true as the former is false. It is the vision of the God-King who reigns quite simply by fashioning and serving eternally and equally to all existence and life, with all necessary supports, salvings and enhancements. It is a vision of the reigning God the service and sonship of whom consists, for those creatures intelligent and responsible enough to see this, in following Jesus. Especially in this: that Jesus led his followers by lording it from the throne of the chair of the one who served at table, the sign and sacrament of the God who acted as the eternal Servant of Life. The God who never under any circumstances coerces anyone in any way by acts of overweening power, neither coercing confession by miracle shows, nor coercing submission by threat of fearsome penalty. A God whose very act of creation takes the form of lovingly forming and fashioning everything that comes into existence in such a way that those made in God's image can see how things are made and then help to make them better in a co-creative act that, like God's own creative act, must be to the benefit of all. The God who, instead of coercing by threat of penalty for non-cooperation or downright destructive disobedience, is content to breathe into the world the love of the Creator Spirit, thereby to inspire the creature to follow the true prophet on the moral road to eternal *shalom*. In Ó Searcaigh's words,

Here it is with his life rather than his words
that whatever God there is makes himself known;
ignoring signs of reverence, veneration.
The source of all energy. Creator of the Elements.

Enough for him to stir, blossom
and push towards the light in every new-grown shoot.
His joy is the lustre of every colour,
he gives life to the air around me with his life.

With every breath I take
I breathe him from the pure air
as fresh as new-baked bread, as cool as wine. *(Sanctuary)*

To the one who follows either of these visions, the one who follows the other blasphemes, is a son of Satan and an idolator (or an adulterer, like Israel lusting after false gods), all amounting to much the same thing. This is evident from many parts of the gospels, but particularly from the altercation between Jesus and Jewish leaders in John 8, and from the account of Jesus before the judgement seat of the High Priest, and it is most easily illustrated from the many disputes and accusations that followed upon Jesus breaking the sabbath law. For his Jewish critics the law of sabbath observance was obligatory because it was laid down by God as an immutable means of acknowledging the one they confessed as the God of their fathers, irrespective of the fact that its observance might deprive some unfortunate of the salving powers that, as Jesus saw the matter, defined God's relationship with his creatures and, as with other parts of the Torah, whether moral or ritual, its violation would be punished by God.

For Jesus this scribal, Pharisaic and priestly preaching and service of this God served simply to turn God satanic, destructive of God's own defining work as Creator. It shrank God to the size of one people's idol and, like any such false depiction of God, it thereby constituted blasphemy. For the opponents of Jesus, quite to the contrary, the God he preached and whose Spirit he presumed to breathe, was no longer, first and foremost, the true God of the truly chosen people whose Temple and Torah had to be accessed, with the permission of the earthly owners, by any outsiders who desired divine salvation. It was Jesus who was the blasphemer, the son of Satan, the idolator. And so the argument went, round and round, with no possibility of resolution short of a conversion, a radical change of heart from one side or the other – the very thing that Jesus had called for from the very outset of his public mission.

So there it is then. Matthew's world famous Day of Judgement scene uses two familiar sets of ciphers, those connected with royal dynasty and those connected with food and drink, with giving and eating and drinking. But while everything we know from the life and teaching of Jesus tells us that the latter set of ciphers, the giving and eating and drinking, should have modified quite radically the former and familiar imagery of kings who as a matter of course lorded it over their subjects, Matthew somehow manages to produce instead from the juxtaposition of these two sets of ciphers a graphic movie of King Jesus, attended by his hosts, coming 'in his glory' to 'sit on his glorious throne'. And what is now the occasion for this particular enthronement? It is so that Jesus should act as The Great and Final Enforcer. One cynic, who shall be nameless, on hearing this account of the matter, was heard to mutter, 'This was the man of whom it was said while he was on earth that he was so gentle, he would not break the crushed reed, or quench the flickering flame! Now he comes back at the head of an army to deal out terror and pain. You'd have to say that his exaltation to the right hand of God did not do him a lot of good, did it?' Cynical as that remark may sound, behind it lies the true perception that for Matthew it is not the crucified Christ who is raised to the right hand of God, but the all-powerful king now savouring the force of his final victory over all his enemies. And coming back on earth for a second time to prove correct those who had always looked on Jesus as a conquering king-messiah.

And yet, it must be wrong to be surprised at this. We have noted how much resistance there was during the public mission of Jesus to what even his closest disciples saw as the excesses of his insistence on having to die for the reign of God rather than enjoy its victorious form. And if we had read Matthew's own gospel a little more carefully, we might have seen how clear attempts to correct these excesses of Jesus were introduced by Matthew into the accounts of the teaching of Jesus. And we might then realise what, once again, we have already noted, namely, that even after the death of Jesus, and even after the early and largely eucharistic epiphanies, his followers kept falling back on revisionary positions concerning what they felt to be the more realistic programme that Jesus was inclined to overlook with his persistent talk of dying instead of just plain winning. All testimony to the primordial and perennial temptation of our race, to have life and the source and support of life at our service, whoever the 'we' may be, with destruction and death being the destiny of others, whoever might prove to be our opponents for the possession of the sources and supports of life.

In the case of Matthew's gospel, two passages would be sufficient to illustrate what is being said of him here. In the first passage there is a truly astonishing juxtaposition of mutually incompatible positions concerning the question of what to do when your brother sins against you, and both are placed on the lips of Jesus. The first position is this: first, confront your offending brother 'and tell him his fault'. If he does not listen, take one or two witnesses with you, in order to convict him as the law demands. If he still does not listen, 'Tell it to the church.' And if he does not accept the church's verdict on the matter, 'Let him be to you as the Gentile and the tax collector', that is to say, an excommunicate and a recalcitrant sinner. Quite an irony there, if not worse than an irony, since it was the tax collector and (other) sinners who were welcomed first and unconditionally by Jesus to the table of the kingdom, and it was Gentiles who played no mean part in persuading Jesus that the faith that opened the way to the kingdom of God was as likely to come from them as from his fellow Jews. And then, without pausing for breath in this very same passage, Matthew faithfully records the position of Jesus himself on this subject of offending brothers: 'Then Peter came up and said to him, "Lord, how often shall my brother sin against me, and I forgive him? As many as seven times?" Jesus said to him, "I do not say to you seven times, but seventy times seven".' In short, limitless forgiveness, and quite in accord with all that Matthew has Jesus preach from the mountain as the code of the renewed covenant and kingdom of God. Those who live under the reign of God must never penalise those who wrong them. Still, at least Matthew had the grace to record the excessive position of Jesus himself, if only in the course of modifying it as any sensible man would surely want to do, for the sake of its successful propagation, you understand. (Matthew 18:15-22)

The second passage that helps explain Matthew's grand Last

Judgement scene, is in fact the very last passage of his gospel. It is the passage in which Matthew supplies the visionary post-death appearance of Jesus that, he clearly felt, was rather inexplicably omitted from Mark's gospel. Remember that these visionary appearances scenes are records of the experiences of his disciples of the continuing and real presence of Jesus with them, still trying to instil into them a full and true sense of the reign of God. And, the records show that it is necessary to add, succeeding with some in a manner in which he still failed to succeed quite as well with others. For these others still experienced the presence of Jesus after his death, as they had experienced his presence in life, as a true prophet and son of God, but one who in life went too far, who was too pessimistic, or too unrealistic or too extreme in some respects, and who was now from his exalted state confirming more of the normal understanding that they all shared of their common Jewish religion. And in any case, the more the death of Jesus receded into the past, the easier it would be perhaps to interpret the death of Jesus as a one-off sacrifice for the sins of all, and not an example of deaths they should be prepared to die, rather than watch their triumphant reigning God kill off those who sinned against them.

So Matthew creates an appearance scene, in which Jesus appears to his remaining eleven disciples in Galilee where, according to Mark, Jesus had directed them. Matthew specifies a mountain in Galilee of which Mark makes no mention, perhaps to evoke the sermon on the mount and a corresponding status for what is now to be laid down for the followers of Jesus. 'Jesus came and said to them, "All authority in heaven and earth has been given to me. Go therefore and make disciples of all nations, baptising them in the name of the Father and of the Son and of the Holy Spirit, teaching them to observe all that I have commanded you; and lo, I am with you always, to the close of the age".' And these are Matthew's last words to us, just in case the reader had forgotten that he had said in the previous passage above that Jesus had given his church the power from heaven to bind and loose, that is to say in rabbinic terms, the power to forbid or permit particular activities. For Matthew loves commands, and the power to command, and the power to penalise those who break the commandments. Or, more mildly put perhaps, no matter what Jesus said or did during his public mission, Matthew, like many another, still cannot hear him say, even to those who have the most abiding sense of his real presence to them after his death, or still cannot accept it if he did say this, that the kingdom of God could be run, either by God or by any of God's appointed lieutenants on earth, without commands and judgement and proper and specific penalties both threatened and then duly applied.

The contrast with Luke's account of the grand commission delivered during visionary appearances of Jesus is instructive. When Luke has Jesus appear in the upper room, 'he opened their minds to understand the scriptures, and said to them, "Thus it is written, that the Christ should suffer and on the third day rise from the dead, and that repentance and forgiveness of sins should be preached in his name to all the nations".' And as he continues that same story of appearance in the upper room in his Acts of the Apostles, Luke adds these words of Jesus, 'You shall receive power when the Holy Spirit comes upon you, and you shall be my witnesses in Jerusalem and in Samaria and to the ends of the earth.' (Luke 24:45-47; Acts 1:8) The contrast could scarcely be clearer between, on the one hand, this summary by Luke of all that we have learned of the way the Creator Spirit always acts, ever creating life and life more abundant, and making that activity itself both the healing of the deleterious effects of sin brought by the errant human race upon itself, and the sending into remission of that sin by inspiring those treated with unconditional grace to treat others in similar fashion. And, on the other hand, the picture painted so resolutely by Matthew, despite his faithful representation in his sermon on the mount of all that Luke has said and seen: a picture now of a God and sundry lieutenants of his who rule by command as much as by inspiration, and enforce these commands by the strictest of judgement and the most terrifying of penalties. So much then for the symbol of kingship or reign of God as Jesus strove to characterise it in the whole course of his mission to spread it, and as Matthew then modified it with his picture of King Jesus as the great judge of the end time.

Much the same results can accrue from a focus on that second key cipher in Matthew's eschatological judgement scene: the symbol of fire. For fire, in its manifold avatars, from the sun to a flickering candle flame, and more so even than water, has proved to be the most ancient, universal, ubiquitous, effective, fruitful and flexible symbol of creation, of the on-going act of creation seen from this side as the on-going creative cosmic process that modern science calls evolution. Fire is, as a consequence, the dominant symbol for the Creator Spirit. For even though the earliest symbol of the Creator Spirit in the Bible is the bird that broods over the dark and as yet sterile abyss, in the words of Gerard Manley Hopkins:

Because the Holy Ghost over the bent
World broods with warm breast and with ah! bright wings
(God's Grandeur),

that dove-avatar is more conventionally directed to evoke the state of *shalom* in which the creation has reached that perfection in which it is ever conceived and created in the mind of God. Whereas fire is the more apt symbol of divine creation inevitably caught up in the uncertainties of creaturely cooperation, the symbol of divine-creaturely creation as a programme in progress – as in the descent of the Creator Spirit on the apostles at Pentecost in the form of tongues of flame. For a kind of divine creation that consists, not in one primordial act of putting the thing there, but in a continuous activity that brings the creation successively through the levels that our modern understanding of evolution reveals, that kind of divine creation inevitably involves the death of old forms of life and existence. It involves their burning off in the very process of bringing on the new and more advanced life, brought forth from the death of older forms.

Furthermore, the Creator Spirit endows the highest creature we know, *homo sapiens*, with the intelligence, the know-how to co-create this universe, thereby acting in the Creator Spirit's own image. So since the Creator concomitantly confers on this spoiled species the freedom of will to create or destroy, we cannot be prevented from acting in adversarial fashion instead, and bringing upon ourselves and our fellow creatures the destruction of life, with all of the misery and suffering that such satanic conduct inevitably entails. And then our only hope is that that misery and suffering with which the Creator Spirit enables us to punish ourselves for all of our wrong-doing, may itself burn out

of us all of the satanic tendencies towards which our self-interest
and lack of care for others so constantly drives us. Fire then is
the symbol of the divine creative agency and act that brings ever
higher life out of the ever-painful deaths of previous forms. Just
as it helps heal us of our sinful, destructive ways both by sustaining us in the natural course of events to punish ourselves for
these, and by the positive force of the constancy of its everlasting
creative love. That two-edged sword of divine creative love in
action is caught, as only the poet-seer can catch it, in T. S. Eliot's
deployment of the imagery of creative fire:

The dove descending through the air
With flame of incandescent terror
Of which the tongues declare
The one discharge from sin and error.
The only hope, or else despair
Lies in the choice of pyre or pyre –
To be redeemed from fire by fire.

Who then devised the torment? Love.
Love is the unfamiliar Name
Behind the hands that wove
The intolerable shirt of flame
Which human power cannot remove.
We only live, only suspire
Consumed by either fire or fire. (*Little Gidding*)

In some myths of the end-time, the new age or the new
creation of this world, that second focus of the imagery of fire
comes into play, in order to highlight our self-punishment as the
finally successful purgation applied by the same Creator Spirit
to all that is evil in us. Paul, for instance, has this usage of the fire
imagery in mind when he writes to the Corinthians: 'Each man's
work will become manifest, for the Day will disclose it, because
it will be revealed with fire, and the fire will test what sort of
work each one has done. If the work which any man has built on
the foundation survives (Jesus is the foundation that Paul has in
mind here), he will receive his reward. If any man's work is
burned up, he will suffer loss, but he will himself be saved, but
only as through fire.' (1 Corinthians 3:13-15) Not quite so strik-

ingly beautiful as Eliot's poetry, but the same point nevertheless put forcefully in honest prose.

This is neither the time nor the place to pause for a meditation on the strategies of cosmic myths. Suffice it to say that whether they be beginning-time myths as in Genesis, or end-time myths as in Paul's brief fire-myth above, their time-imagery coinage cannot be cashed in terms of inner-cosmic time – in the time we count on clocks and that only comes into existence with the material universe. 'In that time,' 'long, long ago,' 'many, many years from now,' as Mircea Eliade use to insist, are ciphers for a time-out-of-time, all part of a strategy for trying to see and say what is forever true of the world. For a cosmic myth tries to see the world in the pristine purity of its coming from the source, as evidenced by the Genesis myth's refrain: 'And God saw that it was good, it was good, it was very good.' But the cosmic myth also tries to see what always happens or can happen in the whole history of the continuing relationship of that world with that source to which its destiny is at once separate yet inextricably linked. In a sense, the Genesis myth, in which the Creator Spirit is imagined as the brooding bird, later the dove, sees the pristine purity of the world which is always there to be recovered. Whereas the end-age myths are there to say that the recovery comes about and will always come about by the same means as those which always produce the pristine purity: by the creative love of the Creator Spirit made real in act and inspiring especially the most co-creative of the creatures to live by it, and by it alone, but this time enabling them to let their self-inflicted punishments purge them of the satanic spirit that so often possesses them.

But then Paul, as we have already seen Matthew do, turns the fire imagery to such a use as to portray God's behaviour in a manner that is diametrically opposed to that of the Creator Spirit who never does anything to or for creation except to create and sustain life, and then to recreate and again sustain life, either under the natural necessities of its evolution to ever more perfect and blissful forms, or for the purpose of reversing once more the reversals that life suffers every time that co-creative creatures turn satanic and destructive instead. So now Paul, in one of the earliest of his letters, to the Thessalonians, uses the fire imagery to portray literally and no longer metaphorically, the behaviour of a vengeful deity who judges and condemns people who do evil, and sentences them to the penalty of eternal torment by fire, a kind of eternal death. 'This is evidence of the righteous judgement of God, that you may be made worthy of the kingdom of God, for which you are suffering – since indeed God deems it just to repay with affliction those who afflict you, and to grant rest (*shalom*) with us to you who are afflicted, when the Lord Jesus is revealed from heaven with his mighty angels in flaming fire, inflicting vengeance upon those who do not know God and upon those who do not obey the gospel of our Lord Jesus. They shall suffer the punishment of eternal destruction and exclusion from the presence of the Lord and from the glory of his might, when he comes on that day to be glorified in his saints.' (2 Thessalonians 1:5-10)

What could be Paul's motive for such a drastic alteration of the import of the imagery of fire from that of its standard import as the symbol of creation and not of destruction, or of destruction only as a mediating element in continuous creation? It is plain that his motive is vengeance against those who are persecuting him and his converts, together with a nostalgia for the hitherto familiar God who ordered the armies of Israel on her way to the promised land to kill every man, woman and child of any people who opposed them. 'Now go and strike Amalek, and utterly destroy all that they have; do not spare them, but kill both man and woman, infant and the one who suckles the breast, ox and sheep, camel and ass.' This is the God whose prophet, Samuel, in his name, proceeded to hack to pieces the king, Agag, of such a people, the Amalekites, that his own appointed king, Saul, had disobeyed his own explicit command and saved: 'And Samuel hewed Agag in pieces before the Lord in Gilgal.' (1 Samuel 15:1-32).

The Great and Final Enforcer is back in business and, quite literally, with a vengeance, and acting now on behalf of Paul and the new chosen people, and acting against any who would oppose or, worse still, persecute the newly elect. Paul had already sounded the same sinister note in his first letter to the Thessalonians, when he reminded them that 'You, brethren, became imitators of the churches of God which are in Judea, for you suffered the same things from your own countrymen as they did from the Jews who killed both the Lord Jesus and the prophets, and drove us out, and displease God and oppose all men by hindering us from speaking to the Gentiles that they may be saved – so as always to fill up the measure of their sins. But God's wrath has come upon them forever.' And he never seems to see the incongruity involved when amongst the exhortations with which he ends this letter he urges its readers: 'See that none of you repays evil for evil, but always seek to do good to one another and to all', thereby urging a higher standard of love on his converts than he expects from God. (1 Thessalonians 2:14-16; 5:15)

Similar judgement scenes seem to be painted, albeit much more briefly, in 2 Peter and in Revelation. The latter simply describes all the dead being brought before a throne. 'And the dead were judged by what was written in the books, by what they had done ... This is the second death, the lake of fire, and if anyone's name was not found written in the book of life, he was thrown into the lake of fire.' (Revelation 20:11-15)

In the former, 2 Peter seems to be reminding his readers of what Paul had to say on this subject, for he also is responding to the discouragement of faithful followers of Jesus at their experience of opposition and positive persecution, with no sign in sight of the coming of Jesus as the divinely appointed judge of the world, to penalise definitively the people responsible for such opposition, and their own ensuing suffering and even death. And their discouragement is all the more exacerbated by the scoffing they hear from their persecutors every time they repeat a threat of divine action against their persecutors that seems longer and longer without any sign whatever of its being carried out. So 2 Peter assures his readers that the comeuppance of their persecutors will come in God's good time. As sure as God once before destroyed with water a world grown evil and corrupt, so 'the heavens and the earth that now exist have been stored up for fire, being kept until the day of judgement and the destruction of ungodly men.' (2 Peter 3)

Now that implicit reference to the flood story and the covenant with Noah, for that is what it is, must surely rank with the most underhand, not so say subversive pieces of exegesis ever to have been invoked in an unworthy cause. For the flood story is a creation story, a story of land being separated from the primeval deep, once more bringing forth living things, being peopled with first couples, and so on. And it is a story that recognises that human evil-doing involves the destruction of God's good world. Further, as elsewhere in the Bible, God here accepts responsibility for his enablement of such human and sinful destruction. But the whole point of this particular flood creation myth – and remember that such cosmic myths are meant to reveal what happens at every time and place – is that God will never, ever allow the good creation to be destroyed by any destructive agents that may well still operate within it. God will not engage in destruction for destruction's sake, nor allow dependent destroyers to destroy creation or any part of it. That is God's covenant with Noah; sealed, not with a sacrifice, and not even with a meal, but with the rainbow that God sets in the sky.

To interpret this myth as if God were to say: 'Well, yes, I did indeed say that I would never destroy my creation, but I only said I would not destroy it with water. I never said I would not destroy it with, let us say for the sake of example, fire.' To so interpret the Noah myth would be to treat God like some sleazy lawyer, trying to twist words out of their common use and import, in order to renege on some legally binding commitment. For fire and water, the high sun and the deep abyss, are different but equal symbols for the source of creation. Out of each and out of both, in our common experience, life comes and is ever renewed and advanced, though both must burn off or wash away the dead and death-dealing forms that accompany renewal and advance of life, or at least wash or burn these back to some lower level of existence where they can begin again to contribute to the birth and sustenance of living things. God does not destroy what God has created, not by fire nor by water, not today nor on any fabled Judgement Day, not in all eternity. And in this respect God makes no discrimination between the evil-doers and the good. Instead God sends the fire and the water, the sun and the rain, to the just and the unjust, equally and alike and always.

That is God's covenant with Noah: God will never (again, as

the story form of the myth has to put it) engage in the plain destruction of creatures, but only in their continual creative transformation or evolution, through death itself. To say that is the same as to say what Jesus so often said or implied on the occasion of meals and healings: your sins are always already forgiven. For that also says to everyone: your very reception of the invitation to this meal, or your very request for and reception of this healing, in the spirit in which both are given, is the sending of your primordial sin into remission. These constant creative acts themselves, together with all that they signify, constitute God's only response to your sins. So you must never even think that God will respond to your evil doing by sitting in judgement on you, passing sentence and then having the sentence executed in the form of the destruction of any creature's life – much less the 'eternal destruction' that Paul promised and 2 Peter based upon a thoroughly subversive, if allegedly implied exegesis of the flood story and the ensuing covenant mediated by Noah. (Genesis 6-9).

And all of that applies also, as a matter of course, to the execution of Jesus. God did not sentence his son, Jesus, to the destruction of that terrible death for the payment of the penalty incurred by the convicted sinners of the race. The God that Jesus called Father does not destroy human life as the execution of a judge's sentence for evil-doing, not on Calvary, not on the Last Day, not ever or anywhere. The death of Jesus was the execution of a prophet by those who resisted the God he prophesied, as he himself testified on his way into Jerusalem for what he knew to be the last time. It was those who executed Jesus in God's name who thereby satanised God, and made God into a murderer, as John explained this matter when he has Jesus say to 'the Jews,' 'You seek to kill me ... you are of your father the devil ... he was a murderer from the beginning.' (John 8:39-47)

It is the ones who make God demand the destruction of those who oppose his rule, his kingdom and his chosen people who thereby make God into an idol. As did that other self-styled prophet of the Lord, Samuel, at Gilgal. As did Paul to the Thessalonians, and 2 Peter, and Matthew, and others, when they could not take the persecution that Jesus told them would certainly come their way for trying to change the hearts of the rich and the powerful and the self-serving – the very ones who

would serve only a god that saw to their own security and richness of life at the expense of the foreigner and the outsider
whose only sin so often was, and still is, to seek the same security
and richness of life that any human being under God should be
entitled to expect.

Jesus died for the sins of our race alright, for the primordial
sin of the race. And he paid the price he had to pay for sending
that sin into remission. But not in the sense of being a human
sacrifice on the cross, which only a satanic idol would demand.
Rather in this sense, that his death was the price he had to pay
for his fidelity to the reign of the God he called Father, who
would never destroy life or kill even those who came to destroy
and kill others, and who distinctly forbade those who would be
his sons to return evil even for such fatal evil. That dying-rather-
than-kill then turned out to be the consummate witness, and
more, the most powerful breathing into a mad, killing world, of
the Spirit of the true reign of the one, true God. That was the
price, and that is what it was paid for, and that is what it gained,
and still gains for those who can take it.

Each of the three so-called synoptic gospels – (Mark 13:3-37;
Matthew 24:4-36; Luke 21:8-36) – repeats a myth, a cosmic myth
of the end or close of the present age. This myth resembles the
myth of the flood and the covenant with Noah (Matthew in fact
draws this very comparison in his telling of this cosmic myth of
the end of the age) and in two ways. First, in that as cosmic
myths the fact that the one is placed at a beginning time-out-of-
time while the other is placed at an end time-out-of-time does
not prevent either of them from offering revelations of what is
ever and always the case with the cosmos. And second, in that
both envisage such an exponential increase of human evil in the
world that the very fabric of society, and indeed the very fabric
of the physical, life-bearing cosmos itself is destroyed, as all returns to the primordial chaos. Yet the sufferings that literally
consummate this current age of the cosmos are but the birth
pangs of the new age of the reign of God that Jesus had announced at the beginning of his mission. This is a point that
Jesus had often apparently made concerning some individual
sufferings of disease and death, when he said that these were
not penalties for sins committed. Rather were they to be seen as

occasions and opportunities for the reign of the eternal Creator Spirit to manifest itself in renewed and ever new creative endeavour by God, and by the sons and daughters of God possessed by that same Spirit. Just as the waters of the flood story, turned into the utterly destructive chaotic depths by the excess of human evil-doing, were once (again) turned by God into waters that let the good earth emerge once more, and make it fruitful for life ever more.

As the myth of the close of this age puts the matter: false prophets will arise and preach false gods. Indeed many of these will come in the name of Jesus 'and they will lead many astray. And you will hear of wars and rumours of wars ... For nation will rise against nation and kingdom against kingdom.' (Where have we heard recently of war waged in the name of the following of Jesus?) And this excess of destructive human violence will coincide with increasing persecution of the sons and daughters of the prophet, Jesus, and of God, until the very fabric of human society is torn apart. 'And brother will deliver brother to death, and the father his child, and children will rise up against parents and have them put to death.' And if only because of the interdependence of the human race and the physical cosmos, with the former as steward of the latter, and the latter the source of the necessities of life for the former, the very fabric of the physical cosmos will also be threatened: 'The sun will be darkened (or send too much heat through a damaged atmosphere) ... and the stars will be falling from heaven, and the powers in the heavens will be shaken.'

And then what? At this point Matthew paints a picture in which 'all the tribes of the earth will mourn, and they will see the Son of Man coming on the clouds of heaven with great power and glory; and he will send out his angels with a loud trumpet call, and they will gather his elect from the four winds, from one end of heaven to the other.' And few readers will fail to remember that, a mere chapter later, Matthew will appear to fill in the rest of this picture, when 'all the nations' are gathered together, then separated, and the rest is pseudo-history rather than a true myth. Mark also talked at this point of 'of the Son of Man coming in clouds with great power and glory. And then he will send out the angels, and gather his elect from the four winds, from the ends of the earth to the ends of heaven.' And even though these verses are part quotation from Daniel (7:13), who is simply describing the coming of the kingly messiah, and even though we may in the overall context of the gospels understand the kingship of messiah Jesus as the rule of the servant, perhaps it is the bad taste that Matthew leaves in the mouth, but we still suspect that the reference to 'the elect' here also elicits a sense of a tribunal of justice and a corresponding suspicion of what is to happen to us poor sinners at the entry point to the new age.

Luke's version of this myth of the close of this age that is ever on the threshold of the new age of the true reign of the one, true God, is probably the version that is most free of confusing imagery. For Luke ends the myth with these words: 'And then they will see the Son of Man coming in a cloud with power and great glory. Now when these things begin to take place, look up and raise your heads, because your redemption is drawing near.' These words could be spoken to anyone at any time or place in this sin-sodden, suffering age that still shows little sign of coming to a close, or of giving way at last and entirely to the new age of the reign of God. At any time we can be freed (redeemed) from our slavery to a destructive evil-doing that seems endemic to our kind, if only we would eat the bread that comes from heaven, and imbibe the Spirit that possessed Jesus the true Christ, who in all of his life and death breathed that Spirit in all of its power and glory, and breathes it still through all who follow him in the Christian churches, or in any religion, or in none.

But it is John, as usual, who is clearest and truest to the historical Jesus, in ridding the faith of Jesus and the keeping faith with him that characterises his true followers, of that pernicious virus of judging, condemning, sentencing and executing the sentence. A virus against which Jesus, no matter what he said and did, could never fully and finally inoculate all of his disciples, and not even some of the closest of these. At the very opening of that farewell discourse and prayer for his closest followers that John composes on the lips of Jesus, you sense immediately that it is bound to be a long one. If only because in the scene painted at the very commencement of that composition, Thomas and Philip, respectively, do not appear to know where Jesus is going and taking them. He said he was 'the way', but to where? Thomas asks. To his Father's house, is the answer. That is to say, to the age and the world of perfect *shalom*. Right then, Philip chips in helpfully, show us the Father, and we will all know where we are supposed to be going. It must have been with some exasperation that Jesus then responds, 'Have I been with you so long, and yet you do not know me, Philip? He who has seen me has seen the Father.' But of course they have not really seen him, and some of them never will; and some will see, and then not see again, and then not want to see. We know that already from all the evidence of the gospels to the effect that they simply did not want to know a messiah who had to die, but only a kingly messiah who would gain a kingdom, and then put on trial and kill or imprison any who opposed him. They simply did not see, or did not want to see – which is much the same thing – the true nature of the son of God, and so of the God he called Father.

So, according to John, Jesus tries again. In a passage or two that repeats much of what is found in the synoptic myth of the end of this evil age, he describes to these still questioning ones the intensification of the persecution to which they will be subjected. Then he describes these sufferings in turn as the birthing pains of the reign of God, and of their own emergence into the new age or the new world of the *shalom* that epitomises the reign of God. And he ends by praying to God to preserve them on this tragic way to that blissful end, with not a word about sin and judgement and punishment, except to say, that 'If I had not come and spoken to them, they would have no sin; but now they have no excuse for their sin,' and to add that the Spirit who moulds his very life will convince the world of judgement, 'because the ruler of this world is (already) judged.' (John 14-17)

What Jesus has in mind with that phrase, the ruler of this world, is precisely what he had in mind when he warned his disciples against the spirit in which the rulers of this world lorded it over their peoples in the course of making their authority felt. This is a satanic spirit, so that the spirit that rules this world in this way is the satan, the great adversary and destroyer of life eternal, in so far as that is within the satan's power. And to a quite dismaying and apparently increasing extent, it is within the satan's power. But Jesus stresses more than once in John's gospel, that the judgement on that inherently destructive kind of rule is already passed by his own coming and his mission. 'For judgement I came into the world, that those who do not see may see, and that those who see may become blind.' (John 9:39) In other words, the coming of Jesus and the true sense and reality of the reign of God he brought with him, enables those who accept him to see what before that they had not seen, namely, that the only power they should wield is the power of the servant to serve the lives of all, as the Creator Spirit does, eternally. But the arrival on the scene of this particular prophet also meant that many of those who were convinced that they had seen it all already and who therefore refused the light that Jesus threw on things – the light of the world – merely became confirmed in their blindness, to the point of wanting to rid their nation and their religion of his very person.

It is extremely instructive to note the terms in which Jesus, according to John, describes his 'hour', the hour that begins with the moment that Judas leaves the last supper they would share, in order to go to those who wanted to kill Jesus anyway, and to expedite his by now certain death: 'Now is the Son of Man glorified, and in him God is glorified; if God is glorified in him, God will also glorify him in himself, and glorify him at once.' (John 13:31-32) Now; at once. Remember that this is the hour, his finest hour in which, again according to John, the Creator Spirit of steadfast creative love breathes most powerfully through Jesus. It is the hour in which Jesus is raised (on the cross) to the status of life-giving spirit, as Paul would put it; or as John so often says, the hour in which God's glory (another image, like the image of God's spirit, used to convey God's effective presence in the world through Jesus) shines unimpeded through Jesus. In other words, this is the moment in which the self-sacrificing love of Jesus, revealed in standard fashion in his breaking the healing and nourishing bread of life to others, now proves to be the moment of revelation *par excellence* of the Creator Spirit who never does anything other than serve life quite indiscriminately to all. Then think of the implications of John's saying that this is the moment that Jesus appears clothed in the glory of God, as the glory of God shines undimmed through him, and see the clear contrast with Matthew. For with Matthew it was on some fear-some Day of Judgement that king Jesus would appear in glory, attended by the hosts of heaven to reward only the good, and to penalise all those convicted of evil-doing with eternal torment.

One more thing is clearly implied and insisted upon by John in all of his imagery of a judgement already arrived on the scene with Jesus himself, and it is this: it is a judgement that involves no condemnation to punishment especially decreed by the judge for the evil-doing of those possessed by a spirit adversarial to the Creator Spirit.

In the words that John places on the lips of Jesus: 'God sent the Son into the world, not to condemn the world, but that the world might be saved through him. He who believes in him is not condemned; he who does not believe is condemned already, because he has not believed in the name of the unique (Greek *monogenous*, meaning 'one of a kind') Son of God. And this is the judgement, that the light has come into the world, and men loved darkness rather than light, because their deeds were evil. For every man who does evil hates the light, and does not come to the light, lest his deeds should be exposed. But he who does what is true comes to the light, that it may be seen that his deeds have been wrought in God.' (John 3:16-21)

That passage in John must be read in conjunction with what John said in the prologue to his gospel, namely, that the light of the Creator Word (another image, like that of Spirit, for the effective Presence of God in the world), a light that enlightens everyone in the world, came into the world, again and quite uniquely, with the Spirit-possessed Jesus of Nazareth. (John 1:1-14) But those who had sold their souls to an adversarial spirit and were in consequence enmired in evil, would not or could not come to the light that shone through Jesus, the light and glory of the Creator Word or Spirit that continually creates the world. And that in itself constitutes their judgement, and their condemnation to life of mutual destruction ever overshadowed by the spectre of death, and by the inevitably incursive despair – a condemnation that would last for at least as long as they refused this new embodiment of the light, the glory of the Creator Spirit that shone through the very person, life and death of Jesus of Nazareth. Whereas for all who, perhaps increasingly disillusioned by the mutual destructiveness of a satanic spirit in action, or scorched by its self-consuming flames, came to the man from whose life there shone the light of a different spirit, however desperate their act of faith in coming to him may have seemed at first – for these the vision opened up of a vista of life and a source of life that could overcome suffering and despair, and light the way through death itself.

As Jesus himself puts the matter, in the first sentence left unquoted from the last-but-one passage from John above: 'For God so loved the world that he gave his unique Son, that whoever believes in him should not perish but have eternal life.' (John 3:16) The giving of the Son, yes, to be understood as the giving up to death on the cross, but not in the sense of sentencing him to death as the penalty for sin. Rather, as is clear from all these other Johannine passages above and more, the death of Jesus is necessary so that the definitive breathing of the Creator Spirit would inspire people to live such lives of healing and serving and enhancing the lives of all, as would in itself continually promote life over death, thereby grounding in life itself, more than in mere words, the growing and blessed conviction that this life that comes from the Creator Spirit is and always in fact has been a life eternal. As Jesus himself put it when arguing against the Sadducees for the common resurrection of all people, the Creator Spirit whose light shines in all of creation is the God of the living, not the God of the dead, the God whom Paul reminded the Athenians they already knew, 'in whom we live and move and have our being'. And is that not enough to show that the truth of this matter is that the God that Jesus called his Father and ours does nothing in all eternity but create life, and heal it where necessary and advance it to eternal *shalom*, and that the only penalty we ever pay or will ever pay for our evil-doing is the suffering and death we bring upon ourselves? The Irish poet, Patrick Kavanagh, put the point most succinctly – and the true poet is always the true seer – 'There are no recriminations in heaven.'

But if even all of that is not enough, then perhaps a thorough reading of the last book of the Bible, and also one of the latest written of the documents that comprise the Christian Bible, could help clinch the case. This biblical document is now known as Revelation, but it was traditionally entitled, The Apocalypse, because it is filled from beginning to end with that apocalyptic imagery of human and cosmic disaster and delivery, so familiar from earlier prophets like Daniel and Ezekiel in particular, and attributed to the end of the age. In short, the whole Book of Revelation is a form of end-time myth. It was written by a man called John who was exiled to the island of Patmos during the reign of the Emperor Domitian (AD 81-96). It was written as a result of one of these visionary encounters with the risen Jesus – otherwise known as appearances of the risen Jesus – who is identified as the Voice, or the Word, or the one through whom the Spirit of God speaks; for, as John himself puts the matter, 'The testimony of Jesus is the spirit of prophecy.' (Revelation 19:10) John of Patmos is a prophet then, in the original sense of one who speaks for God and speaks God's eternal truth about the world, rather than one who predicts the future instead of describing the present. A prophet, and therefore a true son of the prophet Jesus, as Peter might have called him, is he not?

From so much of this book by John of Patmos it would certainly seem so. For example, he describes the trials and tribulations that his people presently suffer from the greed and violence of the Roman Empire, the Great Beast, the Whore Babylon, in the precise terms that are so familiar from these end-time cosmic myths that, like all cosmic myths, are really about everytime. The imagery is of death-dealing and destructive warring amongst peoples, of ever-attendant pestilence and famine, of the very earth itself laid waste, and the heavenly bodies themselves deprived of their life-giving light and heat, or made to produce too much of the heat. And in any case the general imagery of fire, the great transformer, even if it seem to be for some a transformation only into the form of ashes. Ashes to ashes, dust to dust. Not a bad description of all wars in their common outcome, including economic wars, and not only because these also sooner or later involve military violence. (Iraq, poor pitiable Iraq, put to the sword by the latest imperialist marauders of the earth, and all accompanied with the mealy-mouthed protestations that they were bringing freedom, just like the imperialist Romans of old proclaimed their gift of the *Pax Romana*, the Roman version of *shalom*. Nobody wanted such pseudo-*shalom* then. Nobody wants it now, except of course the military marauders themselves.)

Would it therefore not seem to be the case after all that these mighty end-time cosmic myths were being used in this book, as all cosmic myths should be used and interpreted, as depth-analysis of every present time of the cosmos, of the persistent penchant for self-destruction and suffering, and with recipes attached for the only form of deliverance that could ever succeed? Indeed, is not the use of the general fire symbolism in such stories to be deciphered in the sense that the fire of such suffering could also purify people from bad minds and treacherous hearts (*metanoia* – a change of mind and heart), and could thereby imprison forever or bind the spirit of evil that had so far caused such apparently perpetual destruction of creation itself? And all of this compatible with the belief that God never punishes evil-doers with any punishment other than that with which they inflict each other and indeed all of human kind?

There is one other striking feature of John's prophecy that would suggest so, and it is this: John's prophecy ends in a description of the new (renewed?) cosmos, the new heavens and the new earth of the end-time – a description that uses the same central images with which the book of Genesis described this same cosmos as it comes from the hands of the eternal God. 'Then he showed me the river of life, bright as crystal, flowing from the throne of God and of the Lamb through the middle of the street of the city; also, on either side of the river, the tree of life with its twelve kinds of fruit, yielding fruit each month; and the leaves of the tree were for the healing of the nations ... And night shall be no more; they need no light or lamp or sun, for the Lord God will be their light, and they shall reign for ever and ever.' (Revelation 22:1-5) In other words, paradise restored is the cosmos as it has been from the beginning of creation. Or, in mythic terms, what exists as it comes eternally from the hands of the eternal God, is always there for those who wish to recover it. If hell for us is always here on earth, for just as long as we punish ourselves by our own satanic spirit and evil-doing, then so is paradise always here and at any moment recoverable with the change of a heart.

As T. S. Eliot, the poet who knew that 'history is a pattern of timeless moments,' put it in the incomparable genre of poetry:

> With the drawing of this Love and the voice of this Calling
> We shall not cease from exploration
> And the end of all our exploring
> Will be to arrive at where we started
> And know the place for the first time.

> Quick now, here, now, always –
> A condition of complete simplicity
> (Costing not less than everything)
> And all shall be well and
> All manner of things shall be well
> When the tongues of flame are in-folded
> Into the crowned knot of fire
> And the fire and the rose are one. (*Little Gidding*)

William Blake is another poet of modern times who sees as clearly as only the seer can, that no eternal punitive judgement is part of the Christian faith. Blake certainly pictured a Last Judgement that destroys all the wrongs and responding ugliness of the created world, a judgment scene in which the Judge is the Divine Humanity. But in this Last Judgement of Imagination, the error of creation is 'Burnt up the Moment Men cease to behold it'; as Kathleen Raine paraphrases Blake, 'It is burned up in the light of eternity.' The very image and idea of a potentially punitive last judgement is a satanic image and idea, based on the kind of judgement so commonly carried out by natural Satanic Man.

However, just as is the case with Paul and Matthew and 2 Peter, John of Patmos also has his ways of preventing us from reading all of this cosmic mythology as if it refers, as by nature it should, to the conditions of all times and places in the cosmos. John does this by turning the myth of judgement into a (hi)story of a certain future time, and in particular by the simple ruse of talking about a 'second death' that takes the form of a condemnation to eternal torture. So, the same mythic imagery of the cosmic myth, when it could be applied to the destructions and sufferings endured during the years of the Roman Empire, was now applied to a later punishment of all of those who, like the

Romans, opposed the promoters of the reign of God and even persecuted them to death. Once again, one can ask, why did John of Patmos bring back an image of God as the Great and Final Enforcer if he remembered at all that Jesus called on all who would hear him to be sons of his Father in this above all, that they would never return evil for evil, but only share life with the just and the unjust alike?

And the answer to that question, in so far as one can glean an answer from John's prophesy also, emerges here in this manner. Notice that the new world is imagined by John of Patmos as the new Jerusalem. The garden in the imagery that John borrows from the book of Genesis imagery of creation as a garden, makes the new Jerusalem a garden city, in which the trees of life (one on either side of the river of life flowing down the main street) provide eternal life for the citizens, the Jews. The leaves of these trees are 'for the healing of the nations' who presumably must come to the city for this divine salvation from their deathly ways. The new Jerusalem has twelve gates named after the twelve tribes of Israel, and for the twelve foundations of its walls 'the twelve Apostles of the Lamb'. Still in this late document, as everywhere in the part of the Bible added by Christians, everybody including Jesus thinks of the renewed kingdom of God as a renewal and extension of Israel. Jesus more or less confirms that when he chooses as the only leadership group he ever personally appointed for his newly-called gathering (*ecclesia*, church), The Twelve. Adding 'Apostles' adds nothing to their leadership description as such, for an apostle is merely one who is sent to spread the good news of the kingdom of God, and so lots of others can be called apostles, and were so called. So this leadership of The Twelve, for as long as it lasted, carried with it the expectation that the renewal of the kingdom of God was to come primarily through a renewed Israel.

But Jesus himself, as far as we can see from his preaching and practice recorded in the Bible, was capable of seeing the continuity of his own company of followers, without transferring to that new community the structures sacred and secular of the historical kingdom of Israel (John of Patmos too says, 'I saw no temple in the city.' 21:22). And in particular without transferring the ethos of worldly kings and kingdoms, with their perpetual warmongering, killing and laying waste. Jesus would die rather than do that; and he did die, in a way, for just that. Yet his followers and leaders of the community that claimed his name thereafter, were far too given to that kind of kingdom and ethos, and have been so to this day. And that is why they and we still promote, alongside the true myths, these other stories of gods who come like earthly kings with their attendant armies to defeat all of those who are hostile and injurious to us, and finally to gather all of them up and convict them to eternal torture.

In sum, those who believe Jesus in this matter must insist that there is and will be no judgement, and certainly no condemnation of the primordial sinfulness, the persisting evil-doing of the race of *homo sapiens*, other than the judgement of condemnation passed on it by the life and faith of Jesus of Nazareth who, as much in his life and death as in his preaching, showed up for what it was the death-ridden and ultimately despairing life of those who seek to assume power over life by amassing as much of this world's goods as they can do, and in the process cause incalculable destruction to others and to themselves in almost equal amounts. And in consequence, since there is not and will not be any judgement and condemnation other than that of the one who came only to salve and promote this precious life, and only in the form of his doing that – doing only good to those who had done evil – there certainly could be no question of any penalty to be paid, other than the intrinsic self-punishment of the satanic spirit of destruction by which this tragic race is still so patently possessed.

It is worth noticing, incidentally, that this interpretation of these judgement stories in the Bible chimes in perfectly with the interpretation of the stories of resurrection: an interpretation that sees resurrection as a raising, for Jesus and for us, to the status of sons and daughters of God, and to a consequent sharing in the eternal life of God. But a resurrection that happens throughout this life and through the death of this current mortal frame, rather than a resurrection that those misled by a combination of the misunderstanding of the particular time-references of myth, and the adoption of a story, alien to the Bible, of the make-up of the human being and the different destinies of its soul and body, must now imagine to be a resurrection of the body. Just in time for the Day of Judgement, and so as to have something that the Judge can sentence to burning? Burning souls, to these ancient Greeks in any case, would be just a wee bit on the unlikely side. But no more unlikely than thinking of the saving activities of Jesus so fully recorded in the Bible as the saving of souls, without mention of bodies. The wholesale adoption by the Christian religion, and from its earliest centuries, of a crude dualism of soul and body, of which only the most unsophisticated of Platonic philosophers could be accused, has done an immense amount of damage to the faith of Jesus, as is everywhere evident down to the present day.

But then what is to be said about the Bible that contains a picture of divine judgement which has Jesus in glory judging in John's sense the sins of this world with his dying breath on the cross, surrounded by the execution party and mostly mockers; all his company of disciples fled, except for John and, oh yes, his mother and maybe one or two others of even lesser importance on that ancient scene? This same Bible that also contains, courtesy of Matthew, that other picture of Jesus in glory, but now the glory of a triumphant king surrounded by a mighty heavenly host, coming to usher in the end of this evil age, and to put all those who had ever opposed his reign and kingdom to the fiery sword for all eternity? So clear a contrast between John and Matthew that the reader must be tempted to think John's effective dismissal of Matthew's account to be quite deliberate. And then of course the reader must further conclude that one of these accounts must be as correct as the other has somehow become corrupt.

Is this the end then of the fabled inerrancy of the Bible? The Bible that tells the truth, the whole truth and nothing but the truth, with the help of God whose Spirit breathed through its many and varied writers, as that same Spirit had breathed through the whole life and work and even the death of Jesus himself? No, it is not the end of any of that. It is just that the Bible tells a larger truth than any of those people can handle who think it tells God's truth only, and nothing of the betrayal that from the beginning until now corrupted the very reception of that truth. And such a view of the matter is quite convenient for such people, when for example they set out with their armies to kill those they have somehow persuaded themselves and their people are their enemies. For they can then quote as divine confirmation of their conduct the very parts of the Bible that are in fact telling of how the truth of God that came with Jesus was corrupted in its very reception by people who listened to Jesus but could not hear him. For the only God they wanted to hear about was a God they had already turned into a satan, an idol who would secure and advance their lives and the life of their nation or religion, at whatever the expense to others.

But the Bible is inerrant in a sense that is larger than that, and whole. For side-by-side with its presentation of God's truth that came, his followers say, in its fullest and most perfect human form with Jesus, the Bible presents us also with the falsehoods that its receivers have foisted upon that truth under the aegis of the age-old and perennial satanic temptation. And so the Bible tells a truth that is as apposite for us today as it was for the first two pairs of disciples that Jesus called by the lake; as apposite as it was for all of the others who followed Jesus during the years in which the Christian Bible was written, and recognised and authorised by that early community of people who insisted that they were following Jesus. Although many, if not a majority, were in fact so blind still to the truth of Jesus that they took the blindness recorded in the Bible, with respect to the real truth of Jesus that is also recorded with consummate clarity in the same Bible, as truth that the Bible recommended to them also.

And so we do to this day, and never so effectively as when we identify Judas as the one who betrayed the Christ, even though it is so very easy to imagine how his betrayal of Jesus was no different in kind, and no worse than that in which any of the rest of the disciples of Jesus engaged. They all, as far as the evidence goes, wanted a king and a kingdom that would favour them over all other peoples, and that would use whatever power it took to achieve that happy result, thereby rendering these others dependent on them in the life-stakes. So all of them were equally and insistently alarmed at and dismissive of any expression of the very idea that Jesus might actually go off half-cocked, facing up to the Jerusalem rulers and risking execution, theirs perhaps as likely as his own, before success could look at least a little more imminent. There is no reason to think that

Judas thought any different, and every reason to think that he thought of a more effective way of preventing that disaster to the coming of the reign of God as he and the others understood it. As the man in charge of the assets of the leadership group, the managing director as it were, it is from Judas that we should expect a more effective response to the crisis, as all of them saw it, that Jesus seemed determined to cause. Certainly more effective than just waiting and waiting for the foolish thing to happen, and then running away as fast as their poor sandals could carry them. So Judas, believing in what he understood was the cause of the kingdom of God that Jesus seemed so successful at promoting, now thought that Jesus himself was losing the plot. He should, like many another leader that loses the way, be got rid of, so that the others in the chosen leadership group could get on with the job. And what better way to get rid of him for the sake of the cause of the coming kingdom, than to help him as quickly as possible into the presence of those towards whom he appeared to be hurrying anyway, convinced that they were going to kill him?

Nor is there any reason to believe that the death of Jesus when it actually occurred, did not bring about in Judas, as it did for others of his closest followers, the kind of repentance, that is to say, the kind of change of heart that Jesus had so significantly failed to bring about in them during his life with them. Any more than there is any reason to believe that Judas, like many of these others, did not even after that resile once more either temporarily or permanently into one or other version of the false views of the reign of God that have continued to plague the Christian community to this day. Either because the vision of that blessed reign was too demanding, or the age-old temptation of a different vision of rule and kingdom was still too powerful in him. Some early communities of Jesus-followers preserved traditions to the effect that Judas did too repent and became a saint, although he did not take up again his place amongst The Twelve. There had to be an election for that. It is once again the poet as seer that can see that Judas, no more a sinner or a saint than most of his fellows in The Twelve, or most of us, most of the time. Another Irish poet, Brendan Kennelly, sees Judas just like that, through this imagined reverie in Judas's own words:

I have never seen him, and I have never seen
Anyone but him. He is older than the world and he
Is always young. What he says is in every ear
And has never been heard before.
I have tried to kill him in me,
He is in me more than ever.
I saw his hands smashed by dum-dum bullets,
His hands holding the earth are whole and tender.
If I knew what love is I would call him a lover.
Break him like glass, every splinter is a wonder.
I had not understood that annihilation
Makes him live with an intensity I cannot understand.
That I cannot understand is the bit of wisdom I have found.
He splits my mind like an axe a tree.
He makes my heart deeper and fuller than my heart will dare
    to be.
He would make me at home beyond the sky and the black
    ground,
He would craze me with the light on the brilliant sand,
He is the joy of the first word, the music of the undiscovered
    human.
Undiscovered! Yet I live as if my music were known.
He is what I cannot lose and cannot find.
He is nothing, nothing but body and soul and heart and mind.

So gentle is he the gentlest air
Is rough by comparison
So kind is he I cannot dream
A kinder man
So distant is he the farthest star
Sleeps at my breast
So near is he the thought of him
Puts me outside myself

So one with love is he
I know love is
Time and eternity
And all their images.
No image fits, no rod, no crown.

I brought him down. (*No Image Fits*)

The point about the inerrancy of the Bible can then be put like this. The Bible is a self-correcting collection of histories, stories, poems and other fictions (e.g. parables) that record God's ways with the cosmos from origin to eschaton, as revealed in the world and its history both natural and human. It records simultaneously the misunderstandings and downright betrayals that have plagued the continuous creative revelation through all the centuries of its composition, increase, canonisation, transmission, translation and busy interpretation down to the present day. And just as the betrayals and misunderstandings of the divine revelation are commonly attributed to the age-old temptation of a race that names itself 'the wise', so the continuous corrective restoration of the truth is commonly attributed to the prophetic voices whose true insights remain even in the very process of disagreement and downright rejection of these that sit beside them, sometimes on the same page. For the followers of Jesus, his is the prophetic voice *par excellence* that definitively restores the true revelation of the one, true God from the beginning of creation. And so it is his voice above all that must be recovered from the Bible, from amongst all the other voices whose messages are forever more congenial to our common fallen state.

Add one other poem, also from an Irish poet, Patrick Kavanagh of happy memory; the poem with the quirky title, *Miss Universe*, from which the words, 'there are no recriminations in heaven,' were taken; and it is possible to sum up all that has been said through the long interpretation of the Bible offered here, about the cosmic reign of a Creator who never does anything but create and care for and recreate life over and over for all eternity; who turns suffering and death itself into salvation, and never in all eternity returns evil for evil; to sum up all of this with the brevity, incisiveness and brilliant clarity that only the poet-seer with the deepest and highest vision of the very fabric of cosmic reality can muster, and thereby to learn all the more easily all that it is never too late even for the last Judas to hear.

I learned, I learned – when one might be inclined
To think, too late, you cannot recover your losses –

I learned something of the nature of God's mind,
Not the abstract Creator but He who caresses
The daily and nightly earth; He who refuses
To take failure for an answer till again and again is worn.
Love is waiting for you, waiting for the violence that she
      chooses
From the tepidity of the common round beyond exhaustion
      or scorn.
What was once is still and there is no need for remorse.
There are no recriminations in Heaven. O the sensual throb
Of the explosive body, the tumultuous thighs!
Adown a summer lane comes Miss Universe,
She whom no lecher's art can rob
Though she is not the virgin who was wise.

IV: The Natural History of Creation

The history of Jesus of Nazareth has been recovered so far from the stories of his birth, of his public mission, of some events that surrounded his execution in Jerusalem, and of the aftermath of that execution, in particular the preaching and conduct of those who found the courage to proclaim themselves his followers and apostles. That story can be said to be set within the story of creation itself. And when that is said, it is not meant simply in the sense that in the Bible as a whole the story of Jesus is to be found in a set of documents that are tagged onto a previously Jewish set of documents that begin with the book of Genesis and its story of the origin of creation. No, rather what is meant is this: the story of Jesus in its central and most essential element is the story of a creation faith that is at the very heart of the Bible from its very Jewish beginning to its equally Christian end. Therefore the mythic images, the metaphors, the ciphers in which the story of this creation faith, and with it the story of Jesus, is encoded, are present, operative and indeed dominant from the book of Genesis to the book of Revelation, the former of which begins with a garden story and the latter of which ends with a garden city story.

When one wants to decipher any code, one assembles as many documents as one can find written in that code, so that seeing the dominant ciphers in as many different contexts as possible, one can be confident that one has arrived at as full and accurate as possible an understanding of the import of the whole body of texts. A brief summary then of the principal images or ciphers in which the story of Jesus is also cast – the images of creation itself, of kingdoms, kings and priests, of life and death, of nourishing and salving, of sin and judgement, of prophets, of fidelity and infidelity, of faith, hope and despair – can strengthen or modify, and certainly enrich the insights so far gained through these same images, and thereby fill out and clarify the story of Jesus to the extent that it is now possible to do.

The Story of Absolute Beginning

The story of absolute beginning at the opening of the book of Genesis itself begins by pressing into service some of the oldest metaphorical imagery that has come down to us from the dawn of human history. And in case some readers of the Bible, enthusiastic or reluctant, approach that work with the prejudice that some of these ancient images of absolute beginnings are simply too primitive and utterly unworthy for use even as metaphors for divine creation, let them be informed that no image drawn from human experience, as all of our imagery must be, no image of giving origin to things comes any closer than any other to the essentially, humanly ungraspable event of absolute beginning. Three pieces of imagery in particular are drawn to this unending task.

First comes the imagery of the dark and vasty deep of the primeval chaos; of depths that are as fertile in possibilities for existence and life as they are 'at first' empty of form and substance. The Hebrew terms, *tohu w' bohu*, are onomatopoeic of a bleak and lonely wind howling through a dark seascape.

The second image is a composite one: wind again, breath of life, *ruach* in Hebrew, spirit; now combined with the ancient cosmogenic imagery of the great bird coming upon, hovering over (overshadowing?), brooding over the chaos, and birthing a formed and beautiful, fruitful and fulfilled cosmos: 'And the spirit of God was hovering over the waters.' In the story of the flood and Noah's ark (Genesis 8), a story of the utter destruction that human kind is capable of bringing upon the cosmos, and a story of God's re-creation and vow always to (re-)create it, the bird is identified as a dove, the image and harbinger of *shalom*, creation at the height of its peace and perfection, the state in which it always comes from the hands of the Creator Spirit. There is in fact in other parts of the Bible another form of imagery that is either combined with that of bird or breath, or replaces these. It is the imagery that is cognate with air or wind in old cosmologies of the four basic elements; the imagery of fire. 'The dove descending through the air/ With flame of incandescent terror.' Or the Creator Spirit coming upon Jesus's disciples at Pentecost in the form of tongues of flame. For fire is one of the most ancient and universal metaphors for creation, always de-

197

forming in the cause of transforming in the course of life's eternal élan.

So then this Creator Spirit, this primordial bird, this dove, this flaring forth of fire, will appear again and again throughout the Bible in one or other of these avatars, always to create anew, for that is quite simply what Creator Spirits do, as the flood story of Genesis 8 states in generic terms. And all of that is illustrated for present purposes in particular when the Spirit overshadows Mary and the child forming in her womb, or comes as a dove on the grown-up man at his baptism, or comes on his followers as tongues of fire. And on every such occasion throughout the Bible, creation is imagined continually renewed. So whenever any momentary prophet-seer says or sees that the dove has come to rest, as it once did for Noah, on humanity's window-sill, with or without the olive branch in her beak, it is creation itself that is seen as it comes always good and beautiful from the hands of God. An ever renewed creation eternally wandering on its way, making whole again and renewing through all unavailing destruction and death whether natural or malicious. Thereby confirming at one and the same time, first, that divine creation is one eternal act that translates into the mathematical language of space-time as a continuous divine activity, and, second, that cosmic myths of their very nature bring the fictional element in all exercises of the 'science' of history to its apogee. In this respect, that when these cosmic myths seem to envision a time in some dim distant past or future, they are really talking of a time-out-of-time, and thereby saying something that is true (or false, of course, since there are false myths) of every passing moment in the cosmos. The cosmic myths always talk of the whole of natural and human history as it comes from eternity, from the ultimate source, the conventional name for which is God.

The imagery of redemption is included within this complex imagery of bird-spirit-fire. It is included in the sense that whatever it is that is envisaged under the metaphor of redemption or buying back is precisely what is otherwise described as re-creation, that is to say, making whole again or making new. That comes clearest of all from Isaiah 40-66, these chapters that are sometimes referred to as Second Isaiah. For Second Isaiah has God the Creator depicted as Redeemer more frequently than has any other part of the Bible. But the accounts of divine redemption are constantly conveyed in the language of the account of divine creation, so the impression is constant that it is by continuing to create a good life for the Israelis, and for all the nations through them, that God redeems. And just as all continuous creation involves the destruction of current forms of things, metaphorically washing or burning these away, so redemption also involves washing or burning creatures clean of the obsolete or self-destructive forms of life to which they are still enslaved. In the case of obsolescent forms of life, it is easy to understand and accept the natural washing or burning away that coincides with the arrival of newer life forms. But in the case of that self-inflicted destruction and death to which the human race as a whole seems perpetually prone, the divine washing and burning away seems to take the form of divine creative maintenance and empowering of those who come to murder, rape and pillage us who have done so to them. That is more difficult to accept, but if that does not purge us of our evil-doing, what will? 'We only live, only suspire/Consumed by either fire or fire.'

It is in the course of accounting for divine redemption in the original imagery of divine creation that Second Isaiah invokes once again the birthing imagery of creation from Genesis. 'Now I will cry out like a woman in travail, I will grasp and pant', (Isaiah 42:14) and the impression is unavoidable that God suffers the pains of the destruction wrought by these creatures on themselves and on the very earth that should always make their lives glad and fulfilled. But then by God's continuous creative presence amongst them, as soon as they recognise it and the life the Spirit inspires, the self-inflicted suffering of the race will purge but not destroy them. 'When you pass through the rivers … they shall not overwhelm you; when you walk through the fire … the flame shall not consume you.' 'For I will pour water on the thirsty land, and streams on the dry ground. I will pour my Spirit upon your descendants, and my blessing on your offspring. They shall spring up like grass amid waters.' 'I will turn the darkness before you into light.' (Isaiah 42:14-16; 43:2; 44:3-4)

The third image pressed into service in the effort to gain some purchase on the matter of the absolute origin of the cosmos is the image of the word. Unlike the other two, this image is introduced more implicitly than explicitly, as we read of God creating by talking things into existence: 'and God said'. The imagery of God creating by word does not necessarily, if at all, refer to a single word, or even to a brief let-their-be like command. That latter does happen in the case of the first creation of all, the creation of the light: 'Let there be light', but that is a one-off. For all the rest of the first creation story at the very beginning of Genesis, the 'word' through which God creates all that then comes to be sounds more like a formula, a recipe almost, for what is then to be made, and what it is then to make of itself. An exercise in know-how rather than just theoretical knowing, an exercise in wisdom in short, rather than mere knowledge. In sum, an exercise in intelligent design. For an exercise that consists in creating according to formulae is really an exercise in forming, shaping things, setting the limits between firmament above from firmament below, between land and sea, then forming land and sea so that each of these in turn can bring forth living creatures. Creating creatures that can then play their part in creating others, and some of these through seeds of various kinds capable of producing an ever-further-forming posterity.

This account, considering its age and ancestry, is not a million miles away from the idea of divine creation that could be seen from our worm's eye point of view as an evolving universe. And much ancient myth and philosophy did have that very image and idea, although they might present it under the title of metamorphosis rather than evolution. And it would in any case be lacking in the extraordinary accuracy and detail in which modern scientists can describe a continually created, evolving universe. Nevertheless, there is no reason for readers of Genesis to have any hand, act or part, in these stultifying contemporary debates between 'creationism' and 'evolutionism', unless of course they have the misfortune to find themselves caught between a group of fundamentalist exegetes of Genesis who could not tell a metaphor from a motor car, and a group of philosophically inept cosmologists brandishing some scientific qualifications.

However all of that may be, here is the mythic imagery of God creating the cosmos through God's Word, understood as it must be in the opening of John's gospel where it occurs in the

Greek as *Logos*. For *Logos*, though translated as 'word,' nevertheless connotes a full rational account or formula for something, according to which something can be made, and then understood. Or better still, it could be said that God creates through God's Wisdom, for wisdom denotes practical knowledge – knowing things by knowing how to make or deal with them for the best outcome for all concerned. Modern science is wisdom in that sense, or it ought to be. So the book of Proverbs says, 'The Lord by wisdom founded the earth', just as John described the Word as the one 'through whom all things were made'. And these attributes of God the Creator, God's Word or Wisdom, are then personified in the manner characteristic of myth, in both John and Proverbs, as a means of arriving at some idea of the personhood of the otherwise impenetrable God. Wisdom addresses the reader directly in order to inform us that 'The Lord brought me forth ... at the first, before the beginning of the earth ... like a master workman', and she is described building the house that is the cosmos, with its fabled seven pillars holding up the firmament of the sky. (Proverbs 3:19; 8:22–9:1) And all of this forms a perfect parallel with the myth that has God create through God's Spirit, also personified according to the same mythic regulation.

And then, at the very pinnacle of this mighty work of cosmos-creation, who should arrive on the scene but our hairy ancestors, a pair of human beings. These humans took their origin out of the earth, the dust, the ground, like all the other animals. (We are still within hailing distance of evolution theory.) Yes, this original pair come from the ground by the power of the Creator Spirit/Word/Wisdom, but then it is by the same power of the Creator Spirit/Word/Wisdom that the earth and the sea bring forth all the other living things that Genesis says they bring forth according to the same divine formula. (Genesis 1:24; 2:7, 19) So what is truly distinctive about these human beings is that God decided that they should arrive on the scene as the spitting image of their Creator Father. 'Let us make man in our image, after our likeness; and let them have dominion ... over all the earth ... So God created man in his own image, in the image of God he created him, male and female he created them.' (Genesis 1:26-27) Humanity is created in the image of the Creator

Spirit/Word/Wisdom, a derivative, secondary, subordinate, yet very real creator spirit, and with the intelligence or, better, the wisdom to go with the job.

The garden story in this opening creation myth of Genesis makes that point about the wisdom of this derivative co-creator pointedly clear, when it pictures God subjecting 'the man' to a rather exhaustive oral examination. God paraded every living creature before the man, and the man passed the exam with flying colours: he named them all. For to name is to know, and to know in such a wise as to be able to manage, and if necessary to rule. Adam, as Luke's genealogy of Jesus recognises, was the son of God, and as such God's plenipotentiary on earth. The man had garnered from his inspection of God's creatures enough of the wisdom of God to be able to act under God as a co-creator and therefore a manager of God's good world. To this day the scientific name of the human species is *homo sapiens*, humanity-the-wise. You can imagine Adam in the first flush of his qualification for co-creatorship carving on one of the trees of the garden – the wisdom tree perhaps – Humanity-the-Wise Was Here. With the past tense in this case, and in hindsight, sounding somewhat prescient, for very shortly now Humanity-the-Wise, with his equally foolish but perhaps more impetuous partner, will be thrown out of the garden of paradise – a tragic event of historic proportions that we shall shortly witness.

For the moment it is necessary only to recognise that humanity's status as creaturely creators, involving as it does the essential freedom to create things new, gives them simultaneously the freedom to destroy instead. A freedom to do good or evil, and a freedom that God cannot withdraw without destroying the creature created most like God's own self. And therefore also a freedom that will implicate God's own self in any destruction in which these wise ones, then turned foolish, do decide to engage. For as God continually creates the world through creatures, God thereby shares in the responsibility for whatever creatures do when they decide to turn destructive. That is the price God pays for the guarantee God gives at the end of the flood story, that God will never destroy what God's Creator Spirit has created. A point that is emphasised by Isaiah when he has God say, in language that is clearly evocative of the opening creation story of

Genesis: '"Forming light and creating darkness, making *shalom* and creating evil, I am the Lord who does all of these things" ... Thus says the Lord who created the heavens ... who formed the earth and made it.' (Isaiah 45:7, 18)

The First Supper in the Garden
An Evil Eating

With the imagery of the well-watered garden paradise, and in particular with the imagery of the tree of life and its life-giving fruit, the imagery of eating and drinking, the cipher of the meal moves into the very centre of the myth of divine-human creation. And make no mistake about it: this myth of the first feasting and its consequences is wholly integral to the encompassing myth of creation in which it is set. For it is a myth that is designed to account for humanity-the-wise's pivotal part in on-going creation, in the evolution of the cosmos, for better or, as we must now be informed, for very much worse. It is a myth that explains how humanity-the-wise has always looked more like humanity-the-foolish, and shows no present signs of improvement. But it is also a centrepiece of the Genesis creation myth that in its own right very possibly merits the dubious distinction of being the most misinterpreted myth in the whole history of hermeneutics, and most certainly over most of the history of Christian doctrine. (Genesis 2:4–3:22)

This enclosed myth of the first recorded feasting in the garden takes the form of a drama. So, in order to come upon the full and true import of this primordial drama, it is necessary first to make the acquaintance of the characters in the play, and to describe the set and some of the main props. The set is the garden of paradise, cipher for the cosmos as it comes true and good and beautiful from the hands of God, a cosmos in which life could be lived to the fullest and with every prospect of eternity. The principal props consist of fruit trees, and in particular – although it is difficult to decide if are dealing with one or two trees here – 'the tree of life in the midst of the garden, and the tree of the knowledge of good and evil', a fig tree, or at least some fig leaves, some animal skins, and needle and thread for sowing them together.

The *dramatis personae* are as follows (in order of appearance):
The Serpent, an avatar of divinity, in this drama a satanic figure.

Eve, a woman, consort of Adam, mother of the human race.

Adam, at once an individual man and father of the race, and Everyman.

God, the Spirit-Creator who creates the cosmos and all that is in it.

As the notes at the beginning of the script of a play often do, it is useful to include some special directions for staging the drama, and some further information on the characters and roles of the *dramatis personae*.

Special directions: the roles of The Serpent and God are to be played by the same actor, undisguised in either part and with only one distinguishing feature to indicate the difference between the characters/roles played: as The Serpent the actor will be dressed in charcoal grey; as God in burnished gold. All trees, leaves, animal skins, thread and needles used in the play must be re-cycled.

Further description of the characters and their roles:
The Serpent, like the great bird, is one of the most ancient symbols for the Creator of the cosmos. Like the bird in this also, the symbol of the serpent can be used in composite imagery, for example the serpent symbol was often used in combination with the bird symbol to yield the winged serpent. Or the serpent image can be combined with that of the ram which, like the bull, has the attributes of power and fertility that can symbolise the one who brings forth worlds: the ram-headed serpent. Or, like the bird also in this, the serpent imagery can be combined with another universal symbol for creation, fire, to yield the dragon. As a matter of fact, in nearby Babylonian mythology, with which the myths of Genesis clearly have so much in common, the fire-breathing serpent, the dragon, symbolises the deep made fertile for creation, just as the bird-spirit in Genesis makes the dark deep to realise all of its fertile possibilities.

On one occasion at least in the Bible, in John's gospel, the serpent reaches its full potentiality as a cipher for God the Creator as such. This is when John has Jesus say: 'As Moses lifted up the serpent in the wilderness, so must the Son of Man be lifted up, that whoever believes in him may have eternal life.' The reference here is to an episode during Israel's journey through the wilderness to the promised land, when the people spoke rebelliously against God and Moses because of their hard, hungry and fear-filled life in the desert, the kind of occasion on which they often turned to other gods. But it is the response of God and of Moses that is of interest now: 'The Lord sent fiery serpents against the people ... so that many people of Israel died.' This divine initiative of letting them be killed in the course of the self-centred idolatrous pursuit of their own welfare, proved capable on this occasion of bringing about a change of heart in the Israelites, and they confessed their sins, and this encouraged Moses to pray for them. And the Lord's response to the prayer of Moses was positive, for 'The Lord said to Moses, "Make a fiery serpent, and set it on a pole, and every one who is bitten, when he sees it shall live".' So the serpent remains for Jesus, according to John, the symbol of Jesus, the incarnate Word/Wisdom of God, raised to the status of son of God in power and as such the redemptive channel of the Creator Spirit's gift of eternal life. (John 3:14-15; Numbers 21:4-8; the Bible reader may notice that the (fiery) serpent, probably borrowed from Egypt, remained a symbol of divinity for the people during the period of kingly rule.)

Now the serpent-cipher is used in the garden creation story in order to introduce most graphically a tempter whose successful temptation of these humans results in the destruction of life rather than its continuous creation. Just as in the story of Moses and the serpent, the serpent-cipher is used for that satanic figure that brings death first and only afterwards life. And that surely sets a question mark after such ambivalent, if not contradictory, use of this cipher for divinity. The principal clue to the answer to that question is found in the fact that in a cosmos that is known to be continually created in an evolutionary or metamorphic mode, the formation of the ever-new inevitably involves at all stages the deformation of the old. That death of the old, of which we are always so endemically fearful, is the condition of the birth of the new, advancing life always coming out of death. So the Creator Spirit is ultimately and equally responsible for both – Lord of life and death. And the mythic story-form can handle this deep truth either by having two divine characters handling respectively the dark and the bright side of cosmogenesis, the one 'creating darkness and creating evil,' the other 'forming light and making *shalom*,' as Isaiah might put it. Or the myth can manage all of this by portraying the Creator through a combination of characteristics that bring together into one the dark and the light side of God. I seem to remember from somewhere an etching I think by William Blake: a quite conventional portrayal of our Father Almighty, Creator of heaven and earth, in the guise of a benevolent old man with flowing white locks, reclining so that the lines of his white garment draws the eye down to its hem, from which there barely protrudes a pair of cloven hoofs.

But the strategy of employing twin characters, or twin versions of the same character of the Creator Spirit, would seem to be the most favoured universally. To take an example of an ancient culture a very long way indeed from Babylon, in the pre-Christian mythology of the religion of old Ireland – which, incidentally, survived hale and hearty the conversion of the Irish to Christianity, and still survives happily intact to the present day – there is a myth that fits this latter mould. The story goes that every Samhain, the quarter festival at the beginning of winter, a fire-breathing *peist* or monster (a dragon) approaches Tara, the mythic holding centre of Ireland and legendary seat of the high king who could rule the whole land. In actual fact no historical Irish chieftain ever actually held that post, except perhaps for Brian Borumha, whose claim seemed verified for a very short time. So the high kingship of all Ireland exercised from the still sacred hill of Tara remained a mythic entity, much claimed but never realised, a feature oddly but aptly illustrated by the fact that the Irish word for province is *cúige*, which means a fifth, although there are only four provinces in Ireland. Four fifths! The fifth fifth takes us into unmistakeably mythic country: the mythic 'fifth' that represents the holding centre and thereby represents the whole. So the ancient story continues, the fire-breathing serpent comes to lay waste the whole land and people, but is met each year at Tara by the warrior god known as Fionn, the fair or bright or golden one like the sun, and is defeated and turned back, so that the land can begin to be brought to life and to life-giving again. Clearly Fionn is the creator of a life-giving cosmos, whose master cipher is so frequently from time immemorial and so universally, the sun.

So, in ancient Irish mythology also this serpent cipher, either alone or with other attendant images, portrays imaginatively and unforgettably the Creator Spirit, the Fire God taking occasion during the darkest, deadest winter-time of every year – for all creation, as the Genesis myth also acknowledges, originates in the depths of darkness, when darkness covered the face of the deep – in order to bring new life burning from the blasted sod, forever transforming what in that very process the same Fire God had deformed.

This Irish myth of the dragon and Fionn finds an even more striking expression in a piece of architectural drama at Newgrange. There is a prehistoric passage tomb at Newgrange, so constructed that at the dawn of the winter solstice, and at no other dawn, the rising sun sends a shaft of light through a slit over the main entrance, down the length of a long, dark passage, until it bathes in light the sacred chamber at the deep heart of the tomb. Thus, as one Irish prose-poet, John Moriarty, put it, laying down a golden path that the dead and buried have only to step onto, in order to make the journey back to the Ur-Source of Light and Life. But equally offering to the living a life-or-death choice. This is the choice: either to worship and imitate the adversarial, satanic, deforming, death-dealing (version of the) serpentine light-bringer, in its burning living things to dust and cinders, or to live in the image and on the path of the Fire-breathing Creator Spirit, 'the dove descending through the air in flames of incandescent terror,' by deforming things ever and only as an intrinsic part of the best efforts of our derivative and limited creative powers to transform life for the better for all.

Further description of principal prop:
It is the case with myth then that, just as two of the principal characters in the drama, The Serpent and God, can represent one and the same person, but in two different modes of being, so the tree of life and the tree of the knowledge of good and evil, or rather the eating of their fruit, can represent one and the same event and its consequences, but in separate

modes of its occurrence. For the tree of the knowledge of good and evil is the wisdom tree. 'Good and evil' is one of these Hebrew couplets that, by dividing all of reality into two categories and then uniting these in one phrase, connote 'everything'. There are two examples in a Christian Creed. God is creator of 'heaven and earth,' that is to say, 'of all that is,' to which, in case you missed the point, is then added another such couplet, 'seen and unseen', for that too covers just about everything. On the assumption that everything that exists is either good or evil, then, attribution of knowledge of good and evil to someone means that that one knows everything. Further, since knowing good and evil represents practical rather than purely theoretical knowledge, the all-knowing indicated here is all-wisdom. As a supplicant at the throne of David who wanted to flatter him in hope of a favourable verdict, said to him: 'My Lord has wisdom like the wisdom of an angel of God to know all things ... to discern good and evil.' (2 Samuel 14:17-20) The tree of the knowledge of good and evil, therefore, is the wisdom tree. Eat of its fruit and wisdom will be yours.

But then in the book of Proverbs, immediately before the passage in which Wisdom is described as the One, like the Word in John the Evangelist's prologue, through whom 'the Lord founded the earth,' that is to say, created the cosmos, it is clearly stated of divine Wisdom that 'She is a tree of life.' 'Long life are in her right hand; in her left hand are riches and honour ... and all her paths are *shalom*.' To which She herself adds, 'He who finds me finds life ... all who hate me love death.' (Proverbs 3:17-18; 9:35-36) The tree of life, again ancient and universal, symbolises the immortal life of God that God shared with us in giving us life, and that could raise the hope that our lives too might be for eternity. But the Wisdom Tree, by Wisdom's own word, is the tree of life. So here we have another twinned pair, a pair of trees that symbolises now a twinned pair of Divine Creators, who are in effect one and the same. We have seen a strategic need for the twinning in the case of God and the serpent, but what is the need for twinning in the case of the tree? An answer to that may emerge as the drama unfolds, and then again it may not.

Myths often run free from the restraints of pure logic, and it is often that freedom that assures the richness of insight that they offer over that which any purely logical excursus could achieve.

A Resume of the drama:
The Serpent, wiser than any other wild creature (bird, bull, ram?) innocently asks Eve if God had forbidden them the fruit of any tree in the garden, and she replied that they were forbidden to 'eat of the fruit of the tree which is in the midst of the garden', with God adding 'neither shall you touch it, lest you die.' Whereupon The Serpent assured Eve, 'You will not die. For God knows that when you eat of it your eyes will be opened, and you will be like God, knowing good and evil.' In short they would become all-wise, and immortal with it. So when Eve looked at the tree again, and saw 'that the tree was to be desired to make one wise (it was the wisdom tree, then, after all?), she took of its fruit and ate; and she also gave some to her husband (enter Adam in a very secondary role), and he ate.' Immediately they felt naked and ashamed, where before 'the man and his wife were both naked, and were not ashamed.' For now they had done something that belonged to darkness, something to be covered up, so 'they sewed fig leaves together and made themselves aprons.' (God himself would later make them more lasting and serviceable garments of skin, as they faced the long journey out of the garden, and back.)

Then, no sooner had they done the dastardly deed than the last of the *dramatis personae* was on the scene: 'They heard the sound of the Lord God walking in the garden in the cool of the day.' They tried to hide, but they were discovered, made to confess their transgression, and the penalties they would suffer as a result of their foolishness were sketched for them: the pain associated with bringing children into this world would multiply, the task of securing the necessities of life would be hazardous and difficult, the very earth itself, the material mother of their existence and life, would be like a thing cursed 'because of you', and the death that they would experience in any case would now be to them like nothing more than a return to dust. Life itself a trauma rather than a joy, and all hope of outliving death gone. And then, finally, the *coup de grace*, humanity-the-stupid is thrown out of the garden of paradise. Cherubim are placed at its gates to keep the garden and to keep the way to it open, but a fiery sword 'which turned every way' is placed there also, so that those who had earned exile from the garden could indeed return, but only through a purifying fire.

The first question that might occur to a person hearing this myth of the fall of human kind, as it is usually known, is this: but what was wrong about wanting to eat the fruit of the tree(s)? After all, the eternal God creates life on earth and offers it without measure to human kind. And as this fact is symbolised by planting for them the tree of life, what could be wrong with desiring the fruit of that tree? And if it is in the very act of offering life and the management of all the earth to a species capable of inspecting and understanding it that God conveys the know-how, the wisdom by which that species can fulfil its role of co-creator, what could be wrong with desiring that wisdom, mythically expressed as the desire to eat the fruit of the tree of wisdom? The answer to these questions, puzzling as they might seem on first hearing the myth, is actually contained clearly in the myth itself. For it is not the desire for the fruit of the tree(s) that is wrong, and its satisfaction sinful. It is that same desire, operating now under the temptation to appropriate the Creator Spirit's own wisdom, 'to be like God' in this respect, to be capable of securing life for themselves, and life immortal at that – it is that desire that is wrong. And yielding to the temptation to fulfil that desire to be their own god, is not merely sinful, it is the mother and father of all sin.

That point can be put in terms of two trees or of one, or in the mixed terms of our present Genesis myth. In two-tree terms the temptation is to consume entirely the fruit of the tree of wisdom, so that one will have taken into oneself the wisdom that allows one to become the absolute source of one's own life and world. Rather than having to gain wisdom from consuming the (tree of) life that God gives, a consumption that would yield only finite creaturely wisdom, as much as would enable one to co-create only in dependence on and trust in God, with whom the final hope of life temporal or eternal would then forever lie. In one-tree terms, the temptation is to want to consume the tree of life/wisdom, to make it so totally one's own that one could act as its very source could act. In either version, or in any mixture of the two, the temptation is to be like God, to be one's own god, and the sin is to act accordingly. Indeed, on second thoughts, it might be a little harsh to describe humankind so peremptorily as humanity-the-stupid, even if that is undoubtedly the name that the species ultimately and utterly deserves. For as a psalmist reminds God, 'You have made (humanity) a little less than the *elohim*,' which the Genesis myth translates as 'God'. (Psalm 8:5) A little less than God then, is what we are. And 'a little less' seen from God's side might easily seem from the side of the man proud of the wisdom that humanity had been taught by the very process of continuous creation, to require but 'a little more' of this wise species, in order that it should indeed equal the creative wisdom of God. Someone a little less than God could surely with a little more effort acquire a truly divine know-how, more than adequate for the creation of one's own world of limitless life and happiness. So it is to some degree defensible, if ultimately indefensible, to say that it is God who tempts humanity to act and be like God, by giving access to so much wisdom: the point of the myth making 'God' and 'the Serpent' seem like one and the same character in the play.

In short, there is something natural about this temptation. At least it comes quite naturally to creatures whose very nature is endowed by creation itself, in both its generative and revelatory modes, with so much god-like wisdom. In this respect, the temptation resembles those genetic conditions that secrete a proclivity to a certain disease, and carry that proclivity across the generations. (This has nothing whatever to do with a theology of original sin that talks of an actual sin committed by our first parents and that is then transmitted to all later members of *homo sapiens* by the mere act of procreation, a scenario nowhere found in the Bible.) Still, whether it seems natural or not, this is a temptation to which free creatures need not yield, and to which creatures that belong to such an inherently wise species might reasonably be expected not to yield. Yet *homo sapiens* seems to have yielded wholeheartedly to this temptation for as far back as we can see into human history.

Worse still, at the point to which the species has now evolved, one can so easily see that all of that evolving increase in wisdom and power, instead of an increase in glory, has yielded and continues to yield ever increasing satanic death-dealing within the species itself, and to the very earth it inhabits, the paradigmatic instances of this being, as always, war. War waged with ever more effective weapons of mass destruction, or with scarcely less effective economic weapons that spread at least as much destruction of life on earth, the starvation of humans and other animals, and all of the deadly interference with the life-supporting stellar fire and waters of the deep. To the point where it seems probable that this species will prove to be one self-destined to die out entirely in its present bodily form, and to live on eventually only in those more spiritual bodies of which Paul spoke. And one could hardly deny with any conviction that the cosmos we know would be any the worse for the extinction of this destructive species. Any more than one has any reason whatever to deny that there are bodily life-forms elsewhere in this universe that are immeasurably more intelligent and wise than *homo sapiens*. It would be a sad thing indeed to contemplate, if in this physical universe, the only one we know, the Creator Spirit had managed to bring forth, to have evolved, no wiser a species than we are proving to be. We should muster enough humility, on further consideration of the natural history of *homo sapiens* so far, to acknowledge the fact that our translation to a more spiritual kind of existence in the creative embrace of the Creator Spirit, will leave this physical universe at little loss, and less trace of our having been here, and with better prospects from wiser species elsewhere.

However all of that may be, the key to understanding how yielding to the temptation to appropriate divine wisdom causes the excess of sinful death-dealing and destruction, and all of the accompanying anguish, suffering and despair, lies in the frequency with which the little word 'self' seems to repeat itself in the description of that temptation. It is the temptation to consume, to appropriate to oneself the know-how to create life and worlds, and to appropriate to oneself as much of that life, its supports and enhancements as one can manage to acquire. It is the temptation of humans to believe that by their own plans and progress they can build up to the status and height of heaven itself the earthly habitat over which they had been given such managerial control, as the myth of the tower of Babel puts it. (Genesis 11:1-9) And there the trouble begins, for 'self' can refer to anything from an individual self to a group, and the group can refer to anything from a nuclear family, to a tribe, to a people, an empire, a church, a religion. In fact the latter two offer paradigmatic examples of such prejudicial self-centredness, for they are wont to claim the status of the one true church, or the one true religion, with the clear implication that God's beneficence is destined for their members, and only available to others by compliance with their rules and authority.

But whatever its social forms, the human self-centredness that appropriates to itself the divine prerogative of creating worlds for itself, inevitably does so at vital expense to others. The groups find themselves talking at cross-purposes, their plans mutually incomprehensible, if not unacceptable; unable to live together as one any more, but only as potentially rival factions scattered over the whole face of the earth, as the tower of Babel myth describes the punishment for their sinful pride. The whole history of the race, even as written by our 'scientific' historians, seems to be predominantly a story of individuals, groups and peoples securing lives and livelihoods either by naked violence against others, or by trade or, as is the case with the first world countries at this time, by an astute mixture of both. And of course such violence, in both forms, breeds more violence as the violated and despoiled seem to be left with no option but to respond in kind. And the vicious circle of man's inhumanity to man rolls relentlessly on its destructive way, wasting the lean earth as it rolls along.

Violence is done to God too when humanity falls for this primordial temptation. For *homo sapiens* now creates gods in its own self-centred image, instead of acting in the image of the Creator Spirit who always creates worlds equally for all creatures, and never destroys anything created, except in the process of transforming life and creation for all, whereas the satanic spirit of humanity destroys and kills for the gain of some over others.

Falling for this temptation is therefore said to involve blasphemy; in fact it constitutes the proper meaning of that term: to use God's name for what is in fact the satanic spirit of human kind, to use that name for an idol that has been created by humans to usurp the name of God. So that this primordial sin, the mother and father of all sins, is referred to in the Bible as either blasphemy, slavery to satan or idolatry, or any combination of these. For by using its wisdom to destroy rather than co-create equally for all, *homo sapiens* inevitably compromises the Creator Spirit, who eternally sustains and empowers its own free spirit, by involving the Creator in that wanton destruction of life that is the essence of all evil, thereby blaspheming, turning the one, true God into an idol – as Saul and more so Samuel did (not all prophets are good prophets, especially those too closely associated with kings) at Gilgal when they put a whole people to the sword in God's name. Paul did it later when he preached the same God of Israel as the eternal torturer of the sometimes murderous opponents of the cause of Jesus. And the Christian crusaders did it later still, when they massacred Muslims in the mistaken belief that as the 'new' people of God they had inherited the right to ethnically cleanse a land no longer promised to 'the perfidious Jews'. And so on, and so on with dismaying regulatory down the sad ages, through the murder and rapine of spreading 'Christian' empires from Spain and Britain, down to the present escapades of so-called Christian nations in the name of their messianic pretensions.

This apparently endemic human sinfulness turns God into an even more satanic spirit than the fiery dragon in its natural deforming mode already symbolises, by adding as it were another lair of malicious destruction to the natural deformation implicit in the co-creation of life in which *homo sapiens* should be a faithful and reliable partner. So the prophets often say that God brings the nations to punish Israel for Israel's own idolatry, thereby holding God responsible, and rightly so, for the retaliation in kind that occurs with dismal frequency when one nation despoils another. But the answer of God, once again, is to add another layer of continuous creation to that already necessitated by the natural deformation of things in the course of their evolutionary transformation. This is what is pictured in the story of

Moses and the Israelites in the desert, when the Fire-Spirit in the form of a fiery serpent re-creates life for those to whom, by the power he has allowed over him in their own spirits freely turned satanic, he has dealt death. This added layer is known also as salvation, for it heals self-inflicted damage done to creatures.

Just as in the case of the underlying layer of natural deformation in the course of the Creator's continual creation of things, the added layer of self-destruction contains two elements. First, a fiery purgative element, for the very prospect of our natural death should always purge us of even the temptation to accumulate material things and the ersatz power they give us – to grasp at finiteness, as Kierkegaarde put it, in order to sustain ourselves. Just as the quite indiscriminate storm of self destruction and self inflicted suffering released in the second layer should purge all of us even more thoroughly of our immersion in such primordially evil behaviour. And if at either level or both we are not purged – for the evidence of history is that we never learn, and worse, that as a species we are seriously retarded – what then? What if the natural fear of death obscures our view of the constant creativity of the eternal God, to the point where we try to deny death in every way, and mainly by accumulating goods as the trappings of power? What if the experience of destruction, suffering and death, at the hands of those who do grasp at finiteness to sustain themselves, tempts us to answer them in kind, rather than purge us of whatever part we play in such evil-doing? What then?

For few if any of us could claim to be entirely innocent of collusion in the original sin of the race. Could I, an Irish person living in a country now listed in the top ten wealthiest countries in the world, and with more than my fair share in the conspicuous consumerism that goes with it, could I claim to be altogether innocent if so many people, and especially the weakest, the little children and their mothers, have their lives stunted and die daily for sheer want of food in a fertile world that can quite easily feed all living things? No, I cannot; and so, once again, what then? Nothing, and yet everything. The Creator Spirit simply goes on creating, offering us at both levels of deformation and transformation, the natural level and the level of supervening man-made evil, both the purgation and the progressive perfection of life, until we manage to get round to taking the former, the purgation, for what it is, and then, eyes and souls cleansed, to see the latter, the transformation, stretch out before us – no longer living with despair ever snarling at our heels, but blessed with endless hope.

And all of this can be conveyed by the master cipher of the meal. If you eat of the tree of life, if you partake of life in the spirit in which God creates life, that is to say, equally for all, then you will serve (the food and drink, the sacrifice of) your life to others as they to you. And you will have learned wisdom, the know-how to live for more and ever longer the life appropriate to your station as a co-creative creature. You will be seated at Wisdom's Feast, Wisdom who assures you that she has always already delivered humanity from its ancient transgression and restored its power to rule all things in God's good world. This is a truly eucharistic feast to which she herself invites you: 'She has slaughtered her beasts, she has mixed her wine, she has set her table.' (Wisdom 10:1-4; Proverbs 9:2) Indeed you may extend the symbolism of this meal cipher in order to say that you will then be eating Wisdom/ Word/Creative Spirit herself, an extension of the meal cipher that goes back all the way, after all, to the tree of life, which she is said to be, and of which you may eat. (Sirach 24:21) For to consume the life-giving sustenance that the cosmos has to offer, in a truly eucharistic, breaking and pouring, sharing manner, is to imbibe wisdom daily, and to live all the rest of your life accordingly. And that same interpretation applies to the eucharistic imagery of eating the Word/Wisdom/Creator Spirit that to his followers was the very soul and spirit enlivening and driving Jesus of Nazareth through all of his life, and sustaining him through the death of this body made of dust. It is that interpretation, available from a full and detailed inspection of the eating-and-drinking cipher over the whole of the Bible, that saves us all from the embarrassment of the grosser interpretation still in vogue, the interpretation of the meal imagery of the Last Supper as the actual consumption of the earthy body and blood of Jesus of Nazareth, however the mysterious 'transubstantiation' account of bringing this about might be hoped to spare us the otherwise consequent images of teeth sinking into warm human flesh and tongues tasting warm human blood.

Should there be any remaining doubts about this interpretation of the myth of the fall from creation as it comes whole from the Creator Spirit, or about the fact that it describes something that goes on at all times rather than something that happened at the beginning of human history, they could all be dispelled by the reading of one chapter of the book of the prophet Ezekiel. Chapter 28 describes the fortunes of the king of Tyre, a one-time ally of Jerusalem, principal city of the kingdom of Israel – first the good times, and then the bad. Tyre itself has just been described as a garden city – 'O Tyre, you have said, "I am perfect in beauty"' – an architectural gem filled with all the goods and valuable things that the human heart could desire, and set 'in the heart of the seas'. Until Ezekiel, the 'son of man,' is called by God to complain and condemn.

'Thus says the Lord God: "Because your heart is proud, and you have said, 'I am a god … yet you are but a man and no god, though you consider yourself as wise as a god – (and) you are indeed wiser than Daniel … (for) by your wisdom and your understanding you have gotten wealth for yourself … by your great wisdom in trade you have increased your wealth, and your heart has become proud in your wealth – therefore thus says the Lord God: "Because you consider yourself as wise as a god, therefore, look you, I will bring strangers upon you, the most terrible of the nations; and they shall draw their swords against the beauty of your wisdom and defile your splendour … Will you (then) still say, 'I am a god,' in the presence of those who slay you, though you are but a man and no god, in the hands of those who wound you? You shall die the death of the uncircumcised by the hand of foreigners, for I have spoken", says the Lord God.'

So far a classic account of the nature of the fateful fall, the original sin of human kind, of the illusion that we can aspire to the wisdom of God as such, so as to be our own creator gods in whatever world we desire. And an equally classic account of the punishment for that sin, delivered in abundance by our fellow humans and on the principle, first coined in the USA, that what goes around comes around; for, to add another adage, this time coined by Jesus: those who live by the sword, by the sword they will die. But it is in the second half of this same chapter from Ezekiel, where that son of man is ordered by the Lord to 'raise a lamentation over the king of Tyre,' as if the final punishment were already delivered, it is here that the persistence of all the significant imagery of the garden story of creation is omnipresent and absolutely unavoidable. Here is the lamentation that the Lord ordered:

'Thus says the Lord God: "You were the model of perfection, full of wisdom and perfect in beauty. You were in Eden, the garden of God ... on the day you were created ... you were anointed a guardian cherub, for so I ordained you ... you were blameless in your ways from the day you were created, till iniquity was found in you. In the abundance of your trade you were filled with violence, and you sinned; so I cast you as a profane thing from the mountain of God, and the guardian cherub drove you out from the midst of the stones of fire. Your heart was proud because of your beauty; you corrupted your wisdom for the sake of your splendour ... By the multitude of your iniquities, in the unrighteousness of your trade you profaned your sanctuaries; so I brought fire forth from the midst of you; it consumed you, and I turned you to ashes upon the earth in the sight of all who saw you. All who know you among the people are appalled at you; you have come to a dreadful end".'

Paradise is an earthly kingdom, ruled in the age of kings by men who, like Solomon in particular, asked for and received from God such wisdom as God can give to such a creature. The earthly king in return for wisdom divinely bestowed, was obliged to rule the earth as God rules creation, as God's son, or as the cherub who keeps the garden of creation for all human kind and all living things. But Tyre's heart was proud; he grasped at wisdom in the very form of God's own self, and thereby corrupted his wisdom for the sake of his own splendour. He did this by the violence of his trading practices, and by the violence with which he was prepared to protect such practices (how very contemporary this sounds!). He profaned also then the very sanctuaries of God in the land. So the original cherub, the angelic form of the presence of God, came now as punisher, but came in the *persona* of the killing and wasting persons of the erstwhile objects of the king of Tyre's violence – came in the shock and awe of the most terrifying of the surrounding nations. And then that kingly cherub that was Tyre now turned blasphemous and satanic, found himself burnt to dust in that awful fire in his own kingdom laid waste, found himself no longer in paradise, but buried in a wasteland where paradise was and forever ought to be.

It is difficult now to keep from leaping to mind a complete contrast between this misfortunate king of Tyre and another one who died, as the sign on his cross proclaimed, as king of the Jews, the messiah of the eschaton, the restorer of the end-time fulfilment of paradise. For this one also, anointed by the Spirit (of) Wisdom and named Jesus of Nazareth, felt the full brunt of the primordial temptation: the temptation to think that his wisdom amounted to, or could be made to rival, the wisdom of the Creator Spirit for it would enable him to rule all the kingdoms of the world – like the British Empire on which the sun would never set. (Matthew 4:1-11)

But this other one, this Jesus, 'who in every respect has been tempted as we are, (was) yet without sinning.' And more, 'because he himself has suffered and been tempted, he is able to help those who are tempted.' (Hebrews 4:15; 2:18). For possessed as he was by the Creator Spirit, this Jesus was and is the true son of God and Lord, as kings were called, in that he was the plenipotentiary through whom the true rule of God was restored to a fallen world. For this is a rule of service rather than command, for the enhancement of the lives of others rather than his own. And by ruling in God's image in this manner he helped others by inspiring them, by breathing out what in every breath he breathed in from the pure air, the Creator Spirit, eternal source of life, and life ever more abundant. This point is put succinctly and poetically (same thing) in a piece that Paul either composed or quoted in the course of urging the Philippians to have that spirit in them which was also in the anointed one, Jesus, 'who, though he was in the form of God, did not count equality with God a thing to be grasped, but emptied himself, taking the form of a slave, being born in the likeness of men. And being found in human form he humbled himself and became obedient unto death, even death on a cross. Therefore God has highly exalted him and bestowed on him the name which is above every name, that at the name of Jesus every knee should bow, in heaven and on earth and under the earth, and every tongue should confess that Jesus Christ is Lord, to the glory of God the Father.' (Philippians 2:5-11)

It is impossible to miss the imagery of the Genesis creation story here also, or so it could be said if it were not so often missed. This Jesus is fully human and, as all of humanity is, made in God's image or form. Yet when that very thing which tempts human kind to act as God's equals, tempts Jesus also, it does not succeed in making him fall into the endemic sinfulness of the race. For instead of exalting himself to the status of the Creator God, as the king of Tyre did, Jesus fully inhabits his human form, and then humbles himself further to the form and fashion of a slave whose whole life is spent in service to his fellows. Obedient in this manner to the rule of God who continually serves up existence and life to all, Jesus remains obedient in thought and act even through his execution for that very cause. And in this way he is manifested true Lord, under God, the true anointed king, God's plenipotentiary on earth, the universal Adam, the whole man. In this way the kingship, the kingdom and the rule of God is distinguished once more from the rule and kingship that is universally practised by the rulers of this world.

The biblical scholars who so often miss the point of this short hymn in Philippians are those who take the self-emptying talk to refer to the divine 'person' incarnate in Jesus, rather than to Jesus himself. This is an exegetical move that had one notable British theologian ask himself the question: if the second person of the Trinity had emptied himself, presumably of divinity, or at least of some divine attributes, what happened to his task of sustaining the cosmos while he was so emptied? His answer was that the other two persons of the Trinity looked after that matter during the *kenosis*. That answer always sounds more impressive if a Greek word is used, as indeed it would need to do, since that whole picture of a divine being emptying itself of divinity, painted as it is on the assumption that the subject of the relevant sentences that make up the hymn is the Word or Spirit incarnate in Jesus, simply defies the whole textual and inter-textual logic of the piece, and so leads to a lot of egregious nonsense under the otherwise respectable title of kenotic theology.

For the image of divine *kenosis* can usefully refer, not to a temporary shedding of essentially divine attributes, but to a certain reservation of the full power of the presence of God with respect to all creatures, so that they should not be entirely overwhelmed, but should be free to exercise their own co-creativity in creation. It is as plain as the plainest of pies that the subject of all the key sentences in the hymn is the one last mentioned before the hymn begins: 'Messiah Jesus, who, though he was in the form (image) of God, did not think equality with God a thing to be grasped' (precisely what the first parents of the race were tempted to think, and did think). Then, when another subject takes over the last long sentence in the hymn, it is God (in Christian Trinitarian terms, as all three 'persons' together presumably) who elevates this one, this Jesus, by giving him the title, Lord, one of the other titles, together with 'son of God,' conferred on kings of the Davidic line. But this title is conferred in this case on one who was and is a Servant King, to whom all peoples should bow the knee, if they had even an inkling of the wisdom they boast of in the very title of their race, *homo sapiens*.

It is the enemies of Jesus that accuse him of thinking that he, the historical man denoted by the name Jesus of Nazareth, was God, when what the man so named was and is in fact a human being 'made like his brethren in every respect,' except he did not fall for the primordial temptation of the race. (Hebrews 2:17) It is his mortal enemies, as it proved, who accuse their fellow Jew of blaspheming, of thinking that he, the human being that seems determined to undermine all they stand for, is God. Most probably their reason for making this lethal accusation was not because he is called or even calls himself son of God, for they would have known that title to apply without problem to other human beings, to kings and to Israel itself. Rather it was because he blithely ignored or overthrew what they regarded as the commandments of God, concerning the Sabbath, for instance, and he also had some dismissive things to say about the temple, the house of their God. All of which made it seem to them that he was intent on setting up alternative rules of obedience to a god that he had created in his own image and likeness, or that he was simply endorsing licentiousness, but in either case acting like a god over against God.

This understanding of the matter of this hymn is portrayed dramatically by John with his usual precision of historical perspective, in one particular scene from the many suspicious and hostile encounters between Jesus and the scribes and Pharisees and priests of his people – or just with 'the Jews,' as John so often resorts to generalising the opponents of Jesus. The scene is set in the temple. Jesus is talking about his relationship to the God he calls our Father, and ends, 'I and the Father are one.' At this 'the Jews' try to stone him. He asks, why? 'For blasphemy', is the answer, 'because you, being a man, make yourself God.' Jesus immediately challenges this claim that he makes himself God, arguing as follows: 'Is it not written in your law, "I said you are gods"? If he called those gods to whom the word of God came, do you say of him whom the Father consecrated and sent into the world, "You are blaspheming", because I said, "I am the son of God"? If I am not doing the works of my Father, then do not believe me, but if I do them, even if you do not believe me, believe the works, that you may know and understand that the Father is in me and I am in the Father.' (John 10:22-39)

Here then the Bible portrays Jesus himself arguing from the Torah, 'your law'. In fact he is arguing from one of the psalms in the Bible, psalm 82. And before turning to that psalm the Bible reader would do well to keep firmly in mind just what Jesus is arguing from scripture here: namely, that as the man he is, he is not calling himself God, not in saying that the Father and he are one, not in accepting or using the title of son of God, not in claiming that the Father is in him and he in the Father – in fact, not at all, in anything he says or does. The psalm he quotes in order to argue this case pictures God, from his place 'in the divine council, in the midst of the gods,' judging those who fail in their duty to bring justice to the world. In particular they fail to 'Give justice to the weak and the fatherless;/ maintain the right of the afflicted and the destitute./ Rescue the weak and needy;/ deliver them from the hand of the wicked.' For the ones who fail in this way 'have neither knowledge nor understanding,/ they walk about in darkness;/(so that the very) foundations of the earth are shaken.' And the judgment passed on these? 'I say, "you are gods, sons of the Most High, all of you (like Jesus is portrayed in Luke's conception story: 'the power of the Most High will overshadow you ... therefore the child to be born will be the son of God'), nevertheless, you shall die like men, and fall like any prince".' And the short psalm ends with the plea: 'Arise, O God, judge the earth; for to thee belong all the nations.' It seems perfectly obvious that these agents, failed here in God's eyes, are the anointed kings of Israel. The ones in the use Jesus makes of this psalm and in his words, 'to whom the word (the understanding, knowledge, wisdom) of God came.' For the judgement passed upon them here is so similar to that passed on the Prince of Tyre, who was indeed godlike in his first reception of the wisdom of God; but then corrupted that wisdom by making himself equal to God; and then had to be told that, because of his unjust behaviour that had the ultimate effect of raping the very earth itself, he would die like any other man, or like the princes of the uncircumcised. Indeed if a psalm could say of everyman, 'thou hast made him a little less than God ... thou hast put all things under his feet,' (Psalm 8:5-6), it is little wonder that the king, the paradigmatic man, in addition to being referred to as lord and son of God, should be referred to as a god, but without the least intent or implication of making him (equal to) God.

How much clearer could it be, that the one or ones in Psalm 82 judged by God are the king or kings, and the judgement is death for their lack of knowledge and understanding; in short, for the significant absence of the wisdom that comes from God, and allows them to channel God's own rule to the earth. It is this wisdom that makes them 'a little lower than God', or in this more robust formula, 'gods'. Or, as Jesus puts it in his defence against those who think he divinises himself, it is 'the word', another image for the wisdom; it is this that makes it possible to describe as 'gods' those, like Jesus himself, to whom (according to John's prologue) the word of God comes, but without in any way making any of these men God. Instead, what such attribution of Word or Wisdom coming to such men allows them to claim, is that they are sons of God, or lords as the Philippians hymn puts it; or as Jesus in reply to his accusers also claims, in traditional biblical terms of the double immanence, that 'the Father is in me and I am in the Father.' True divinity belongs to the Father, the Creator Spirit, the Word, the Wisdom – the latter three being attributes of God now personified as the myth's way of asserting the personhood of the otherwise incomprehensible One, as the note to Proverbs 8 explains, where Wisdom describes herself as the one through whom God creates the world. True divinity characterises the One God who worked his true creative rule through the man Jesus, through the whole of his existence, his life and his very death. It does not characterise as such the men, the historical kings of Israel, nor the man who proved to be the rather anti-king, Jesus. That is quite plainly the case that Jesus makes, according to John, against those who wanted to execute him for blasphemy, and who, by a collusion of king (or comparable ruler) and priest, eventually managed to do so.

Is it in order to avoid that conclusion to the query about the meaning of the psalm that Jesus quoted, that so many professional biblical exegetes find in Psalm 82 an altogether different meaning? For example, the note to that psalm in the *Oxford Annotated Bible* reads as follows: 'Making use of a conception common to the ancient Near East, that the world is ruled by a council of gods, the poet (presumably a priest or a temple prophet) sees, in a vision, the God of Israel standing up in the midst of the council and pronouncing judgement upon all the other members.' It is true, of course, that the Bible does make use of the plural in talking about God. This usage is already implicit in the opening creation myth of Genesis, in recipes for creation itself which take the form: 'Let us make man in our image,' and so on. So if God creates the cosmos in council, as it were, it would be no surprise if God also rules it from a heavenly court composed of the One God and his 'sons' or offspring.But this ancient mythic conceit does not result in the *personae* of the heavenly court being mortal rather than immortal; they are immortals and do not 'die like men' no matter what they do, even if like Lucifer they are thrown out of the heavenly court. The mythic conceit of 'God in council' or God as 'we' therefore cannot support the contention that in Psalm 82 God is chastising other gods for not ruling the earth as the heavens should; and then threatening them with the deaths that humans die if they fail to do so. And Psalm 89, which this note to Psalm 82 refers to as corroboration of its odd interpretation, paints the quite conventional picture of some king in the line of David, who presumably thinks that he is innocent of injustice, pleading for God's intervention to prevent him and his line from being wiped out by God's enemies and his.

Therefore the prayer with which the psalm ends is for God to judge the earth, not the heavens. The myth pictures God doing this, as God long ago issued the creative formulae for the cosmos, from the midst of the council of the immortals. And so, as one might expect, Jesus has the correct exegesis of the psalm, when he takes the phrase, you are gods, to refer to those human beings to whom the Word/Wisdom/Spirit of God came. And he then clinches his case by interpreting the term, son of God, as a means of connoting a human being who imitates the Father in 'doing the works of my Father'. In fact that particular part of the contretemps in John 10 contains a further phrase that clinches the case that Jesus is arguing from the scriptures. 'If I am not doing the works of my Father. then do not believe me (that I am the son of God, one with God, mutually immanent); but if I do them, even though you do not believe me, believe the works, that you may know and understand that the Father is in me and I in the Father.' Surely this amounts to saying: leave me out of the equation altogether, if you must; no belief in me personally or in any claim about me is a necessary prerequisite to the cause for which I live and die. It is the works that I do, the works of healing and creating well-being for the good and the bad alike without discrimination that point to the working of the Father of all. And if you see this and keep faith with it you will follow the true rule of the one true God into eternal life, whatever you believe or do not believe about me. Although, to be fair, if you do see all of this through my human work in life and death, you should then be able to allow, not that I am trying to make myself out to be (equal to) God, but that God is indeed working in and through me, and that I am indeed filled with God and emptied of self-regard, so that I am a true son of God in the sense in which you have always understood that phrase.

It would indeed be no exaggeration to say that the maintenance of the distinction between God and humanity is crucial to the whole biblical message from beginning to end. Just as, the whole Bible also insists, it is the efforts on the part of humanity to collapse that distinction between humanity and God that is the mother and father of all the evils that are perpetrated over the whole tragic history of the race – evils perpetrated on itself directly, or indirectly through the destruction of the good earth that this proud race occupies. All human evil-doing is, at source, a form of idolatry of self, a form of satanism, an age-old and seemingly perennial blasphemy. Of this his enemies accuse Jesus also, 'You being a man, make yourself God', and this Jesus quite explicitly denies.

Readers who remember the scene in Acts where Paul faced some Athenian philosophers may find in that same scene implicit confirmation from Paul of the argument of Jesus himself, that he is not to be called God in any manner that might make a god of the man, Jesus, or make him equal to God. Paul was in Athens arguing in synagogue and marketplace, 'provoked ... as he saw that the city was full of idols.' That is what brought him to the notice of the philosophers, who thought that Paul himself was a 'babbler' preaching foreign divinities, and one named Jesus among these, so that he needed to be asked some serious questions, and not least this: if their gods were idols, what was this god called Jesus? Paul's very politic answer points to the God who cannot be named, the unknowable God in whom all live and move and have their being. And instead of calling this God by the name, Jesus, he goes to quite some lengths not to mention the name of Jesus at all to these people; introducing him instead, anonymously, simply as 'a man' whom God has appointed to judge the world. But that judgement, we know, Paul thought would take place at the general resurrection. So he does not introduce Jesus as a divinity, foreign or otherwise; but he is in worse trouble with his resurrection talk than if he had insisted that Jesus was a god. (Acts 17:16-32)

Looked at from another angle, what all this is about, indeed what the whole Bible is about, is the quest for the true Messiah. Who is the anointed one, who is the king, who is the priest (for around the time of Jesus there was some talk of a priest-messiah), who is the one who truly relays God's rule to all creation? The altercation between Jesus and 'the Jews' that John just now described, begins with the impatient request of 'the Jews': 'How long will you keep us in suspense? If you are the Christ, tell us plainly.' Now, in order to gain some insight into all that is going on here, put yourself in the role of Jesus; feel your heart sink, like it sank when some of his closest disciples asked him, 'Show us the Father', 'Show us the way,' and (here we go again) 'Tell us plainly about you and the Messiah.' Ask yourself, still playing the part of Jesus, how could you ever get the truth of this matter into their thick, self-centred skulls, both the ones who said they were for you, and ones that were plainly against you, all equally full of images of power-play messiahs? But lift up your weary heart; try one more time, and one more time again, and again ... Yes, do it by constantly increasing the distance that must be kept between God and humanity. Start by saying that, far from grasping at equality with God, you were to be found an ordinary man. Distance yourself yet further from normal perceptions of divine status by pointing out that the form of ordinary man that was yours was the form of a slave to all – two ideas that, if you could then foresee it, at least Paul in his Philippians correspondence would pick up on.

Then take yourself further still and further from divine status; you know you must if you are ever to make the tiniest crack in the thick skulls of *homo sapiens* (God help us all), and make that sad, self-destructive species better. Efface your human self itself; efface completely now this very self that every human being seems constitutionally constrained to divinise; as John will remember you did when he writes about that pivotal altercation with 'the Jews,' remembering you saying, 'Then do not believe me, believe the works.' Tell them not to bother with you yourself at all, if they cannot abide you. Tell them quite simply to focus on the works done. Their prejudice against you will not matter as long as they believe the works, the works of creatively advancing life for all, of saving life from all life-threatening conditions and behaviour. For if they keep faith with such works, they will recognise the God of infinite promise working there, and through you all will then be blessed with mutual happiness and eternal hope.

For it is to enable them to encounter again that eternal Creator Spirit that you came, and in contrast to that encounter you, the mere man named Jesus of Nazareth, are of no consequence. You are just the human channel of the benign rule of your Father and theirs. As you said to 'the Jews', 'The Father is in me and I am in the Father', for the Father it is who does the eternal creating that is also salvation and will be fulfilment. And it is so that the Father can do all of this with the fullness and ultimate perfection that only the Creator Spirit can achieve, that you must empty yourself, to echo the language of the Philippians hymn, of all self-regard, and even, if need be, of all self-reference. So that anyone who should hear you or others calling you son of God, or speaking of God and yourself in terms of mutual immanence, or if anyone should say, either in complaint or compliance, that you called yourself God, either in set terms or in equivalent language about what you did, what was done through you, then they must know, or be reminded that the God in question is the one eternal Creator Spirit and not the human person bearing your name.

In order to make that crucial truth finally clear, you the human person called Jesus of Nazareth, are prepared to undergo the final form of self-emptying, as the Philippians hymn so pointedly puts it, the death of Jesus of Nazareth on the most cruel and humiliating instrument of terminal torture, the cross. In this you will lead as always by example of the general principle that you constantly pressed upon a host of disciples reluctant to the end to listen to it: the principle of the reign of God, dramatised in eucharist; the principle that one must give of one's very life for others if we are all to save life for all, rather than deal death to all. One must lose life in order to gain it. And this you will do, even though when you finally come face to face with such a terrible end, the old temptation will come back to plague you one more time, the old temptation, now with the force of the primordial instinct for self-preservation itself, to do whatever it takes to keep your self alive. And you will have to cry to God through blood and tears to save you this last time from falling as all mere humans fall. 'Lead us not into the trial,' you will have to cry, or as you will put it on this occasion, 'Let not my will, but thine be done.' Another version of the prayer for the kingdom that you taught your disciples, 'thy kingdom come; thy will be done on earth as it is in heaven.' For as ever, the reign of the eternally benign Creator God can come through human kind only if the human will does not set up in selfish and ultimately foolish opposition, if it does not turn satanic and idolatrous and thereby bring nothing but disaster on itself and its world.

It might suddenly dawn on someone reading all of this, that a question has been forming itself and may already have begun to hover over all of it. And the question is this: what is to be said now about the traditional talk of the divinity of Jesus? A very long answer would be required in order to fully and adequately answer this question. And that would then throw the whole of this book out of line and out of shape. But this much can be said. The statement, Jesus is God, is at best misleading, unless it is immediately followed by some explanation. For Jesus is the name, a very common name indeed in that time and place, for a human being who was as fully human as any of the rest of us. Jesus names the man; it does not name God, who has no proper names. So all talk of the divinity of Jesus really has to do with a presence of God in Jesus, 'reconciling the world to himself,' as Paul, who ranted against named gods as idols, somewhere put it. It has to do with the degree of that divine presence in Jesus, and that degree in turn depends on the degree of self-emptying by Jesus of all purely selfish regard and aim, so that he should prove an absolutely unhindered and uncluttered channel of divine creative power in creation. Which makes that ancient hymn in Philippians 2 the most complete and powerful expression of 'the divinity of Jesus' in the whole Bible.

The statement, Jesus is God, is therefore a permanently potentially misleading one, for it tempts us to think that the man Jesus is as such God. Whereas all statements about the divinity of Jesus should be so fashioned and expressed as to let it be clearly understood that the reference is not to the divinity of Jesus, but to the divinity *in* Jesus; so permanently, powerfully and unobstructedly present in Jesus that everything human that the fully human Jesus did and said and thought became the very model – sometimes, admittedly, after a bit of a struggle – of the eternal creative-salvific activity of God's own self in the world. This is what the ancient Council of Chalcedon tried to express in what have long become the commonly unintelligible metaphysical concepts of Greek philosophy: a divine and a human nature operated on creation through the one person of Jesus of Nazareth, the latter ever freely providing the fleshly forms of thoughts, words and actions, while freely removing any impediments to the flow and direction of the indwelling divine Spirit/Word that in-breathed his whole life; the former being as fully and truly divine as the latter was fully and truly human.

In one brief passage in a letter he wrote to converts to the cause of Jesus in Rome (Romans 8:14-23), Paul provides a perfect paradigm in miniature of the manner in which the Bible sets the story of Jesus into the cluster of powerful primordial images that weave the story of creation from origin to eschaton. Brief yet crystal clear and deeply insightful as only poetic diction can be, Paul reprises the rich imagery of the story of creation that opens the Bible: the creator spirit, the birthing of continuous creation, the fall with its curse of continuous destruction and pain, the creator spirit-bird birthing still, sonship recovered and paradise-kingdom inherited evermore.

The passage opens with a clear and simple definition of what makes a son or daughter of God: 'Everyone moved by the Spirit is a son of God.' That short and sharp definition on its own should prove quite sufficient force to deter Bible readers from treating John's 'the Word became flesh,' as *the*, if not the only incarnation text in the Bible. At the very least it should help readers to set that Word text securely in the complex of frequent, indeed common sonship texts that talk instead of the Spirit coming on and remaining in the ones who thereby become true disciples of true Messiah Jesus. For, as Paul's Romans argument continues, it is the Creator Spirit coming on and remaining in any human being that enables that one to call God 'Abba, Father'. For that one, moved by the Creator Spirit within her, acts in and with this whole continuously creative world through which that same Spirit comes to her, cooperating in salving and re-creating this evolving creation, to the point of imaging that Spirit to others. Daughter of God, son of God, acting in the image of the Father. And if sons and daughters, Paul continues, then 'heirs of God (God's kingdom) and co-heirs with Christ, sharing his sufferings so as to share his glory.'

Sufferings? These are shared not simply with Jesus the true Messiah, but with all of creation, and they are of two kinds. The first kind appears as Paul evokes the powerful image of creation as birthing: the bird-spirit bringing about the birth of creation. Not in any one-off act of parturition, but in one continuous – from our earthworm's-eye point of view – act from eternity to eternity in which the creation becomes partner in the creative act, empowered by the Spirit to bring forth successive forms of existence and life. 'From the beginning till now,' in Pauls' own words, 'the entire creation, as we know, has been groaning in one great act of giving birth.' As close an image to the idea of evolution as one could expect from so early a myth, evoking the experience of the birthing of the new through the pain and loss of ever-obsolescing forms.

Then there is the second and supervening echelon of destruction suffered by the creation. This is the decay and futility, in Paul's words, brought upon the earth itself by a fallen humankind acting as its own fount of creative wisdom, its own creator god. It represents the level of wilful destruction dealt out equally to creation and humanity itself, to both alike, that God has in mind when issuing the judgement in Genesis, 'cursed is the very ground because of you.' Indeed, God in the Genesis story might just as well have repeated to the earth the words he had just spoken to the Woman, 'I will multiply your pain in giving birth.' And for liberation from this level of destruction suffered, Paul adds, the creation as a whole can only await and hope 'to obtain the glorious liberation of the sons of God'. For just as God cannot avoid taking a share in the responsibility for the higher level of destruction that fallen humankind wreaks upon its mother earth, neither can God force a change of heart to the status of sonship and daughterhood that would see this fallen race return once more to the path to universal and eternal *shalom* for all of creation. And unfortunately, it seems to be as true today of us self-admired members of *homo sapiens* (God help us all), that we are as far from realising creation's hope as we were when Paul penned the words, 'We ourselves, who have the first-fruits of the Spirit, groan inwardly as we wait for adoption as sons and for our bodies to be set free.' So, it is still true to say today, only when we are liberated, inspired in the ways of true sons and daughters of God, can creation itself hope to be freed from the increasing and now near terminal destruction to which we subject our only habitat, the mother earth that brought us forth and still every day offers life in abundance to all.

Paul and John are the two biblical writers who appear most apodictic in their insistence that nothing in the life of Jesus did so much as the death of Jesus on the cross to reveal, and to inspire his fellow humans with, the Spirit that entered into and moved Jesus to the point at which the powerful image of incarnation was called into service. Paul actually uses the phrase, 'the Word of the cross,' with a force that indeed suggests that the incarnation of the Creator Spirit reached its apogee on Calvary, and then goes so far as to say that 'I decided to know nothing among you except Jesus Christ and him crucified.' (1 Corinthians 118-2:4) And John throughout his gospel conveys the clear impression that the Glory, a partner-image with Spirit, Word and Wisdom for the special and effective presence of the creator-saviour God operative in the world, points with great power and precision to Calvary as the finest hour in the career of Jesus, the prophet *par excellence* and the son of God. To that death-scene then it is necessary to return once more in order to complete the story of the life of Jesus in the fullest sense possible.

V: The Trial and Death of Jesus

It is conventional for biographies to begin with births and end with deaths. Yet in the case of any truly historic figure it is never enough to position the birth at one end and the death at the other, with little more than details of time and place and a few other interesting details of circumstance or incident to complete the drama of their entrance on the stage of life and their exit from it. This is particularly true in the case of those truly historic persons who died for the causes to which they devoted their adult lives, and who occupied or claimed roles and titles in human society which would justify them in taking the lead in whatever the cause it was for which they each lived and died. For such people it is necessary to go before birth in search of genealogies and other forms of precedent for roles and causes; as it is necessary also to go beyond death in order to describe and estimate the destiny of such pivotal agents in the twists and turns of human history. And then the act of dying or being killed for a cause, more than being born to it, can bring a relentless focus on what is really going on, beneath all the usual bluster and special pleading from the prosecution and the defence teams alike.

In the simplest of historical terms, the death of Jesus was by crucifixion, a death sentence handed down by a Roman Imperial Governor with the collusion of a Jewish High Priest, and carried out by Roman soldiers who also on that same Friday executed two 'brigands'. (Mark 14:53–15:47; Matthew 26:57–27:61; Luke 22:54–23:49; John 18:12–19:30) One might almost say 'two other brigands', for the name 'brigand' refers to one who fought against the Roman occupation of the land of the Jews. These were the IRA of the time, the kind of people who are called freedom fighters by those who believe in their cause or if they win, but are called bandits, brigands and terrorists by those who oppose them or if they lose, for it is the victors who write history. And Pilate, against his own better judgement, had gone along with the High Priest's suggestion that Jesus was a messianic pretender in the usual sense of one who wished to restore the kingdom of Israel. Like Barabbas, the bandit who has a walk-on role in that same trial scene, and whose name also means 'son of Abba, son of God the Father'. It seems to have been freedom-fighters' day on that Friday morning at Pilate's court in Jerusalem. Barabbas alone escaped, on a technicality. (Mark 15:6-15) But the point of this biblical story, whether Barabbas was a true historical character or not, is to tell a truth about some Jewish leaders, namely, that on the fateful day they would favour a man in the traditional mould of a follower of a war-like king, to the kind of messiah that Jesus had portrayed so consistently over the whole course of his public mission. And that tells us how implacably hostile they were to what Jesus was doing and saying. We do not know if the closest disciples of Jesus would have joined their fellow Jews in the clamour for the release of Barabbas over Jesus, because by this time they had all turned the coward's heel, and were well out of earshot when the vote was called. But Judas had already shown where his vote might well go, and it is very likely from all that we know of the others' expectations of the kingdom, that they could very well have followed Judas in voting for the release of Barabbas, so as to remove Jesus who was proving a liability to them. One way or another every one of his closest followers betrayed Jesus, and left him to his fate. He was crucified that afternoon.

The execution of Jesus of Nazareth resulted from a cynical collusion of temple and palace, of sacred and secular rulers. And these two, especially in the matter of the kind of collusion that is demanded by realpolitik to keep both of them in power, had form in this matter, as those who bet on racehorses would put it. So that it is more than merely interesting to note that Israel in its most formative years had neither royal palace nor temple. It is of great significance to our current concerns to realise that the God of Israel had original objections to each of these institutions in turn. And, in view of the fact that the execution of Jesus was in essence the killing of a prophet, it is also worth taking some time out to note that it was a prophet in both cases that relayed both God's objections and the relaxation of these. It is worthwhile then to take a moment to look at the origin of these institutions in Israel.

First, the king in his palace: 'In those days there was no king in Israel; everyman did what was right in his own eyes.' Those were the days when 'Samuel was established as a prophet (formerly known as a seer) of the Lord ... for the Lord revealed himself to Samuel at Shiloh by the word of the Lord. And the word of the Lord came to all Israel.' But when the people clamoured for a proper king, like the ones that led surrounding peoples, the Lord God let them know, through the prophet, that this was the last thing that people under the reign of God's own self needed, reminding them for good measure of what kings did to their peoples: lord it over them, take from them everything from their land-holdings, their natural resources for building and other purposes, to their very man-power for standing armies or for virtual slavery in forced labour as required. In spite of this, Samuel the prophet conveys the divine acquiescence in this scheme to have kings like the surrounding peoples, and anoints Saul, whom he says God had picked out for the job. And we get the collusion of the two principal characters in the roles in which, together, they will shortly be responsible for the savage and completed massacre at Gilgal.

A strikingly similar story accounts for the origin of the temple. Solomon it was who added a temple to Israel's royal palace. For Solomon was the one in that line of kings who saw the greatest riches and extension of the now kingdom of Israel, 'from the Euphrates ... to the borders of Egypt.' This the Bible suggests is due to the fact that when God asked Solomon what Solomon would like to receive, Solomon replied: 'Send me the Wisdom that sits by your throne', sits like a divine consort, like the Widsom goddess through whom the world is created, like the Sovereignty goddess as she is called in old Irish mythology. Solomon asks for 'an understanding mind to govern ... that I may discern between good and evil.' And because Solomon asks for wisdom, rather than land and riches, God promises him all of that and a reign for his 'house' that will last for all ages.

So Solomon built a temple for the Lord God, despite the fact that when his father, David, first proposed to house God in such a man-made building God, again through a prophet, Nathan, demurred and pointed out that God had never been domiciled, much less domesticated, in a house. God was always with God's people wherever they wandered on the earth. An anticipation of what Stephen, the first man executed after Jesus in the same cause, said to his judges in the temple at Jerusalem: 'The Most High does not dwell in houses made with hands; as the prophet says, "Heaven is my throne and earth my footstool. What house will you build for me, says the Lord".' (Acts 7:48-50) Solomon acknowledges all of this in his dedication prayer for the temple he has nonetheless built: 'Behold, heaven and highest heaven cannot contain thee, how much less this house that I have built.' Yet Solomon continues to pray 'that thy eyes may be open night and day towards this house, the place of which thou hast said, "My name shall be there".' So that when God's people, either at home or abroad, turn towards that house, God will always hear, forgive and help them, for that house will be the locus, the principal domicile as the taxman might put it, of God's Presence on earth.

There are a number of features of the origin stories of these two institutions in Israel, of kings in their palace and priests in their temple, that continue up to the time of Jesus and help explain his fate. The first of these features has to do with the character of the prophets involved, in particular, Samuel and Nathan. These were indeed seers in that they could see what God's reign in the cosmos really was and really required of the sons and daughters of Adam. Yet they belonged to a sub-section of prophets in general, the sub-section that contained those prophets who, if they were not formally installed as court prophets or temple prophets, were nevertheless close enough to priests and kings to want to tell these, whenever they felt they could do so, what the latter most obviously wanted to hear. It would always be so easy for prophets who operated closely with kings and priests to believe that God's word on a subject that affected priests or kings, despite God's own demurring, would be such as to contribute to their own long life, health and happiness. And these, for kings and priests alike, would be counted true prophets, unlike other claimants to the title of prophet who seemed to spend an inordinate amount of their time pointing out to both priests and kings their failures, indeed their sins in the eyes of God, in whose name they had been anointed. Now Jesus, even a blind man could see, was a prophet of the latter ilk.

The second informative feature to be noted in these origin

stories, is what might be called the twinning of these two institutions: the house of God and his priests, and the house of the king. This twinning took the most physical of forms when Solomon had the temple built in his palace compound, so that temple and palace sat threshold to threshold and doorpost to doorpost in the same compound. This was merely another feature of the aping of the other kings and royal compounds at the time in the ancient Near East. For since the king was God incarnate in this ancient ideology, as son of God and Lord of the earth that God had given him to rule, it made excellent sense to have sacred persons of both royal and priestly persuasion who had such direct access to God to live and rule together, however their divisions of labour or separation of powers might otherwise be drawn, or not drawn. Indeed we have a fairly detailed description of the administrative offices and officers who ruled Israel from the temple-palace compound that was Solomon's headquarters. They are listed as: priests, secretary-recorders such as were called scribes in Egypt, the generals of the standing armies, enforcers and overseers of such forced labour as royal projects required, twelve provisioners from twelve districts whose job it was to keep up the supply of food and other materials fit for a royal household – all the things that God warned the people would come with their kingship – and so on, and so on. (This story of the origins of the two houses of God and of his king is compiled from the following: Judges 25; 1 Samuel 3, 8, 9; 2 Samuel 7; 1 Kings 3, 8.)

So God did not give up on earlier objections, but rather added another to this twinned institution erected by humanity-the wise in God's name. For always, from the very start, this twinned institution seems to have been made in humanity's own image rather than God's. A 'real' prophet, Ezekiel, put this on-going objection in the following words as they came to him from God: 'Son of man, this is the place of my throne and the place of the soles of my feet, where I will dwell in the midst of the people forever. And the house of Israel shall no more defile my holy name, neither they nor their kings, by their harlotry and by the monuments of their kings, by setting their threshold by my threshold and their doorposts by my doorposts, with only a wall between me and them. They have defiled my holy name by their abominations which they have committed, so I have consumed them in my anger. Now let them put away their idolatry and the monuments of their kings far from me, and I will dwell in their midst forever.' (Ezekiel 43:7-9) In the time of Jesus, of course, there was no king of Israel in Jerusalem, and no palace in the temple compound. But the man in the place of the king, the Roman Governor, had a seat a short distance away, and the imagery of threshold to threshold and doorpost to doorpost still provided a powerful metaphor for a very real twinning of the powers of priest and imperial lord. For each depended for the continuity of its power and authority, if in a different degree and manner, on the cooperation of the other.

The powers of lording-it-over being so similar in nature – as in the later case of pope and emperor in Christianity and Christendom – the priest could as like corrupt the king, as the king the priest. For this is the kind of power that corrupts, as all good fall stories illustrate, and absolute power corrupts absolutely. This the prophet Jeremiah proclaimed: 'Will you steal, murder, commit adultery, swear falsely, burn incense to Ba'al, and go after other gods that you have not known, and then come and stand before me in this house, which is called by my name, and say, "We are delivered!" – only to go on doing all these abominations? Has this house which is called by my name become a den of thieves in your eyes? Behold, I myself have seen it, says the Lord. Go now to my place in Shiloh, where I made my name dwell at first, and see what I did to it for the wickedness of my people Israel.' (Jeremiah 7:8-12) God will destroy their temple, just as utterly as Shiloh was destroyed. For priests use the temple to give themselves a better life, to amass wealth, and even to kill off their more effective critics, overlooking the sins of the people who use the temple, or pretending that the temple will deliver them from the pillage and murder that they too commit in the worship of Mammon, all the while committing a kind of idolatry themselves, as Jesus accused them of doing. And in this way they encourage kings to act as kings are only too often tempted to act in any case.

In the case of Jesus, it was the priest that corrupted the king. But before coming to a closer analysis of that particular piece of historical collusion, it might be well to clarify the issue of the precise charge on which Jesus was tried and found guilty at the court of the High Priest. As the Bible relates this matter, Jesus was first charged with having spoken words against the temple, and hence of course, against its priests. This charge refers no doubt to statements of the kind elsewhere recorded in the Bible. For example, a statement made by Jesus during his 'cleansing' of the temple echoed precisely the terms that Jeremiah, just quoted above, had used when he proclaimed such divine punishment on the temple of his time: it had 'become a den of thieves'. Or sundry other statements of similar intent, statements to the effect that the temple would be destroyed, like Shiloh. (Matthew 24:1-2) Or the statement made to the Samaritan woman at the well, that the time is coming when 'neither (at the temple) on this mountain (Gerizim) nor in (the temple at) Jerusalem will you worship the Father ... But ... true worshippers will worship the Father in spirit and in truth.' (John 4:21-23) All adding up to the impression that the temple in Jerusalem and its priesthood, as Jesus saw them in his time, counted for very little, if indeed in the future they would count at all in the coming of God's reign, as Jesus preached and practised it.

In explaining his own reasons for cleansing the temple, Jesus implicitly quotes another prophet of the past, in addition to Jeremiah. Jesus gave as his reason for cleansing: 'Is it not written, "My house shall be called a house of prayer for all the nations"? But you have made it a den of thieves.' The second part of that explanation is quoted from Jeremiah; the first from Isaiah. And although we have seen it already above, the passage from Isaiah is worth quoting again here if we are to understand as fully as possible the charges on which Jesus was condemned to death on the cross. 'And the foreigners who join themselves to the Lord, to minister to him, to love the name of the Lord, and to be his servants, every one who keeps the Sabbath, and does not profane it, and holds fast my covenant – these I will bring to my holy mountain, and make them joyful in my house of prayer; their burnt offerings and their sacrifices will be accepted on my altar, for my house shall be called a house of prayer for all the nations.' (Isaiah 56:6-8)

Now it cannot but add to the significance and seriousness of statements concerning the destruction or irrelevance of the

Jerusalem temple, if Isaiah envisages the accession of the Gentiles in terms of their coming to the temple at Jerusalem to offer their sacrifices, thus validating the power and privilege of Israel's priesthood. Whereas Jesus envisages the Gentiles coming from all directions to sit at table with the Lord Jesus, the table from which he and The Twelve would preside over the renewed kingdom of God. But Jesus and the leaders of his followers would preside over the people of God, not by laying down commands about cult and conduct and thereby lording it over the people in God's name and under pain of special punishment for those who did not obey all the commandments of God's covenant with Moses. Rather would they lead by serving the needs of all, as the eucharistic meal both symbolised and put into effect, and all would then be expected to serve the needs of each other. This vision of the accession of the foreigners to the fellowship of Jesus came to Jesus when he saw the faith of foreigners. The case has already been noted of the faith of a Canaanite woman. On another occasion it was the faith of a Roman centurion who asked for healing for his paralysed servant that prompted Jesus to query the exclusivism of his religion. As Jesus himself is reported to have put it: 'Not even in Israel have I found such faith. I tell you, many will come from the east and the west and sit at table (not in the temple or the palace) with Abraham, Isaac and Jacob in the kingdom of heaven, while the sons of the kingdom will be thrown into the outer darkness.' (Matthew 8:10-12)

However, this first charge of speaking words against the temple, words of Jesus which when all of them are put together, would see the temple and its priesthood drastically reformed, or marginalised, or even destroyed, does not seem to be the charge on which he was found guilty and condemned, however much harmonious background noise it may have contributed to the eventual condemnation. For as Mark observes of the witnesses called to prove this charge, 'Yet not even so did their testimony agree.' (Mark 14:55-65) And indeed it is easy enough to see how a good lawyer for the defence could handle this charge: Jesus was saying no more than prophets like Jeremiah had said. If the leadership of the people behaved idolatrously, God would bring down the temple itself, but it would be restored when Israel and its priests and kings returned to the their part in the reign of the true God. And as for all of this talk about the eucharistic table as a central ritual for the followers of Jesus, this did not of itself preclude their attendance at a temple run by a priesthood that understood that God's house, like God's reign, filled the whole cosmos, as Stephen reminded his judges when he was tried on much the same combination of charges as Jesus himself. (Acts 6:11, 13) The first followers of Jesus felt no compunction in attending the temple as usual after the execution of Jesus. After all, God's original demurring against the temple, through the mouth of the prophet Nathan, was mainly concerned with any attempts that a human group might make to confine God's especial salvific presence to houses made by men (or church buildings or tabernacles housed in church buildings).

But if it was not the word against the temple on its own, what precisely was it then that constituted the capital charge on which Jesus was found guilty by the High Priest? The only other charge brought against Jesus at the court of Caiaphas, the one to which Jesus immediately confessed, though with a thinly veiled threat that his accusers would see him vindicated by God at some future judgement, was that he claimed to be 'the Christ, the son of the Most High'. Yet neither the pretension to the title of messiah, nor to the title of son of God would constitute in and of itself a capital crime. Certainly if the messianic claim came in the strict form of pretension to the status of the king-messiah, the charge under which the High Priest sent Jesus to Pilate's court, it was never likely to succeed without coercion or blackmail. And so events proved when Pilate, who could tell such a militant threat to the throne of Israel at a thousand yards, dismissed it out of hand. But neither, of itself, could the claim to be a royal successor to David and as such a son of God constitute a criminal charge before the court of the High Priest. Similarly, the claim to the title of son of God on its own, so widely conceded in the cases of kings and commoners alike, could offer without more ado no grounds for the capital charge of blasphemy. In fact, in a text from John just recently analysed above, Jesus had himself explained to his Jewish accusers what they should have well known in any case, namely, that neither a claim to be son of God nor any of its possible equivalents like 'I and the Father are one,' or 'the Father is in me working the world through me, and I am in the Father,' could justify a charge of blasphemy/(self) idolatry/satanism, through a suggestion that the claimant to such epithets was thereby claiming *equality* with God, claiming in effect *to be* God. For all of these epithets, as Jesus further clarified, simply meant that the one to whom they were applied either by self or by others, was by God's eternal creative initiative simply doing God's own work in word and act, in life and death, and was thereby the very image of God, who was and is his true Father.

Just what then is going on here behind this terse description of charge, confession and condemnation at the court of Caiaphas? The most obvious way to get an answer to this question is to recognise the fact that the title 'son of God' can actually apply to many people in many different walks of life, and then to ask: if Jesus was not a kingly messianic pretender in the strict mould, what was he in terms of office, profession or role in life and, more crucially still, what did he do in that role in order to incur the charge of blasphemy (idolatry, satanism)? That is the right question to ask, and asking the right question is always the best way of getting to the right answer. And sure enough, once that question is asked, one notices immediately that this account of the trial before Caiaphas, brief and almost peremptory as it is, offers a strong clue to the correct answer. This clue is contained in Mark's remark that when the sentence is passed and Jesus is handed over to 'the guards', the temple police, they and others begin to beat him and mock and humiliate him as a false pretender to the role of prophet: 'Some began to spit on him, and to cover his face, and to strike him, saying to him, "Prophesy!"' This clue is strengthened when one notices that when Pilate, quite cynically and purely as a matter of realpolitik, condemns Jesus to death as a pretender to the title of king of the Jews, and Jesus is handed over to his soldiers, they in their turn mock and beat and humiliate him: 'They clothed him in a purple cloak, and plaiting a crown of thorns they put it on him. And they began to salute him, "Hail, King of the Jews!" And they struck his head with a reed, and spat upon him, and they knelt down in homage to him.' (Mark 14:65; 15:17-19) Apparently the kind of conduct towards the condemned prisoner that disgusted most of the world in the case of the execution of Saddam Hussein was common, if not *de rigueur*, at the time and place of the trial and execution of Jesus. But for present purposes it is necessary only to notice that such reprehensible conduct does contain the clue that the form and content of the humiliation indicates the nature of the charge on which the accused was sentenced to death. So, if before Pilate the charge was that Jesus was a pretender to the throne of David, then before the High Priest the charge was that he had conducted himself as a prophet, but was in fact a false prophet. Which could only mean that, in the course of his self-proclaimed prophesying he misrepresented God's word, God's will, God's self. In other words, he blasphemed.

Jesus before Caiaphas then was charged, confessed, and sentenced to death on the charge of being a prophet, but in the eyes of his judge, a false prophet. This part of that answer to our question should cause no surprise whatever. It has already been obvious that Jesus understood his role in life to be that of a prophet. Remember the two particular occasions in his life story that made that clear: when at the beginning of his mission he came to his home town synagogue and used the self-same words Isaiah had used to describe his divine election as a prophet of God, and incurred such hostility that his hearers tried to kill him. He simply said, 'No prophet is acceptable in his own country.' And as at the end of his mission he approached Jerusalem and certain death he cried out, 'Jerusalem, killing the prophets and stoning those who are sent to you.' (Luke 4:14-30; Matthew 23:37)

Remember the so-called transfiguration scene when Jesus appeared with Moses and Elijah. (Mark 9:2-13) Clearly from the commentary that follows, this scene was a way of presenting Jesus as prophet like these two, whom God speaking from heaven identifies as the beloved son of God. But no ordinary prophet son of God, rather a prophet like Moses – the prophet like himself that Moses himself had predicted that God would send (Deuteronomy 18:15-16), the Moses-like prophet that Peter and Stephen preached persistently after his death to those who had killed Jesus as a prophet. (Acts 3:22; 7:37) And in that same commentary that follows the transfiguration scene, it is hinted that John the Baptiser, whom the people recognised as a prophet, was in fact Elijah returned, the expected precursor of the one who was to come. John who was treated as Elijah had been treated, in that the ruling house sought his death, and as Jesus would be treated. (see also Matthew 11:27-33) And finally, Jesus himself claims to be the prophet like himself that Moses predicted would be sent by God. In one of his many altercations with 'the Jews', sometimes specified as 'the chief priests and the scribes', Jesus responds to their claim to be true channels of the Torah of Moses with the counterclaim that he is the Moses-like prophet that Moses himself spoke of: 'If you believed Moses, you would believe me, for he wrote of me.' (John 5:46)

But that leaves the last part of our question still unanswered. Yes, Jesus was tried and condemned to death as a prophet like Moses, but the charge of claiming to be a prophet of the Lord, and as such a son of God, does not of itself constitute blasphemy, and is not of itself cause for condemnation to capital punishment. So what was it then that Jesus said or did that, in the eyes of the priestly powers in the land, made him at one and the same time a false prophet and a blasphemer, and punishable by death? The entire answer to this final question is given briefly but succinctly by John the evangelist, as you might expect, for John is the most historically insightful and accurate of all the writers of a life of Jesus or occasional recorders of some of it, in the whole of that part of the Bible that Christians added on. John gives the answer in words that he places on the lips of 'the Jews', elsewhere identified as priests and scribes from the temple authority, on the occasion of Jesus having healed a cripple on the sabbath day by the Sheep Gate pool in Jerusalem. 'This is why the Jews sought the more to kill him, because he not only broke the sabbath but also called God his Father (that is, called himself son of the Most High), making himself equal to God.' (John 5:1-18) All of this is tantalisingly similar to the charge brought against Stephen before the same temple authorities, of which he like his leader was found guilty and executed: 'This man never ceases to speak words against this holy place and the law (the Torah which they believed came definitively from Moses on God's holy mountain) ... We have heard him speak blasphemous words against Moses and God.' (Acts 6:11-13) Unpack either or both of these admittedly densely packed formulae, and you have the fullest, and most compelling answer to the question as to the real charge on which Jesus was executed. For shortly after Moses himself promised that 'the Lord God will raise up for you a prophet like me,' the Lord God says, 'But the prophet who presumes to speak a word in my name which I have not commanded him to speak, or who speaks in the name of other gods, that same prophet shall die,' (Deuteronomy 18:15, 20)

Begin with sabbath observance, for that seems to be what stuck most stubbornly and most frequently in the craws of the temple authorities and other religious leaders. Notice that it is mostly by healing, by salving that Jesus is deemed to have broken the sabbath rest. To Jesus this is merely allowing God to do through him what God always does from eternity to eternity – creates life ever anew and restores life when it is damaged or set back, creator/saviour as the Bible from the beginning regards God. To the temple authorities this is Jesus replacing with some rules of his own one of the most central commands that God through Moses had enjoined on his people, the law of sabbath rest. Jesus, in short, is playing God, acting like God's equal, and his stubborn defence of such conduct amounts then to little more than 'blasphemous words against Moses and God'. It is as simple as that: two positions that could not be clearer, or more contrary to each other, or more extensive in their ramifications. For at the end of the day they involve, not just a knock-down drag-out argument about particular divine commandments, with sabbath observance mostly to the fore as the prime paradigm. No, they involve rather quite contrary views of God, as one can see clearest once again from John's gospel – chapter eight is a good example – where Jesus responds in kind to 'the Jews' (this time a mixum-gatherum of temple police, chief priests and Pharisees seem to be involved). These say that Jesus is possessed by the devil; Jesus says, quite to the contrary, that it is they who are sons of Satan; each party denying that the other is made up of sons of the true Father.

The law of sabbath observance and its breaking for the sake of creation/salvation, together with the consequences in terms of sonship of the true God, rather than blasphemy/idolatry/satanism, is paradigmatic with respect to other laws, and their keeping and breaking and the consequences that ensue. This becomes clear from the following biblical considerations. First, John has Jesus counter the claim of the Jews that he should be killed because he healed on the sabbath day, by reminding them that they allowed circumcision to be performed if the eighth day fell on a sabbath. 'If on the sabbath a man receives circumcision so that the law of Moses may not be broken, are you angry with me because on the sabbath I made a man's whole body well?'(John 7:23) In other words, if you circumcise on the sabbath in order to bring the child into the ambit of the people of God to whom and from whom salvation comes, how can you possibly object to someone, anyone bringing salving to anyone else on the sabbath day?

Then Jesus offers an example of another law that was justifiably broken when the creative healing of a human ill required such. When the Pharisees complained about the disciples of Jesus plucking ears of corn on the sabbath because they were hungry, Jesus reminded them that David and his company when they were hungry actually entered the temple and ate the Bread of the Presence (as a group of Catholics might break into a church tabernacle and satisfy their hunger from the reserved hosts). With the implication that these men were justified in breaking that law also, but always to the same end: that this particular law should not be allowed to interfere with the higher and more universal law of the reign of God, namely, that life must be continually healed by humans who, in the image of God, must bring that reign or rule of God into all of their world. (Mark 2:23-28) For it is at the end of that little speech about David that Jesus really shows the law of sabbath observance to be a paradigm case for our attitude to all laws laid down in the name of God, as he issued this thoroughly humanist general principle: 'The sabbath was made for man, not man for the sabbath.'

That general principle governs every rule or practice or programme proposed by any group of people in any faith or religion that presumes to the following and fellowship of Jesus of Nazareth. For the sabbath rule, as the paradigm of all rules, is written into the covenant of creation, and the seven-day creation myth of Genesis is especially designed to make that clear. It is a rule designed to keep *homo insipiens* ever mindful of the precise place that belongs to that perennially self-admiring species in the continuous creation of the cosmos. In relation to the Creator Spirit, humanity is to recognise that the whole cosmic creative enterprise, and even humanity's part in it, comes from the eternal God and from nothing and nobody else. In relation to fellow creatures, humanity is to recognise its perennial obligation, based in the wisdom conferred on it through the eternal act of creation itself, to play its derivative role in creatively advancing existence and life, and in particular in salving fellow creatures from the effects of destructive deformation, whether natural or inflicted by humanity's own evil-doing.

The recognition of the first side of the Creator-creature relationship is dramatised and ritualised by setting aside one day in the week on which *homo insipiens* will keep his greedy, grubby little hands off the creation altogether. No better way of acknowledging that the advance of creation is entirely in God's hands and will go just as well, and more likely much better, without humanity's perennially bungled cooperation.

The recognition of the other side of the relationship, the creature-Creator relationship, has two parts to it. First, the general task of co-creating in favour of all of God's creatures, in so far as this is humanly possible, is and should be set aside during the sabbath, for only so can the chief purpose of sabbath observance, the recognition of God as the all-creator be dramatised and continually brought home to humans who are perennially tempted to think of themselves as the real creator gods of creation. But second, humanity's role particularly in salving life on this earth, most of the threats to which come in any case from humanity itself, should never be postponed any more than it already is habitually postponed by man's indifference and inhumanity to man and to every other creature that comes within its greedy reach in the whole of the cosmos.

That would seem to be a fair account of the principles that Jesus applies to the law of sabbath observance. And since that law is clearly a paradigm for any law issued in God's name, it would have to apply equally to any such law. Stated more simply it would then read: the observance of any law issued in the name of the Creator Spirit must be for the benefit of God's creatures; and in so far as it proves to be contrary to, or even to postpone unnecessarily that benefit, particularly in cases of set-backs such as hunger, or illness, or injury, it may safely be set aside on such occasions. This is just an expression in legal mode of the principle of the reign of God as Jesus understood and interpreted that process for which he lived and died: the reign of God is there for man, not man for the reign of God. For God rules only by eternally creating and advancing all of the existence and life of the cosmos. The eternal advancement of existence and life, and the goodness, the greatness and the glory thereby achieved for all, is God's only purpose in creating the cosmos. God's purpose in creation is not to lord it over creatures in a manner that demands continual self-abasement and prostration before the throne, and the kind of glorification that 'the rulers of the Gentiles' demand from their subjects; the kind that fathers never ask of their children. (This admixture of rest (*shalom*) and salving work that Jesus enjoins on the sabbath, provides also an apt symbolism of the rest, the *shalom*, of God's own self that is not in the least disturbed by the eternal work of creation – as Jesus said somewhere, 'The Father works until now, and I work,' – the still centre at the heart of the whirlwind of continuous creation. The co-operative multitude of symbols are sometimes replaced by the multivalence of a single symbol, in this case the single symbol of sabbath rest.)

All of these rules in the Bible are habitually presented as rules of a covenant between God and humanity. The image of covenant comes from arrangements, say between an over-king and a client-king, which define the privileges and obligations to the other that each will incur, and the rules by which they will conduct themselves. The image of covenant (*suntheke*) is therefore not the best metaphor for this aspect of the relationships between Creator and creature, for the creature brings nothing of benefit to the Creator and cannot bind the Creator to any obligations. Another image, close cousin to the image of covenant, is better: the image of a will or testament (*diatheke*) also used in the Bible, suits better the relationship of the One who gives all, without any obligation to do so, to the creature. For the simple recognition of such unrestrained giving must make the wise ones feel the obligation to care to the best of their abilities for all that is always given to them. Just like the family that inherits a great house and estate from their ancestors, rightly feel obliged to keep it up, and if possible to add to it and further enhance it. The rules then are the guidelines that this family adopt in order to pursue the best advantage of all that has been handed down to them. And the rules will be revised, or sometimes subjected to sets of exceptions, or even set aside altogether and replaced, as the inheritance evolves or its managers grow in experience and, one must always hope against hope, in wisdom.

There are many examples recorded in the Bible of great men who tried to reformulate the original covenant between God and humanity. But the only one of these that is of immediate concern here is the covenant mediated by Moses from God's holy mountain. For the book of Deuteronomy ends with the words: 'There has not arisen a prophet in Israel like Moses, whom the Lord knew face to face, none like him for all the signs and wonders which the Lord sent him to do in the land of Egypt, to Pharoah and to all his servants and to all his land, and for the mighty power and all the great and terrible deeds which Moses wrought in the sight of Israel.' And so say all of us, you can hear the echo from the temple priests and scribes and other religious leaders of the Jews at the time of Jesus. So heartily and unreservedly that they often unwittingly attributed to Moses rules and arrangements that came at other times. All gathered together now under the name of Moses, as the eternal rule of God, the Torah, to which all of humanity would have to subscribe. Even if that meant, as it meant to Isaiah, that they should all in the end come to the temple at Jerusalem and have their sacrifices there accepted, and keep the sabbath holy to the one Lord of Creation.

You have seen how these temple authorities reacted to Jesus when he broke the sabbath observance. Can you even begin to imagine how these same men from the temple would have jumped up and down and torn their garments, if they had been present at the mythical scene on the mountain, the scene composed by Matthew as background to his famous composition, the Sermon on the Mount, when Jesus, the new Moses, handed down the renewed terms of the renewed covenant of creation? (Matthew 5-7) The very shock of his repeated formula, 'You have heard that it was said of old (by Moses from the other mountain), but I say to you', must surely have shaken the very mountain itself, never mind a few priests and scribes and Pharisees trying to keep their footing through this howling breath and thunderous voice of what must have seemed to them to be a man possessed entirely by a demonic spirit. 'You have heard that it was said to the men of old, "You shall not kill".' The scribe is already calculating in his well-stocked mind just how many causes there are in the Mosaic code for executing those who break the law, and he is just about to add to this the number of occasions on which God ordered, or acted through Moses, and Joshua, and David and Saul and ... to kill in war the enemies of 'his' people, when the next burst of utterly implacable words strike his unfortunate ears (to paraphrase): 'But I say to you that, far from killing anyone at all, you are not even to be angry with anyone, you are not to insult anyone, you are not to make any-one look like a fool, and you are certainly not to approach the altar of God with your gifts if you have done any of these things and not yet been reconciled to any of those you have injured in any way.'

Nor, as Matthew has Jesus hand down this new Torah from God, like the new Moses on the new mountain, is anyone who is injured by another in any way to respond by punishing that other for such offence against the person. Rather is the injured party to do some extra good to the offender, as the most effective way of showing the offender that forgiveness has anticipated the evil deed, and indeed to love the offender also as one loves one-self. 'You have heard that it was said, "An eye for an eye and a tooth for a tooth." But I say to you, do not resist one who is evil ... if anyone would sue you and take your coat, let him have your cloak as well; and if anyone forces you to go one mile, go with him two miles ... You have heard that it was said, "You shall love your neighbour and hate your enemy." But I say to you, love your enemies and pray for those who persecute you.' And then, to cap it all, immediately after he has legislated for human behav-iour in these most demanding terms, Jesus justifies all of this by appealing to the way in which the Creator Spirit behaves, as any one with eyes can see from the daily exercise of that divine con-tinuous creation – 'so that you may be the sons of your Father who is in heaven, for he makes his sun to rise on the evil and on the good, and sends his rain on the just and the unjust.'

Sun and rain, fire and water, are symbols for the ultimate Source-Creator of all existence and of all life in the cosmos. Just as in Genesis the Creator Spirit is symbolised by the mothering bird brooding on the watery deep, and later by fire, like the flames of the sun transforming life on earth – symbols together of the Ultimate Source whose eternal creative power is always at the equal service of all, no matter what they have done or do, or omitted to do, good or bad. This view of God's ways with the world is further stressed by Jesus on these occasions on which he tells anyone who would listen that disasters that befall people, whether natural or man-made, are never to be interpreted as God's own punishing penalty for sins committed by those who suffer such misfortunes. Rather are these occasions for that salving to occur that the rule of God exemplifies for all people without distinction, in all circumstances, and at all times, sabbath included. All converging on the same principle of the reign of God: you must heal and enrich the lives of those who injure you, just as much as you do for those who are good to you; and you must never injure in turn those offenders against your person, either on your own authority, or through the legal affordances of your society. For only so can you be sons and daughters of God, and broadcast God's true image to the world. The true image of the one, true God who never adds any penalty of punishment to the punishments that we in our fallen world and our evil ways inflict upon each other, legally and illegally, indiscriminately, daily and apparently interminably.

No degree in theology is necessary in order to recognise that two very different images of God faced each other across the divide between accuser and accused on that fateful night at the house of Caiaphas the high priest. The one is the image of the God who creates the world, probably by command – 'Let there be!' And then, within that command creation, God created the species most like himself, and the members of that species he also commands with respect to its actions and obligations towards him, and with respect to its actions and obligations towards each other and towards other creatures. From amongst that species God then makes a choice: from amongst the tribes, peoples or nations he picks his especially chosen ones to whom he especially communicates all of these commands, together with the rewards and punishments that follow on their observance or non-observance. For God takes personally any offences committed, as defined by his do's and don'ts, and will punish both now and in some future age or world those who disobey his commands. As indeed he authorises his appointed rulers, from sacred temple and royal palace alike, to punish transgressors also in this life and world. And as this God has decreed that all others should come to his chosen people (or church) in order to avail of the eternal revelation and rewards on offer, and to avoid the eternal punishments that await those who deliberately refuse to join his chosen people in some manner or form. So he has authorised his chosen people to make war on those who deliberately oppose and attack them, to eradicate such enemies with his aid, if need be, and he will add his own eternal punishment to these enemies in due course.

The other is the image of the God who creates by lovingly fashioning things of beauty like a potter fashions the beauty of a vase out of a lump of clay that he moulds and fires in accordance with a vision he has in his mind of something good and true and beautiful in itself. A joy for God's own self to behold, a joy to be reciprocated in whatever ways prove suitable for any offspring of such a good and beautiful progenitor – birds singing from the budding and then flowering branches of spring, people singing psalms of praise. This is the God who continually creates those creatures, and most of all the human species, by empowering them to create their likes, thereby continually forming, reforming and transforming them through all necessary dyings during all of that *élan vital*. It is the God who inspires rather than commands, leaving it to the wise ones to come up with and continually improve sets of rules, of do's and don'ts, that will help them co-operate as best they can with God's own reign and project of ever advancing existence and life for all into eternity. And above all the God of Jesus is the God who never, ever returns evil for evil done, but is entirely occupied in this respect with healing and overcoming the evils that the wise ones in particular bring upon themselves and on the world that is within the range of their influence when they fall. As they seem to be forever falling out of the existential condition of grace given and of gratitude and grace returned.

It is only too easy to see how the teaching of Jesus from Matthew's mythical mountain, and the practices of Jesus that follow upon it, for all of Matthew's insistence that it represents the fulfilment of the Mosaic Torah, would appear quite differently to Israel's official upholders and interpreters of the Law of Moses. (Matthew 5:17-19) To the latter it would appear to be nothing short of a series of contradictions, sometimes in set terms, of the unalterable commandments of God for the cosmos that God had given on the real holy mountain of Sinai through God's incomparable prophet, Moses. To any fair-minded judge sitting in the highest court of Israel at that time, Jesus was guilty of uttering blasphemous words against Moses, that is to say, against the Law of God, and thereby against God. Jesus, Caiaphas had no doubt, was a false prophet promoting another self-serving law in honour of some other god made in the image of the unacceptable behaviour of Jesus himself and displacing the one, true God definitively revealed to Israel through Moses. It was as simple as that. From the perspective of the philosophy and faith, the custom and law by which the nation of Israel at that time lived and died, the trial of Jesus was thoroughly valid and legal and fair. Jesus was indeed guilty as charged, and his execution an unimpeachable outcome of these straightforward features of law and of fact.

Put in terms of covenant, the renewed covenant that Matthew sees Jesus mediate, through the imaginative conceit of having him hand down Torah from the mythical mountain, the point of all of this could be expressed, as it is expressed in the Bible, as follows. Jesus was condemned and executed for his promotion of this (re)new(ed) covenant. So he himself is said to have asserted in scenes of a last supper: his blood would be shed, his body would be broken for the coming of the reign and covenant of God as he understood and lived it out. And so the food and drink, necessities of life that his followers shared, both symbolised a life lived under God's true reign and covenant – their solemn commitment to which in this sacramental act meant that their bodies and blood also would be broken and shed, their very lives given if need be. Each one internalising this ultimate undertaking in pursuit of the reign of God, to the clunk of earthenware wine goblets and the soft sound of the breaking of bread:

my body broken, my blood shed. Of course, in actual historical fact, the disciples at that last supper did not internalise the symbolism of saying over the shared cup and loaf, my blood shed and my body broken. Or if they did, they negated that solemn symbolism again when faced with the prospect of having to make it real in act. They ran away, and waited for Jesus to come back even after his death, to bring on a real kingdom of God, one like that of their real father, David, once more.

For things to have turned out differently, nothing less than a complete *volte face* would have needed to take place in that historic courtroom. The temple authorities would have had to accept that it was they themselves who had failed in their service to what they called the Torah of Moses and of God; and in the end that it was Jesus who should have been sitting where Caiaphas sat, and Caiaphas and his priests and scribes should have been sentenced to death instead of Jesus. For Jesus, according to John, had already passed upon them the precise sentence that they now passed on him: 'You are of your father the devil, and your will is to do your father's desires. He was a killer from the beginning.' (John 8:44) In short, in seeking to kill Jesus these leaders were sons of Satan, not of the Father. They were fornicators (i.e. idolators) and blasphemers, and as such prime candidates for capital punishment according to the Torah. Except of course, if Jesus were really to take the judgement seat from Caiaphas, neither Caiaphas nor anyone else would ever be condemned to death, nor indeed to any life-diminishing penalty applied particularly to any offence committed. Jesus put this matter most plainly to those about to execute a woman caught in the act of adultery, when the scribes brought the unfortunate woman before Jesus as he taught in the temple. The scribes reminded him that the law of Moses stated she should be stoned. Jesus handed down the sentence: 'Let him who is without sin among you throw the first stone at her.' And when, predictably, no such person stepped forward, Jesus then said to the woman: 'Neither do I condemn you; go, and do not sin again.' (An alternative section of John 7:53-8:11, or after Luke 21:38)

But that comment only hardens the impression that the terms of the covenant that Jesus handed down from his mountain contradicted the terms that Moses handed down from Mount Sinai.

So Moses was a blasphemer, an idolator, possessed by satan and not by the Spirit of God? For endorsing so much legal killing off or serious damaging of human life? That seems to be the correct impression we get from the words of Jesus. And it is a long way from the impression we would surely get if Jesus were, as Matthew has him say at the beginning of that famous sermon from the mountain, merely fulfilling the Mosaic law. It is difficult, from the few comments that the gospels record Jesus making on the subject of his relationship to Moses, to decide with any certainty where on the line between the extremes of contradiction and fulfilment of the law of Moses Jesus himself thought he stood. We have heard him say that if his opponents really followed Moses, then they would accept him, because Moses wrote of him. That could be interpreted to mean that Moses foresaw the need for a prophet like himself sent by God in the future, because the world moves on. But that moving on, so liberally illustrated in our day by our knowledge of the evolution of life, cannot be understood in a warm, reassuring and totally optimistic sense. If only because of what our rapidly accumulating knowledge of the details of evolution and history prove beyond any doubt, as better and higher prospects for life appear daily, and not least in the form of our own human powers to make life on this planet better for all, there seems to be a corresponding increase in our tendencies and abilities to destroy our own lives and even the life of the planet itself. Evolution moves forward, it seems, only to threaten constantly to go into reverse, most especially since we came on the scene.

Therefore, as Moses did the best he could in his time to formulate the terms of God's covenant in creation so that the people could abide by them, then at some future date, a (more) final age of the world's development, another prophet would come and make the law itself more perfect than Moses had managed to make it. The covenant of creation, for example, can be interpreted to contain a ruling against divorce, because God had united the first man and woman, the first parents of the species, in the unity of 'one flesh', to be bound together in a unity of steadfast love in which the procreators would imitate the creator in the steadfastness of their love for each other and for their own special creations, the children of the race. So Jesus ruled: 'What God

255

has joined together, let not man put asunder.' Jesus then explained that when Moses, quite contrary to the very spirit of the reign of God, legislated for divorce, it was a concession to hardness of heart, the common image for human resistance to the reign of the one, true God. But Jesus also felt quite strongly that those inspired by the rule of God that he was commissioned to introduce anew, should be capable of the steadfast love that always lies at the heart and substance of that reign. (Mark 10:1-12) Therefore the prohibition of divorce written by God's loving providence into the fabric of creation itself should be re-introduced into human legislation, Moses to the contrary notwithstanding.

Similarly with another rule that is even more at the heart of the covenant of creation between humanity and the God who does nothing but continue to create and re-create life: thou shalt not kill. Jesus could be said to have been fulfilling that rule when he extended it beyond simple killing, either lawfully or unlawfully, and then to all life-diminishing activity. That represents a perfecting of the moral sensitivity as expressed now by addenda to the simple ruling, thou shalt not kill; addenda such as: you must not even harbour hostility in your heart, must not mock and demean. But it also leaves one with the impression that terms like fulfilment and perfecting are being elasticised to the point at which they can cover plain contradiction. In the end, all that can be said is that one man's fulfilling is another man's contradiction, and that the second will kill you for it, and the first never will. So you may at some stage have to die for it, rather than kill, as Jesus never tired of explaining to his would-be followers, albeit mostly in vain.

Now no sooner do we recognise these kinds and causes of one group of a faith community splitting from the parent 'people of God,' than we realise that it happens again and again in human history. And we recognise also that all too often it happens with the added irritant of the parent people persecuting the ones they see as their divisive critics, and sometimes being persecuted by these in turn. Jesus and his early followers, allowing that their fellow Jews had the true revelation from God through Moses, then accused their erstwhile leaders of corrupting the terms of that revelation, and were persecuted even to death for so doing. These Christians, as they came to be called, then in their own turn not only persecuted the Jews as best they could themselves but, like Paul, they called down on God's originally chosen people God's eternal punitive wrath, a kind of eternal death as punishment for persecuting the Christians.

Mohammed and his followers, when their turn came, allowed that the Jews and the Christians once had between them the book of the true revelation of God's truth through the good offices of their prophets, particularly Moses and Jesus. But then, although the Holy Qur-an itself records initial acceptance by Jews and Christians of the revelation that came through Muhammad, and even speaks of the prophet Jesus in terms sometimes more fulsome that those used of Muhammad himself, the three-way persecution, attack and counter-attack soon broke out, and continued and increased in the sad centuries since. And then, much more recently, the Bahai's allowed that Muhammad had the true revelation of the one, true God, but that his followers gradually misinterpreted it and introduced corrupting elements, and God sent the prophet, Baha'ullah, and the Muslims then persecuted his followers, the Bahai's. Although the Bahai's have declared that they cannot and will not persecute anyone, and they also have had the wit to follow the logic of the scheme so far outlined, so as to propose that, if the past is anything to go by, then the renewed revelation that came with their prophets will last for only a couple of thousands of years, before it too becomes corrupted or obsolete in some ways, and God will then have to send another prophet. Thus they accept the pattern of prophecy for the future as it appears to have shown itself in the past.

And all the time, underlying that particular pattern of how the world moves on, or rather moves on-and-back, on-and-back, on-and-back ... there is another pattern, deeper lying, that our evolution scientists, and in particular those involved in socio-biological evolution, persist in trying to describe to us by means of ever more compelling stories. And that pattern, we can easily see from what has been said above about the complex relationship between Jesus and Moses, applies also to the Mosaic version of the Jewish religion and to the renewal and revision of this that Jesus much later attempted. The story of this deeper pattern is the story of what evolution science would call the story of the evolution of the religio-moral sense of our species. This religio-moral sense seems to have first evolved with our species, and there is evidence to the effect that it continued to evolve further during the ages of our tenure of this planet earth. From cruel and savage systems, dripping with the blood of human sacrifices made for the placation of cruel and savage gods to, ultimately, the system preached by Jesus in which the rule of the God he called the Father of us all required consistent pro-life behaviour, with no reversals of life-forms countenanced, other than those that were an integral part of the deformation that must always form part and parcel of the continuous transformation of life for the better.

But that evolution of the religio-moral sense of human kind, it is clear from the fullest and clearest story told about it, does not consist in a steady and smooth rise from the cruder imagery of the behaviour of gods and humans that attended the early and much greater vulnerability and fear of human beings before the death-dealing forces in their world. For the wiser these ancestors of ours became, and the more competent in controlling the forces and vagaries of nature, including their own human nature, the more tempted they were to see themselves as gods. So that, as the matter has already been explained in the Bible, they found themselves reverting to the old savage ways of the earth, which in consequence they made to look, not like a paradise holding out eternal promise, but like a patchwork of killing fields. And the pattern of onwards-and-backwards, onward-and-backwards, reproduces itself at this deeper level of cosmogenesis, just as it is seen at the social level at which the three (now four?) members of the so-called family of monotheistic faiths from the Near East related to each other.

So Jesus did die then in defiance to the last of the satanic spirit that still had hold over the followers of Moses, as expressed both in some of the terms of the covenant of Moses itself – mainly the killing terms – and in the further deteriorations that the temple authorities or their predecessors had introduced into the terms of that covenant. And in dying thus, rather than resist in the killing spirit that inspired his accusers and executioners, Jesus breathed into a still dying world, in consummate fashion, the spirit in which he had lived all his life, the spirit of faith in a God who is always and forever the God of the living and of life, and never the God of the killers and the dead. And before anyone begins to jump up and down at this point and raise the cry of anti-semitism, we must point out that we have already seen above a resume of the sad story of how Christians who take the name of Jesus, in this case in vain, revived this satanic spirit, not only by their own endorsement of killing, but by their main traditional interpretation of the death of Jesus himself.

For the death-sentemce of Jesus was the death-sentence of a prophet, judged to have been a prophet who played false to the point of continuous and contumacious blasphemy, and duly condemned to death in accordance with the rule for dealing with such a prophet, as laid down in Deuteronomy 18:20. Because he taught – can you believe it? – that God, through nothing more than what God revealed in the on-going act of divine creation, issued guidelines that were purely for the service and benefit of creatures, and not, as the conduct of virtually any known earthly king or cognate kind of ruler could illustrate, commands for the showing of obedience to his royal person. Commands first and foremost for the provision to the king of all the power and authority, and then of all the wealth and rich sustenance and grandeur and other forms of service that he needed in order to keep his subjects safe and fed and housed and, well yes, to some extent entertained. So that the people did benefit after all, however indirectly, from their obedience to all of the demands and commands of the God-King and his earthly plenipotentiaries; and the people should therefore not be so ungrateful for this benefit as to disobey and risk imprisonment and, in some cases, execution. The God that Jesus preached, and in whose name he spurned laws designed to make people subservient to God and to God's plenipotentiaries, both royal and priestly on earth, was and could only seem to the priests of such peoples – an idol. And so it was as the self-styled prophet of what his priestly judge perceived to be an idol that Jesus was condemned as a recidivist blasphemer, and sentenced to death.

So the priest condemned the prophet to death, quite legally and validly in accordance with the understanding of the terms of the true Torah of the one true God, as the priest understood and administered these at that particular time. But then, instead of having the death sentence carried out by the priest and his minions, by stoning Jesus to death as Stephen was later stoned, the story takes a sudden and, in hindsight at least, a quite unexpected turn, one that the biblical stories of these matters fail to take the trouble to either prepare us for, or to explain properly. For here and now the king takes over, or at least that equivalent of kingship, Pilate, the Roman Governor who had taken up residence in Jerusalem for the often turbulent period of the Passover festival. And he takes over to such an extent that subsequent history takes the trial before Pilate, together with the sentence handed down and the execution of that sentence, as the real trial. In comparison to which the goings-on at the house of the High Priest the night before are of relatively minor importance, both for our understanding of the reasons for the killing of Jesus and for the assessment of the historic, not to say cosmic significance later claimed by his followers for that death.

Now this apparent lacuna in the biblical story cannot simply pass without question, not even in justifiable haste to produce an example in the age-old realpolitik relationships between priests and kings that shows the priest corrupting the king, forcing the latter to hand down a judicial decision he clearly considered unjust. The questions that must be asked, and some attempt made to answer them, are at least two. First, did the priestly party now standing before Pilate change the charge, or at least alter significantly the balance of material in the capital charge, when Pilate was asked to condemn Jesus as a true messianic pretender to the Davidic throne, even though he had been sentenced at the other court as a false prophet? And second, and perhaps even more crucially, what precisely was the priestly purpose in having Jesus, already duly condemned to death, exposed to hazards for both himself and the priest, of risking another trial before another authority who was as much an enemy as a colluder? What if Pilate were to let Jesus go (as we now know he tried to do)?

It is not a good answer to the first question to say that, yes, the priestly party did alter the charge on presenting Jesus before Pilate, for they knew well that Pilate could care less about their prophets, true or false. So they charged him before Pilate as a messianic pretender to the Davidic throne, knowing full well that whatever Jesus himself had to say on this matter – in the synoptic gospels, readers will remember, Jesus himself had specifically denied, and quoted scripture to prove this denial, that he was a son of David (Mark 12:35-37 and parallels) – the crowds that welcomed him to Jerusalem for the Passover, and indeed even his most intimate disciples, looked on him most hopefully in just this light. Yet it does seem excessive to accuse the priestly party of such a cynical move to pervert the course of justice. If only because, to put the matter rather cursorily, the job description of a Davidic messiah and of a prophet like Moses could be deemed to overlap in significant ways.

Remember that Moses as prophet, long before this people had a king, in addition to bringing what his followers believed to be the definitive Torah from God, also liberated this people of God from the power of Egypt. And in the course of this liberation, by the power of God, the people of Egypt had all of their first-born males massacred, and the army of the Pharaoh wiped out. And Moses also by God's power fed and watered the people on their way to the promised land, and with his brazen serpent he healed all the illnesses they had brought upon themselves through their persistent idolatry. So Moses did everything that his successors, like Joshua and the judges and their future kings would do in pursuit of possession of the promised land. And because of this overlap of the role and duties of the arch-prophet, Moses, with that of future kings, it would be not unfeasible for contemporaries of Jesus, both his followers and his accusers, to mix references to him as the prophet like Moses, with references to him as a pretender to the throne of Israel, a kingly messiah. Any more than it would be pure cynicism on the part of the priests to substitute for the title of prophet for Pilate's benefit, a title that the latter would more immediately recognise and to which they hoped he would react in a predictable manner.

However that may be, Pilate's official judgement was that Jesus was not guilty of that charge. Pilate accepted what Jesus told him in his own defence, namely, that the reign of God which he preached and enacted was not like that of the rulers of this world, not a rule of lording it over others, not a kingdom extended and protected by military power. This self-defence by

Jesus chimes perfectly with all that he had ever said about the manner in which the leaders of his company should conduct themselves: like him they were to be the servants of all, not lord it over others, and never, ever kill them. In a scene that Luke alone adds to this story Pilate, on hearing that Jesus was a Galilean, sends him to Herod, the puppet king whose writ ran in Galilee, in the hope that Herod could be persuaded to try Jesus, presumably on the self-same charge that he, Pilate, was hearing. But Herod also refused to try Jesus on such a charge, preferring to believe that Jesus was probably a foolish fellow, but no credible pretender to a throne. Interesting, to say the least, that the two 'kings' in the case, the ones whose prime business it was to see pretenders to thrones coming from miles away, quite simply rejected the view that Jesus was a messianic pretender in the most generally accepted meaning of that phrase. Pilate's verdict then was, and remains to this day: not guilty as charged.

Yet the story goes on to say that the priestly party blackmailed Pilate into having Jesus executed by his own soldiers after the manner reserved to the Roman authorities in the land, crucifixion, while ostentatiously attempting to wash his own hands of responsibility in the whole messy affair. And that leads inexorably to the second question: why on earth did the priestly party want so badly to have Jesus tried and executed by the Roman overlord, when they had a perfectly valid and legal process of their own by which to achieve both verdict and execution on the charge of false prophesy and the blasphemy that entailed? Especially since the effort to involve Pilate resulted, by all accounts, in what for them must have looked very much like a pyrrhic victory?

The reader may read all the relevant parts of the Bible as thoroughly as possible, and it may still remain unlikely that any clear answer to that question is to be found. We may have to be satisfied in the end with the kind of educated guess that scholarship commends. For it is established that the idea of a show-trial is by no means a modern invention. That is a trial that depicts the accused in the worst possible light, whatever the nature of the deeds the relevant authorities think worthy of capital punishment. It is worth observing also, in the case of our present *dramatis personae*, that it is always dangerous to execute a prophet, especially an inspirational prophet, precisely for being a prophet. Jesus once asked questioners of his authorisation for what he did, what they thought of John. They were afraid to answer, because the people took John for a prophet. And despite the fact that so many took Jesus to be a messiah in the Davidic mould, it would be a sure bet that the majority of the people, especially those who were well off and produced the ruling class, would be glad to be rid of Jesus if he were linked to the IRA of the era.

That matter may never altogether escape from the realm of conjecture, though one must hope that the conjecture may always be educated. But it must never be allowed to distract the inquirer into the death of Jesus from the important and assured findings that matter most for the answers to two questions that really matter. Namely, for what did Jesus really die, for what precisely was he actually killed? And, in consequence, what precisely did his death in particular achieve? The full and correct answers to these questions will follow only upon recognition of the fact that the trial and sentencing of Jesus which resulted in the death penalty was the trial before Caiaphas, and that the actual carrying out of that sentence – for no guilty sentence was passed at the Roman trial – by a Roman execution was an arbitrary add-on for reasons that inevitably require a degree of guesswork. All of that must inevitably also affect our understanding of standard claims concerning the crowning episode of the death of Jesus, such as that Jesus died for our sins, and that his death was a sacrifice, and so on. And all of that in turn can best be summarised by a final, comprehensive summary of the roles and bearers of the titles of prophet, priest and king, such as we find in masterful fashion in the Letter to the Hebrews.

Jesus of Nazareth: Prophet? Priest? King?

The Letter to the Hebrews was written reasonably early in the history of the followers of Jesus, certainly before the temple was destroyed in 70CE. It was written by an apologist for Jesus, and it was addressed in particular to those followers of Jesus who now appeared to be tempted, in face of well founded fears of meeting the same fate as Jesus, to slip back under the protection of the Mosaic Torah. The opening note to this letter in the *Oxford*

Annotated Revised Standard Version offers a wonderfully anachronistic picture of this situation: 'The recipients of this letter were on the point of giving up their Christian faith and returning to the Jewish beliefs and practices of their ancestors.' This is anachronistic because nobody whose views are represented in any document of the Bible had as yet any inkling that they belonged to a different, 'Christian' faith or religion, or indeed to any faith or religion other than that of Jesus the Jew.

So no, this is not a member of the Christian religion writing to fellow members of that new religion who, in fear of persecution by the Hebrews, threaten to return to the Jewish religion they had left. This is, rather, a card-carrying member of the Hebrew faith writing to fellow members who have opted to follow Jesus, but now, in fear of a fate similar to his, are tempted to return to the safety of the covenant with Moses, its Torah and its priesthood, that Jesus had at the very least heavily modified. It is a letter to Hebrews; it is a part and a document of an affair strictly between Hebrews. How else explain how much of the letter is taken up with an elaborate case for the superiority of Jesus over Moses, for the superiority of the prophet Jesus that Jesus himself claimed Moses predicted? A case supported by an even more elaborate case for the end of the Levitical priesthood and its temple sacrifices? The very kinds of case that were fashioned into charges against Jesus, and against Stephen. The only difference is that here in this letter the downgrading of Moses and of the Torah that bore his name, together with an announcement of the end of the temple priesthood and sacrifices, achieves a finality and a level not witnessed earlier either from Jesus himself or from the earlier disciples of his as we see them preach and behave in the opening chapters of Acts. And so the Letter to the Hebrews is part symptom, part harbinger of a separate religion that within another century or so will sever itself irrevocably from its true parent, the Jewish faith and religion – an event that was never envisaged by Jesus, as far as one can tell, and that might very well not have met with his approval if he had foreseen it. For it has proved to be so very tragic for both religions in so very many ways.

Moses then is the direct target of this letter's opening contrast: 'God spoke of old to our fathers by the prophets; but in these last days he has spoken to us by a son.' (1:2) And the contrast is specifically directed at Moses when the title of son of God (*'uios, filius*) accorded to Jesus is quite deliberately contrasted with the title of domestic servant (*therapon/famulus*), the best that our author can offer to Moses. (3:5-6) Although he softens the blow somewhat by insisting that Moses was as faithful to his God in his time and circumstance as Jesus was in his.

Then the contrast is heightened further when the letter eulogises the sonship of Jesus as one in which God has raised Jesus higher even than the angels. Angels, like the gods (*elohim*) of which humanity is said to be only a little lower, are in reality respectively hypostases of divinity in its role of sending or revealing its messages to the world, and yet not so as to appear to be themselves fully comprehended or grasped by humanity the wise. So by use of this imagery, Hebrews offers us the very same analysis as we found in the Philippians hymn, of the self-emptying of Jesus that consisted in his obedient slavery, even to the point of dying on the cross for that way of living – the very means of his being raised by the God who could then work unhindered through him, to the status of son, as no other had been son; *monogenes*, unique of the kind. Although, it must be said, in Hebrews this same analysis and argument is found in a much more verbose, rambling and convoluted manner, scattered over the first two chapters of that letter.

Jesus, as Hebrews puts it, 'reflects the very glory of God and bears the very stamp of his nature, upholding the universe by his word of power' (the Word, the Spirit that made him son of God in power, that spoke and breathed through him as the perfect prophet). Yet, Jesus 'partook of the same nature' as all who 'share in flesh and blood,' and he was 'made (still) lower than the angels,' when 'as the pioneer of (our) salvation,' he was made 'perfect through suffering', reduced to dying the death of a slave on a cross. So that 'when he had accomplished the purgation of sins (*purgationem peccatorum, katharismon 'amartion* – purging sin like a physician sending cancer into remission by excising the visibly diseased parts), he sat down at the right hand of the Majesty on high, having become as much superior to angels as the name he has obtained is more excellent than theirs.' The name is Lord, as the Philippians hymn states clearly, son of

God in the fullness of the divine power working in and through his utterly human frame, and never working more powerfully than when the divine Spirit dissolved that mortal frame as Jesus endured and triumphed over the cruel torture of the cross. Breathing forth, as he did so, the Spirit embodied in him, as powerfully as any human being could ever breath it, onto the killing and dying fields of this fallen world. These opening chapters of Hebrews do echo faithfully the content of the Philippians hymn to the lordship of the self-emptied one.

However, if one wants to use Hebrews to show how the Bible adds the second motif, that of the king-messiah, to the first motif that is already used to explain the charge on which Jesus was condemned to death, then one has to notice that there is something distinctly odd about the manner in which Hebrews does this. The oddness consists in this, that the manner in which Hebrews introduces the king-messiah motif consists in the evocation of an ancient convention by which the kingship motif was linked to the motif of priesthood in the very job description of one and the same person. This looks odd to those readers of the trial accounts, in which priests and kings are quite as separate as Caiaphas and Pilate. Yet the historical figure through which Hebrews develops its argument further from the Philippians theme, is the figure of a certain Melchiz'edek, king of Salem, who is also a priest. Salem is *shalom*, in a form that occurs in the name, Jerusalem, so Melchiz'edek is king of *shalom* as any ruler of Jerusalem should be, and his own name suggests that he is also king of justice, that his rule will be characterised by justice, by truth or wisdom.

The idea of a king-priest would seem even less strange if one read a little further in the biblical books that record the customs of the age of Melchiz'edek. For then one would notice that kings of Israel did as a matter of course exercise the office of cultic priest in these far off times, offering sacrifices and so forth. 'And David's sons were priests,' one text proclaims; and we see one son of David, namely Solomon, on the occasion on which he asked God for wisdom, offering the burnt offerings at the sacred shrine of Gibeon. On reading a little wider still, one discovers that in an enthronement psalm, the one in which the king, David it is thought, is conferred with the title of Lord, it is also said of him by God, 'You are a priest forever after the order of Melchiz'edek.' (Psalm 110:4; 1 Kings 3:4; 2 Samuel 8:18) At this point the ideal of a king-priest should no longer sound at all odd. Least of all to Roman Catholics, who should at this point realise something that otherwise might not occur to them, namely, that they have an absolute ruler against whose decrees there is no appeal, as the Code of Canon Law puts it, for he is the highest earthly wielder of legislative, judicial and executive power (no separation of powers here).

Yet he is at the same time a high priest of our worldwide church, a priest in the sense of one who offers a blood-sacrifice on an altar, albeit in this case 'in an unbloody manner'. Indeed, he may well be called the High Priest in that he can control and dismiss from the exercise of their priestly office his bishops who 'have the fullness of priesthood' and, *a fortiori*, all those 'ordinary' priests who, by definition, do not have the fullness of priesthood. And below these serried ranks of clergy, it goes without saying, he can lay down absolute rules for the lives, both cultic and common, of the massed *laos*, the even more ordinary people of God. So that the manner in which Hebrews deals with the theme of king-messiah, twinned with the motif of prophet, is of perennial and present interest. And not least because it is in the anonymous author's description of the sacrifice that Jesus makes in emptying himself of precisely the kind of self-aggrandisement and conspicuous lordship over others that kings are wont to acquire, that he addresses simultaneously the question of the kinds of sacrifices, the kinds of leaders and the kinds of priests, if any, that should characterise any community of people, local or international, that claim to follow Jesus of Nazareth.

It is while he is still heavily engaged in drawing ever more clearly the portrait of Jesus who is superior to Moses, that our author first introduces almost incidentally his idea of Jesus as a priest. 'Consider Jesus,' he urges us, 'the apostle and high priest of our confession.' (Hebrew's 3:1) This is the context in which he contrasts son with domestic servant, and follows that up with the contrast between the promised land that Moses, and eventually Joshua, led them to; for that was only Canaan, after all, as it was called at that time. And it can bear no comparison with the paradise of God that humankind had destroyed for themselves through their fall, and to which they could be led back by Jesus, the pioneer of salvation, through the fire, the flaming swords, through which alone that paradise could be regained. Two chapters later our author ventures that the high priesthood he has already attributed to Jesus without any explanatory comment, is the priesthood that God confers on him, in the same terms as God had conferred it on David: 'a priest forever – that is, an eternal priesthood – after the order of Melchiz'edek.' And just as our expectation rises that he will clarify that simile, he informs us: 'About this we have much to say which is hard to explain.' He has much to say alright, but this reader at least finds that, rather than the matter being of itself hard to explain, his rather disorderly and rambling explanation makes it hard to understand. The other point he makes, to the effect that people who have drifted away from the truth for self-interest will prove 'dull of hearing' is fair enough, but that would explain how we might not be able to *accept* what he has to say, not that we would not be able to *understand* it, if he had taken a few lessons in clear and consecutive exposition of what my edition calls, rightly, 'the longest sustained argument of any book in the Bible'.

But this much at least of his explanation of the Melchiz'edek theme is clear, and it is more than sufficient for our present purposes. The king-priest, king of justice and peace, is already prophetic of the ones who should rule over the people of God from Jerusalem. Melchiz'edek is as prophetic-messianic a figure as David was. Hebrews then uses the fact that no genealogy of Melchiz'edek is given in the Bible, and no line of successors in his twin office, in order to see him as a true prophetic symbol of the true Jewish messiah, Jesus. For of the latter it can be said that all that he is and does comes from God and not from any royal ancestry: there is something of eternity in and about him. In addition, so perfect is Jesus in resisting the primordial temptation of the race, as image and son of God who thereby channels God's creative spirit unhindered into the world, that his followers will always be just that – followers who must always acknowledge his pioneering leadership, his lordship. And his followers should need no succession of messianic prophets, for they can forever experience the presence of the Creator Spirit that made him the messianic prophet of the age of perfection, by letting the Spirit that fashioned him in life and death, fashion them also as in memory of him they partake of the eucharistic meal and are thereby inspired to make it into the eschatological meal of the world. No need for genealogies or successors; Jesus, the pioneer, perfecter and (relative to God) source of our faith shares in the eternity of God, to which all who follow him have equal access, without the mediation of any other priests of the traditional cultic kind. Jesus the messianic priest without predecessor or successor.

This leads into the second strand in the current stage of the argument of Hebrews: the obsolescence of and replacement of the blood sacrifices offered by mortal priests. The paradigm case here is the sacrifice with which Moses ratified the covenant of Sinai, with extension of the reference then to the sacrifices offered by the Levitical priesthood, still in business in the temple at Jerusalem. The business of the High Priest in particular, who condemned Jesus to death. This part of the argument now proceeds as follows: these blood sacrifices, of bulls and goats and *a fortiori* of human beings, or anything of that ilk, although they might well have been said to ratify a covenant, certainly could not consummate it. These cultic sacrifices never could consummate a covenant in the sense of seeing its terms realised and the favour of the initiating covenanter restored. That quintessential deficiency was true of the sacrifice that Moses offered, and equally true of the temple sacrifices. This is in line with the view, often expressed in the Bible, to the effect that no sacrifice offered in the temple could expiate (make reparation for, i.e. repair, restore) the sinful state of humankind, but could only seek reconciliation with God for sins committed unwittingly, by mistake or in ignorance. (Numbers 15:25-30)

But Jesus not only ratified, he consummated the renewed and improved covenant, the terms of which he had expounded according to Matthew's Sermon on the Mount. He consummated that covenant by the emptying, the sacrifice of self that was itself consummated in the shedding of his own blood on Calvary. Then, perfected through such suffering he became the perfect image of God, allowing the Creator Spirit to breathe eternal life into others, making them co-creators rather than destroyers of life, repairing and restoring their erstwhile satanic spirits and broken bodies, so that they too become temples of the Holy Spirit. In this way Jesus gave to these others, human as he was human, direct access to the source of eternal life, the Throne of Grace. This enfolded imagery as it is unfolded reveals the following vista: the channelling of the Creator Spirit to humankind in the most perfect way in which the Spirit can be channelled to human beings – that is to say, through a human being utterly and entirely as human as themselves, as Hebrews repeats over and over again – gives them their own access to the Creator Spirit simply as the human beings that they are. This right of return is pictured by Hebrews in the follow-the-leader imagery that sees Jesus re-entering paradise, the true and only sanctuary of the eternal Father. For this is the Father who sent Jesus to bring to his human brethren the defining grace of the same Creator and Father, who creates life eternally, repairing and restoring spirits turned satanic, and reversing the sinful destruction that human beings bring upon themselves with seemingly perennial persistence. And now Jesus returns to the inner sanctum, the blessed place of paradise, showing his spilt blood as the symbol of the behaviour by which he let the Creator Spirit breath into those who now follow him back to the paradise that this Spirit creates for them from the beginning of the world.

In short, Jesus is presented as a priest in a metaphorical sense. As a metaphor, the image, in this case the image of a priest, has something in common with its commonly experienced instances. But it is applied to something that exhibits some features different from these common instances. In some cases these differences are incalculable, when images of Father, Creator, Spirit and so on are used for God. But in the case of the image of priesthood used first of Moses and the temple priests, and then of Jesus, the differences are calculable. Jesus was like Moses and the temple priesthood in that he carried the blood of the sacrificed into the sanctuary of God. He carried into God's house the blood he shed in the process of inspiring and inspired, empowering and empowered, that brings Creator and creaturely co-creators together again. But immediately after this restricted range of similarity, both the differences and the new insights that metaphor brings begin. Jesus did not kill in order to provide sacrificed blood to bring to God, not another animal and certainly not another human being – even the ancient ancestors of the Israelis had given up human sacrifice from at least the time of the story of Abraham and Isaac.

Nor did Jesus kill himself, nor did he ever pretend to be a priest in that sense of a sacrificer of any living thing. Nor did he ever 'ordain' any such cultic priests. No document in the Bible shows any knowledge whatever of there being priests amongst the officers of any of the communities of Jesus-followers. Nor did any priest collect his blood and present it to God in any man-made sanctuary, in completion of a kind of sacrifice that the Bible is in any case adamant could never expiate, repair, restore humanity from its deliberately incurred sinful state. Instead of the blood of Jesus being splattered on some altar in some man-made sanctuary, it is splattered on the earth itself, the true house of God, and in particular the blood is splattered on the killing hill of Calvary, the place especially designated for the age-old ritual in which sinners kill other sinners in the spirit of their common satanic gods, thereby turning the paradise that God continually creates into a hell on earth.

So the one image that brings Jesus and the temple priesthood together in the disclosure-light of the metaphor, is an image that of itself marginalises the temple, any temple. And it does so in the same double movement with which it links up with other familiar imagery of salvation through the death of Jesus. Jesus, the giver of his life to the point of giving his very life-blood for others, so that the Creator Spirit could again rule the hearts of humans, and through them the world itself, making it the paradise it always was and is as it comes fresh every morning from the hands and in the eyes of God. But Jesus is now bringing and sprinkling the blood of his sacrifice, not into the temple-house of God in Jerusalem but sprinkling if onto the earth, the house of God which is thereby the heaven, the house of the eternal creator of paradise. And more specifically and significantly still, sprinkling his blood on the hill of Calvary, the very epitome as part and symbol – that is to say, sacrament – of paradise turned to hell by the primordial sin of the race. As Jesus said to the 'good' brigand, 'This day you will be with me in paradise' when, actually, neither of them were going anywhere on that particular day, but back into the earth from which they both came, as is the case with all of us. 'Dust you are, and to dust you will return.' For the hill of Calvary, cleansed by the blood of Jesus of the dark detritus of the killing fields, was on that black day, as in essence it always is, as much a part of paradise as anywhere else on earth. And so for those whose dust is breathed into by the Creator Spirit, and especially for those who die even the cruellest of deaths for and in that Spirit, death itself can be experienced as the passage-way through the same fiery Spirit, the sword of fire, that keeps the garden of paradise now regained.

All of which must remind the reader of the gospel stories about the trial and death of Jesus, of the run of imagery in these stories that in fact runs exactly parallel to this imagery of Jesus going into the heavenly sanctuary to pour out there the blood of his saving sacrifice – on Calvary. Mark, at the very moment of the death of Jesus when he 'breathed his last,' has the veil of the temple torn in two, from top to bottom. To which Matthew adds that many of the dead were also then raised to eternal life. (Luke 23:39-43; Mark 15:38; Matthew 27:51-54) This is a story of the escape of the Glory, the Presence, from its domestication in the man-made sanctuary closed off by that veil, closed off to all others except the High Priest who dared to enter once a year bearing the symbols of an essentially useless blood sacrifice. And where, according to this amazing myth, does the Glory go? To where it always was and always will be. But first and foremost onto the hill of Calvary, the very image and epitome of a fallen world, into and through the body broken and blood-letting of this dying man. John is the most powerful persuader on this, in his description of Calvary as the hour of the Glory.

And one more insight is now unavoidable and utterly in line with all that the author of Hebrews has to say about Jesus and Moses. It is an insight into the covenant that is always as old and as young as creation itself, the covenant God made with humanity in its very creation and its simultaneous endowment with the Word or Wisdom that would enable it to co-create the world. It is an insight that takes the form of the realisation that the mountain on which the covenant of creation itself is especially renewed, formulated, delivered, ratified and now also consummated is not the impressive mount Sinai, but the nondescript, blood-stained hillock called Calvary. That is why Paul says that he wishes to know nothing except Jesus crucified; and why the identifying symbol of the followers of Jesus to this day is the scene of that crucifixion. For that is the place, for them, on which the Glory especially descended and consummated its benign creative reign. And from there, through the cowards clinging together in an upper room, it went out from Jerusalem, and out into the whole world, its only true house and sanctuary, its heaven, its paradise and ours. If we could but let it change our fallen hearts and minds, and so let it be so – as the early chapters of the Acts of the Apostles describe the pilgrim's progress of the renewed reign of God through Jesus of Nazareth, God's prophet, son and messiah.

If any further biblical licence is necessary for explaining and interpreting in this way the true line of the argument of Hebrews concerning Jesus bringing the blood of his self-sacrifice into the heavenly sanctuary, it can be found in all the biblical talk of new heavens and a new earth, or a new age instead of another world. And it can be found especially in the description of paradise at the end of the last book of the Bible, the book of Revelation, where it is pictured in exactly the same imagery as that in which Genesis describes the world as God (first) created it – paradise regained.

The death of Jesus was a sacrifice, then, in that it constituted his acceptance of the shedding of his blood as his final fidelity to the God who never kills but only creates life and life ever more abundant for all. The God who, far from ever requiring us to kill in his name, absolutely commands us not to kill at all, to die rather than do so, and for the rest to exert ourselves in the cause of life better and better for all. Therefore the sacrifice of Jesus on Calvary was the price that Jesus paid for his part in sending into remission the sin of the world, by letting the Creator Spirit breathe into the world in a manner as consummate as any human being could achieve. It was not a payment-in-penalty exacted by a vengeful divinity intent, like some heavenly Shylock, on having his pound of flesh for the satisfaction of his justice in recompense for offence to his person and status. A primitive idea still alive in the medieval theologian Anselm's day, dressed up in the feudal ideology current at that time. The idea of the death of Jesus as ransom-price or redemption from sin paid for the human race is therefore as metaphorical as is the image of Jesus as a cultic priest.

The eucharistic meal is then also a sacrifice, in the sense that there is a self-sacrificial move at the very core of that symbolic drama: when we take the necessities and supports of life, symbolised in food and drink, and break and pour them out to others and receive them from the others again, in part realisation, part earnest of the giving of our lives for life and life ever more abundant for all. The eucharistic meal does not involve the offering thousands of times every day of a blood sacrifice, in this instance a human sacrifice, no matter how un-bloody it may be made to seem by some abstruse and currently unintelligible piece of medieval metaphysics.

There is a scene in John's gospel in which John allows us to eavesdrop on a general discussion between the people themselves, the temple authorities and the Pharisees, concerning the claims of Jesus to be either the king-messiah or the prophet. Claims that some people ardently accept since, as they explain, 'no man ever spoke like this man', but claims that the others involved in this disputation as ardently refute. Because of this perceived uniqueness on the part of Jesus, some of the people were inclined to think that he could well be the king-messiah or the prophet of the age of fulfilment that Moses was thought to have promised – or as we have seen possible above, a bit of both, the best bits of both. But the erudite ones sought to put an end to all such speculation by arguing from the Bible. First, these argued that Jesus could not possibly be the king-messiah, because a descendant of David would have to come from Bethlehem, 'the village where David was'. Whereas, as his full name suggests, Jesus of Nazareth came from Nazareth. (Is this why Luke has such a complicated infancy story that included a census and a visit of Joseph and the pregnant Mary to Bethlehem, so that Jesus perhaps could have been born at Bethlehem, and be Jesus of Bethlehem after all? Another twist to the genealogy stories, this time in order to shore up rather than undermine the case for the messianic kingship of Jesus? Luke 2:1-6) Second, and this time in a sarcastic comment from the aristocratic folk from Jerusalem: 'You can search the scriptures all you like, but you will never come across the idea – the very idea! – that a Galilean peasant would be chosen by the Most High as his prophet like Moses, in order to inaugurate the new age of the perfect reign of God in the world.' (paraphrasing John 7:40-52)

If it had occurred to any of the participants in this wide-ranging discussion that Jesus in his words and actions might also have had a claim to the office of priesthood, even an implicit one which, unlike the case of the other two claims, he had never been heard to express, the answers of the erudite would have been even more dismissive and much more easily argued. The only valid priesthood, by God's own law, had for long now been the Levitical priesthood. And any other kind of claim to priesthood that Jesus might be thought to have harboured, to be a priest for example as kings and the prophet Moses had once exercised the essential sacrificial cult of that office, such a claim would certainly then be destroyed by the same careful exegesis of the scriptures that scotched any claims this deluded Galilean peasant might entertain to be the king-messiah or the prophet of the new world.

So if Jesus did claim to be the king-messiah, as his followers still call him a king, he was and is so in a sense that is quite the polar opposite of the sense in which such monarchs then and thereafter understood and exercised that office. He rules like God the Creator, his Father and ours, by serving up life to all without distinction, and never by lording it over people and making his authority felt. And if Jesus did claim to be the prophet – and he certainly did, without any doubt – as his followers still call him the prophet, then he must be seen as a prophet so much superior to Moses that the issue of deciding whether he was perfecting the prophecy of Moses or contradicting it is always likely to draw a line between those who believe in him and follow him, and those who persist in thinking that he set himself up against the law that God gave through Moses, and then proceed to execute him quite legally according to that law.

And if Jesus claimed to be a priest, and there is not the faintest whiff of evidence that he ever did so, but his followers, beginning with the anonymous author of Hebrews, claimed that he was a priest, then his priesthood is even more different from the priesthood of those who offer cultic sacrifices on altars, than is his kingship different from the kind of kingship exercised by monarchical-type rulers before his time, and during it, and down to the present day, even in some so-called democracies. And it is the same difference in both cases, the case of the king and the case of the priest. In that the polar oppositeness of service to monarchical-type rule makes us all, Jesus and all of his followers, either kings or non-kings, depending on the ideology of kingship – either that of Jesus or that of his opponents – that we use. Just as the polar oppositeness of self-sacrifice for the benefit of others, to the sacrificial killing of a human being or indeed any other living creature to satisfy the justice of God, means that all are priests, Jesus and all of his followers, or that none is a priest, depending on the ideology of priesthood – either that of Hebrews or that of Torah and temple – that is used.

Amongst the followers of Jesus, then, all are priests in the metaphorical sense of those who are eucharistically committed to the offering of their daily lives and livelihoods for others. None are priests in the old traditional cultic sense of those appointed to offer the life of another human being, a life taken to make satisfaction to God's justice for human sin. For, as the whole of the teaching, life and death of Jesus reveals, the God who comes into view through his true and consistent sonship is the polar opposite of a god who would apply special punishments for particular sins, as a special penalty is applied for wrong-doing in human systems of penal justice. The spirit that inspires human beings to kill other human beings is the satanic spirit, and those who kill their fellows rather than give of their own lives that others should live, are sons and daughters of that satanic spirit. And those who kill their fellows rather than give of their own lives that others should live, are sons and daughters of that same satanic spirit; even if they were to kill in compliance with an alleged divine requirement of human death in satisfaction for sin. That Jesus should have abhorred such a notion, that his death engineered by the temple priesthood could be taken by God as required satisfaction for sin, is made blindingly clear in an account in John's gospel of one particular altercation between Jesus and 'the Jews'.

Jesus knew that the authorities in Jerusalem wanted to kill

him: and he came to realise that they would succeed. So he tells them plainly – spades are spades here and no one's sentiments are spared – that in doing so they will prove themselves sons of Satan. 'You seek to kill me ... You do what your father did ... You are of your father the devil ... a murderer from the beginning.' (John 8:39-46) Now if Jesus himself saw Calvary, as it turned out, as the outcome of the ethos and death-dealing reign of the satanic spirit working through the temple priesthood, he could hardly agree with later Christian dogmaticians that it was the result of the providence of the God he called Father dealing out death through cooperative human beings in order to take satisfaction for human sin. Quite to the contrary, the God who is the true Father to the true son of God, Jesus of Nazareth, never deals out death as such. Rather does he deal out life continuous-creatively and always to all; and most especially at the point at which all of us mere mortals go through the most critical threshold that corresponds to our birth, the death of our current material forms. As Luke adds to the story of Jesus, in response to the Sadducees' challenge to resurrection belief, that the God of Abraham, Isaac and Jacob is not God of the dead, but of the living, 'for all live to him' eternally, that is to say. (Luke 20:38)

Jesus never showed the least intent of founding a new religion, or even a new church that would fall outside the range of institutional structures already envisaged within his own Jewish religion in his time. But that fact should not in itself be taken as a permanent deterrent to the followers of Jesus creating some new institutional structures to serve growing numbers. Especially since, due to their own infidelity to the teaching of their master, as much as to their violent rejection by their fellow Jews – this infidelity took the same concrete form for both, namely, the portrayal of a god who required the infliction of deprivation, suffering and even death, whether on battlefield or altar, and both here and hereafter – these two originally and equally Jewish communities drifted irrevocably apart into separate and increasingly hostile camps. At this tragic point of apparently irreversible parting, as it rapidly revealed prospects of expansion throughout the Roman Empire, the scattering Jesus-community badly needed institutional structures that would hold it together and advance its prospects without dilution or disintegration. It could not opt for the reigning structure of monarchy (in this case, emperor) combined with priesthood that had served the Jewish people in the past, and a version of which could still be made to work in parts of traditional Jewish territory, as with the Herodian dynasty for example. For the Jesus-followers saw that the rulers of the Roman Empire ruled and expanded their rule by dealing out death, while claiming to be incarnations of divinity in one way or another, as had the Davidic line of Jewish kings, and so they rightly regarded the emperors as idolators. And the emperors could not countenance this attitude in a community that seemed well on the way to making the whole empire its home, and beyond. As emperors could do and did for the other Jews who seemed to want to have their ways in a small piece of territory only, for which some accommodation might always be made.

So this community of Jesus-followers, now called Christians because they took Jesus to be the true Messiah who was to come, did the next best thing. They formed an institution of *episcopoi* or overseers such as would imitate the offices and divisions of the empire: with the *episcopos*, the bishop who was the *papa*, the father in Rome setting out his stall reasonably early as the *primus* of provincial counterparts. That this was a good thing to do, if not indeed the best, can be argued from the perception that the best way to influence the 'secular' powers in human society, the most effective means of getting them to act in the spirit of service to all rather than as self-serving, coercive and often brutal overlords, is by the example of a twinned type of institution operating always in this spirit of service.

Much the same could be said of priesthood, when Christians in the years after the biblical texts were completed began to refer to their overseers and elders, *episcopoi* and *presbyteroi*, as priests. They could do this, and it seems did do so at first, by making a metaphor out of the language used of the cultic sacrificer of living things. And the justification for so doing, as it could still be stated to this day, reads somewhat as follows. Despite the fact that in the eucharistic drama each one is the priest-offerer of his or her own self-sacrifice, and the community gathered round each table of the Lord therefore exercises their communal priesthood – 'built into a spiritual house, to be a holy priesthood, to offer spiritual sacrifices acceptable to God through Jesus Christ' (1 Peter 2:5) – it still makes sense to refer to the one who presides over the eucharistic meal, through whom the assembled people of God speak and act at the most significant points of the sacrament, as the priest in the special sense of the priest-president, or the presiding priest at each eucharistic celebration. Particularly when the bishops and presbyters who took on the task of preserving, handing on and teaching the truth in word and act, of which this eucharistic meal was the crowning expression, were also the ones who regularly presided over the eucharistic meal, itself now regularly celebrated, not in people's homes, but in the new temples and basilicas, the local churches of the Christians. For now, as each eucharistic celebration also incorporated the preaching of the faith of Jesus of Nazareth, the one who would preside over the eucharistic meal would be expected to be one who had had some special training in understanding and preaching that true word. Yet every age should guard against the image of the Christian priest slipping back again into the image of the priesthood of the old, savage gods who required the taking of life for the remission of sin.

In both cases then, that of the monarch and that of the priest, the Christian ideal of the office and the Christian form of its exercise as self-sacrificing service, could have been thought well designed to inspire their Roman Imperial counterparts with the same ideal of office and the same form of humanitarian praxis. The whole expanding Roman empire could have been converted to live by and propagate the true faith of Jesus of Nazareth, its original sin by which it aggrandised itself in the twinned violence of war and trade now sent into permanent remission. But instead the true and abiding insight of original sin imagery was neutered by mystifying doctrines of guilt transmitted by human conception from some act of disobedience by 'first parents' in a long lost garden. The true faith of Jesus, a keeping faith with the God he called Father of all of us, was resisted by even his closest followers during his lifetime. Even though they did hear and remember the words and kept in mind the unforgettable pictures of it, so that it seemed to be seen at last for what it truly was, and put in practice for a while after his death. But soon, too soon after that again, the old ersatz influence of the ethos of the kings of the nations infected the new-fangled rulers of successively Christianised territories, just as had happened when Israel first demanded kingship, and got what it wished for. And, doorstep to doorstep, the kings corrupted the priests, or was it the priests who corrupted the kings? Hard to say once both adopt the same ethos of overlording coercive power, secured by 'just' penalties of pain and death inflicted on battlefields and instruments of execution and altars, both here and, allegedly, hereafter.

Epilogue: The Future of the Faith of Jesus of Nazareth: Fidelity and Infidelity

Such a topic as this would take a book to itself, and more than one volume at that. But all that needs to be done in order to conclude this present book is to list, in the most summary form, what has happened to the original faith of Jesus the Jew during all the centuries between, and to say what should happen to it now, if the same Bible that shows us what that faith *was* is to guide us to what it should once again become. And for much of that list it is necessary only to point back to previous chapters in which the story is told in some detail of how the misconceptions of the kingship and kingdom of God in which the closest followers of Jesus persisted, virtually from the moment of their calling, re-emerged after the death of Jesus, after a brief period of renaissance of the truth of the matter. And how these misconceptions of the messianic title were then consummated, and seem now as if they were set in concrete in subsequent centuries, when the royal imperial ideology that is still in pristine condition in the little independent kingdom of the Vatican, embraced war just as closely as that royal ideology was itself embraced by the Emperor Constantine. Thereby reversing in the most complete manner the reversal of the interpretation of the moral principle, thou shalt not kill, that Jesus had dealt to the interpretation previously attributed to Moses – a principal plank of the platform on which Jesus stood, and for which he was hanged, as a claimant to the title of a prophet greater than Moses.

Yet, if for no other reason than that it lifts and delays the impending encircling gloom, it is worth dallying a little longer on that honeymoon period described in so picturesque a fashion in the early chapters of the Acts of the Apostles – a section of the Bible, incidentally, that seldom tops the bill in any of the marshalled theological tomes that undertake to explain the faith of Jesus. So, rather than read them for research, take the time to meditate on these few chapters of Acts. For if you do, the impression will come, and gain in clarity and revelatory power, that you are looking at a first renaissance – well, really, a first naissance in his followers after his death, of that which was born in and of Jesus himself as he first appeared in Galilee proclaiming the reign of God, and subsequently made his way (quite literally, fashioned his way in life), preaching and breaking bread and healing, all the way to the cross of Calvary and his greatest triumph on that blood-stained hill.

In the story of Acts, his followers gathered in the upper room, the room in which they had celebrated a last meal with Jesus; but now terrified and dismayed at what could not but seem to them to be the end of the kingdom they believed he would re-introduce. Yet soon they began to sense his abiding presence with them, starting again to do what he had started to do in his earthly life with them: starting again to teach them the true reign of the one, true God. This would be a forty-day trial for them. But then he had had to go through a forty-day trial in his own desert place, fighting off, as they would now have to do, the temptations to set up just another satanic kingdom on earth. Both episodes, his and theirs, mirrored the forty-years in the desert during which Moses helped his people to overcome constant and similar satanic temptations, so that they should finally be enabled to enter into a covenant with the reigning God, and enjoy the promised land.

Through this sharing of hospitality with him in his new, more spiritual presence with them, they did overcome at once their temptations and the fear that makes people fall for it, the oldest and most persistently successful temptation of the race. And they went out and, like a re-run of the story of his own life on earth, they preached the new covenant of the renewed reign of God, simultaneously presenting him as a prophet greater than Moses. And they engaged in the twin strategies for making that reign real for them: table-fellowship or the breaking of bread, as they came to call it, and healing, exactly as he had done. And so they clashed with the temple authorities just as he had done, and on precisely the same grounds. And, as the paradigmatic story of Stephen shows, they went to their deaths when that is what was called for, in a consummate breathing of the same Spirit through whom they too, like him, lived and died, having that mind or spirit in them, as Paul would put it, which was also in Jesus, the one true Christ. It is all a perfectly parallel re-run of the life, death and destiny of Jesus himself.

And it copperfastens the impression, so often conveyed in the gospels and letters of the Bible, to the effect that the Holy Spirit, the Most High, never breathed so fully into the world through Jesus, was never so fully embodied, incarnate in Jesus, never possessed Jesus so completely as to inspire his fellow humans to the greatest extent of one man's inspiration of another, as happened at and through the death of Jesus. John has Jesus-on-the-cross raised to what Paul calls the status of son of God in power, locus of the revelatory and empowering glory of God. Paul sees the utter human self-emptying of the cross as the condition of that presence of God in and through Jesus in the world that allows Jesus to be called Lord; *'o logos gar 'o tou staurou*, the word (incarnate) of the cross. (1 Corinthians 1:18 – for paradoxically enough, when it comes to becoming human, one does not become fully human until one dies: all men are mortal, as Aristotle long ago reminded us.) So it is not at all surprising that the mission of Jesus to bring all to the status of sons and daughters of God for life eternal, the calling to which he had dedicated his earthly life, should not have begun to be fully effective until after his death. Nor was it at all surprising that the realisation of its full effectiveness should have taken the form of their experience that the one whose continued but more spiritual presence to them at the meal, was none other than Jesus Christ and him crucified, as Paul puts it, something that is corroborated by so many of the other post-death appearances and meal stories.

The opening chapters of Acts, then, describe the kind of human community in this world that most adequately embodies, in spirit and in letter, the human side of the covenant with the true reign of the one, true God. These chapters describe how that community, potentially a united community of all people, should be constituted and, most particularly, how it should be led. It is to be a eucharistic community, through and through. That is to say, it is to be organised as a meal-table is organised, at which all of the supports and enhancements of life, both material and spiritual, are to be put equally at the disposal of all. Just as the God of life eternally puts all of these equally at the disposal of all. The leaders of that community are therefore to model themselves on those who take the lead in serving at table, as they take their place at the table of the world, to which all the nations of the earth are to be invited with equal and unconditional access. This is precisely the kind of community or commune that the first ones, who for the first time were really and truly converted to the reign of God, under the leadership of The Twelve, set up in Jerusalem. It was communism in its purest form. And that was the springtime of the faith of Jesus, budding and growing in the hearts and gatherings of his first community of followers. The eyes of all of them opened at last, and their hearts burning with desire for the vision of eternal life that the Creator Spirit ever gives and promises, a life instantly and always available if only they could keep faith with the God whose effective presence was seen and heard and felt in the life and death of Jesus, and of Stephen, and of …

However, that first experiment in having God's reign run on earth as it did in heaven did not last. In Acts itself there are hints at its breakdown, rather than a blow-for-blow account of that actual and, as it would seem, gradual process. Ananias and Sapphira are the first ones we meet who hedge their bets on God providing for them for all eternity, through their fellow sons and daughters of God also, with the wherewithal for life. These two keep some of their material possessions hidden just in case, and lie to Peter and to the Holy Spirit for good measure. Thereafter we meet those who flaunt their conspicuous consumerism and simultaneously their contempt for the poor, during the very eucharist itself, thereby undermining eucharist. So that Paul has to tell them that it is no longer the Lord's supper that they eat. And Paul, in some of his letters, has to criticise those congenital dossers who join the community so that they can live well without working, thereby undermining the eucharistic life from the other end of the social spectrum. In short, the oldest temptation continues unabated in this garden-world that could be paradise: the temptation for people to grasp at finiteness in order to sustain life as long as possible, and to put at risk in the process the lives and livelihoods of others, as well, eventually, as their own.

It was some time after the early years covered by Luke in Acts, indeed it was after all of the years covered in the remaining documents that make up the Bible, that the most dangerous and long-lasting undermining of the eucharistic community model that Jesus clearly had in mind for his fellowship began to take effect. This happened in the course of the process in which the followers of Jesus organised the faith of Jesus into a religion other than the only one that Jesus himself ever had in mind. And it coincided with the emergence of the Jesus fellowship from the status of a persecuted faith, and in particular its emergence from the catacombs of Rome into the light of a favourable gaze cast upon it by imperial power, and finally into the benign gaze of the Emperor Constantine. This brought about a coupling of eucharistic table-leadership with imperial leadership, for which the old prophetic warnings about temple and palace lying threshold to threshold and doorpost to doorpost seemed supremely applicable. Except that this particular age, the fourth of the centuries hereafter to be called Christian, lacked any prophet of the stature that could hurl that metaphorical criticism once more, and with the hope of any serious effect.

Not long at all after the year 303CE, when the Emperor Diocletian ordered the destruction of church buildings, threatened Christians in official positions with loss of all of their public privileges, and ordered Christians to hand over their holy books to be burnt, another emperor, Constantine, began the process that soon resulted in the establishment of the Christian religion as the religion of the empire. So Christians had their public buildings back again, more numerous than the synagogues of the religion of Israel, and eventually more impressive than the temples of the religion of the Romans that they now seemed set to supersede. Temples with altars and all, and with their popes and bishops and presbyters recognised as priesthoods, just like the divinely sanctioned priesthood that Israel had in the days of their founder, and the Roman temples still had. For after all, had not Constantine been vouchsafed the vision of the cross, the symbol of Jesus, Son of God and Saviour of the world, set within the circle of the sun, the symbol of *Sol Invictus*, the high God of Rome. So that Christians and (other) Romans really served the same one, true God, something that had been concealed, albeit in differing degrees from each side, until Constantine saw the light.

This collusion of temple (or basilica, the house of the Cosmic

King) and imperial palace quite rapidly became as close as the metaphors of thresholds and doorposts could ever have imagined and feared. And the consequences of this that the prophets of old had foreseen – the prophet as seer – continued to be verified for this Near-Eastern faith that went on to become the dominant religion of the West, and was then spread by Christian colonists to the rest of the world, new and old alike, and down to the present day – as the potted histories used above to illustrate the original misconstrued messianic assessments of Jesus of Nazareth serve to show in some detail. The secular ethos of the palace continued to seep into the temple, as the prophets of old had warned it would. For these latest imperial rulers, like the ones that Jesus called 'the kings of the Gentiles', fashioned a god in their own image, as kings of the peoples had always done. These were rulers who would kill in order to secure a better life for themselves and, well yes, for their people also, in ever extending territories. Yielding a god who would kill or at least torture for eternity any who would resist his own will and reign, as expressed through earthly plenipotentiaries, sacred and secular – man was made for the sabbath. Instead of the ethos of the sacred seeping into the secular, the ethos of the one, true Creator God who never does anything except to continuously create existence and life in ever better and more wonderful forms, who never destroys anything so created, although forms of it must consistently be shed in the course of such continual transformation – the sabbath, symbol of the eternal *shalom*, was made for man. Made for everything else also, of course, but since we say even this in our fallen state, we cannot help distorting it in the most self-serving of fashions, as if the eternal *shalom*, like everything else, was made exclusively for the use and benefit of *homo sapiens*.

Reformations of this Christian religion were attempted many times in the course of its history, reformations large and small. Each a little more or a little less successful than the others, but all eventually experiencing the alienation and, more often than not, the abiding hostility, sometimes quite brutal, of the part of the universal Christian community most immediately affected by them. The reform movement led by Luther, that most substantially realigned Christian communities here in the West, was the

Protestant Reformation of the 16th century. The subsequent attempt to reform the remaining Roman Catholic Church, mainly through the Council of Trent, was mostly reactionary. That is to say, instead of going back to the pristine origins of the Christian faith, as Luther had done, the Vatican was content to secure all of its traditional positions against a frequently quite proper Protestant critique, while doing a relatively minor clean-up job on some of these positions. The news that renaissance time was blooming and spreading over European culture failed to penetrate the Vatican compound.

The Protestants might wish to count as one of their major successes their replacement of the lordly episcopal leadership of the Roman Catholic Church, indistinguishable as that lordship had become from the secular feudal lordship of the time. But read a good book on Calvin's Geneva, and you will be left with some serious doubts as to whether the ethos of rule differed much from the side of the Christian pastor to that of the civic magistrate, much less in the interchange between them. The same vengeful God presided over both together, waiting to greet with eternal punishment those who might have escaped earthly punishment or who might not have properly repented of the crime that brought that punishment upon them. In fact and ever since, the Protestants have been even more notable than the Catholics in what one of our finest Irish poets, Cathal Ó Searcaigh, called, 'the brutal piety of the pulpit' – even more lurid than the Catholics in their preaching of hellfire and damnation, a petrifying scenario that a Protestant doctrine such as the doctrine of double predestination did nothing whatever to soften.

But move towards the other side of the distinction-in-unity of secular and sacred, and a much more deserving success can be recorded for the Protestant cause. The Protestants rejected outright the view that the eucharistic meal was by any manner of means a repetition of the cultic sacrifice of Jesus required by and offered to God to make satisfaction for the sins of the race. Therefore they rid their communities of priests after the manner of the Jerusalem temple priesthood, taking heed at long last of the argument of Hebrews to the effect that, after the sacrifice that Jesus offered on Calvary, there would be no place for a cultic priesthood like that of the Jerusalem temple in the communities of Jesus followers in the world. But then they lost to modern Christianity most of the good ground they had gained in that much overdue move. For they failed to notice that it was in purely metaphorical manner, and not at all in a manner univocal with the meaning of priesthood and cultic sacrifice in the Jerusalem temple, that Hebrews continued to evoke the image of Jesus as the High Priest of the Christian faith and religion. So they persisted with the assessment of the death of Jesus as itself a cultic sacrifice, and a human sacrifice therefore, as punitive pay-back or ransom, required by God's justice for the sinners of the race. And then they put the finishing touches to that gruesome picture with the doctrine of original sin that they held in common with their Roman opponents, and which made sure that all members of the human race from its beginning to its end would by divine dispensation be sinners, whether they ever did anything to deserve that bleak distinction, or not.

And we are straight back once more in the dark shadows of a God who kills those who resist his reign, back under the ethos characteristic of the rulers of the nations of the world – so far back that it almost seems as if we had never progressed beyond Gilgal. And there is simply no point in trying to soften the edge of that conclusion by protesting that God required the death of one man only, and furthermore, that the man God sent to pay the price demanded was God's uniquely beloved son, who went willingly to that penal execution. All of that kind of pleading is but a little less pathetic than the young girl hoping to soften the blow for both of them when she tells her mother that she is pregnant, by adding that she is only a little bit pregnant. And it is always necessary for the Bible reader when dealing with this kind of material, to call to mind again and again that paradigmatic row between Jesus and the temple authorities in John 8, when Jesus accuses his opponents of being sons of satan, that is to say idolators, worshippers of a false god, and why? Because they are going to kill him. And Jesus passes this sentence on them knowing fine well, surely, that they will execute him in accordance with the Torah that they attribute to God's revelation through Moses. The God that Jesus addresses as 'our Father,' does not kill, does not destroy anything created, but only transforms all.

So anyone who pictures God requiring the killing of anyone, creates an idol in his or her own image, and anyone who deliberately kills another in God's name or in the name of any alleged moral rule of God, blasphemes.

Because the eucharist was instituted by Jesus in his lifetime as the central strategy by which to spread the Spirit of the true reign of God to all of humankind, the damage caused to eucharist by the application of these regressive ideologies of sacrifice was and continues to be of the most serious and threatening kind for the faith of Jesus in the world. And yet that persisting damage should not be overestimated. For every priest who abuses his power in any way to the detriment of the faith, there are a hundred lay and religious people who work in the healing mission so central to that faith in the world. They provide education and health services to the poorest of the earth, as well of course as food and drink and shelter, especially in times of disaster. And there are a thousand instances in ordinary Christian lives of similar service of life and the necessities and enhancements of life to the sick and the needy. And indeed, if one were to look beyond the boundaries of the Christian communities scattered round the world, one could well get the impression that the core values of the faith of Jesus of Nazareth had made their way in significant forms into what is known as civic or secular society. The image of the governing leadership of democracies as ministries provides a key example. For the one who ministers to others is their servant, and the social counterpart of the faith of Jesus would seem to be perhaps even more intact outside of some structured Christian churches than it is within these.

It is necessary to remind oneself not to get carried away here however. One might well do, if one forgot for a moment the fact that it is the most advanced democracies in this world that, on the back of their advanced science and technology, colonise by economic rather than military strategies, though occasionally by a combination of both, what they deviously but, they would hope, reassuringly call the developing world. They do so with earth-raping, life-stunting, life-destroying, dehumanising effects on the indigenous populations that can rival similar results achieved by the older, straightforward brutal military means used by their predecessor *conquistadors*. It is all in a way but an extension of what happens in the internal affairs of these advanced democracies. For since the main purpose of the governments of these nations seems to be to increase the wealth of the nation, their very government programmes and laws are designed to favour capitalist entrepreneurs. And that inevitably means that the gap between the rich and the poor increases all the time; and most, if not all of these countries have to try to hide the shame of substantial percentages of their own populations also having to half-live below even their own generously drawn poverty lines, without proper access to the basic means of well-being. The words that God spoke to the king of Tyre through the prophet Ezekiel could be applied to any of these so-called advanced democracies, without changing a single one. And that goes for Christian Ireland also, as its favourite predatory nickname, The Green Tiger, acknowledges in a most unsubtle manner.

The reference to science and technology above, in a paragraph that also recalls the words of Ezekiel to the king of Tyre, suggests that this whole matter fits quite snugly into the ideology of original sin. Because the wisdom gained from creation for which Ezekiel rightly praised the king of Tyre – it was his pride in that wisdom that made him act as if he were God, and the ensuing violence of his economic strategies, that is condemned – is now in this so-called scientific age widely thought to be, almost in its entirety, the gift of our scientists. As a consequence, that wisdom stretches beyond the traditional output of the empirical sciences themselves, as it reaches with surprising ease towards what can only be called a metaphysics of the whole of reality: a total view of the universe, its origin, evolution, future evolution and possible options for ending or not ending. And finally, here is the crunch, a view that its total make-up is material through and through, so that any perceived element of consciousness in us must be accounted a mere *epiphenomenon*, a fleeting appearance around and about certain complex material substances like human brains and nervous systems, that will simply desist as soon as these disintegrate. This phenomenon of consciousness has not as yet found its full scientific explanation, our scientists in moments of rare humility freely admit, but there is no prospect of its being evidence of minds or souls or spirits such as pre-scientific ages misgoverned by religion and superstition (the same thing, really) imagined.

This is not the place or the time to explain how this thoroughly materialist worldview, far from being the true outcome of the empirical sciences as such, is rather a dogma. And just as much a dogma as any of the most mistaken doctrines of any of the world's religions, and equally as much a seed-bed for a despairing and rapacious destruction of self and planet. Suffice it to say here that contemporary physics has actually removed the concept of matter itself from the fundamental role it played in science even up to the time of Bertrand Russell, who still accounted for the origin of all things that have come to be in our universe in terms of 'omnipotent matter rolling on its relentless way'. And with that demotion of the idea of matter has gone the last vestige of credibility for the kind of Darwinian explanation of the evolution of all that makes up our world through the operation of mindless material entities such as genes. But what is of interest in our present context is the manner in which this dogma of absolute metaphysical materialism has penetrated all levels of Western society, and is spreading with the influence of the West to the rest of the world. At the very outset of a recent BBC series on the mind-body problem, the presenter warned viewers that he would occasionally use the word 'mind', but that we should be careful not to think that he referred to anything other than the brain and nervous system. The mindless heart of Richard Dawkins, the modern missionary of this destructive dogma – for that is what he is and that is what it is – must have jumped for mindless joy at that announcement, as he realised how his gospel was now being spread by the mass media, reputed to be the most powerful popular persuader in the whole of the long history of our race.

What is of interest here about all of that is this: it is the manner in which such a thoroughgoing materialist dogma fits the perennially fallen mentality of human kind. It is the kind of outlook on the world that best accompanies a person's prideful decision to take over God's part in creation, and to secure life ever better and indefinitely for oneself. Quite simply because grasping at and accumulating the material supports and enhancements of life is the only way the human person on its own can enhance and prolong life, being able neither to create life nor to prolong it in any other way. And popular metaphysical materialism also provides the kind of worldview that can initiate and encourage the original fall of human kind. For if the material world is all there is, then most people are bound to feel that the sooner the *carpe diem* philosophy of life is formally and wilfully adopted the better. But then all the sooner will the violence increase in competition for these finite resources, and the opposite of all that Jesus promised in the imagery of paradise regained will quite literally materialise.

It would be fitter for missionaries of this materialist dogma to take heed of such dastardly existential inter-connections, instead of striking pseudo-poses of the false courage of men and women who can fearlessly face the indifference of the universe and the extinction to which it condemns us all. Indeed Ireland, like other economically advanced countries, could well ask itself if there is not some real causal connection between this well-fostered materialist philosophy, secured on the excessive prestige of modern science, and the increase in violent crime (often as mindless as the materialist philosophy itself) and the rapidly climbing suicide rate amongst young males and females that have accompanied the recent decline of the influence of Christianity, however flawed its current forms in this country. For the human spirit which, as Feuerbach pointed out at the beginning of his book, *The Essence of Christianity*, has as its distinguishing mark the capacity to conceive of infinity, can scarcely be satisfied to encounter only matter on the road to its own fulfilment.

What then is the future from now on for the faith of Jesus of Nazareth, the prophet and son of God? Two thousand years after the execution of the prophet, it seems as if the primordial fallenness of human kind, with the ensuing and perennial destructiveness of self and earth-world, has increased almost exponentially rather than decreased. And this is in no small part due to the increasingly constructive but equally destructive technologies that science has put in our power, in combination with the materialist metaphysics and philosophy of life that are preached and popular in the name of the same science. It certainly does not seem as if the prospect for eternal *shalom* for *homo sapiens* will be realised in some 'new age' of the existence of this earth-world-home of ours, a *shalom* of the kind that the early followers of Jesus were so sure would soon arrive. After two thousand years it becomes increasingly impossible to believe that this species, *homo insipiens*, will ever arrive (back) on this earth-world at the age of the happiness and fulfilment of the paradise it really is as it comes fresh daily from the hands of God, and from there to be transformed so smoothly at the death of individual or species to a form of life higher and more spiritual still. It seems far more likely that we shall destroy ourselves together with all life on earth by the simple continuation of our current fallen conduct. In the course of such self-devastation we must, individually and as a species, go through more hells than we have as yet managed to create for each other, or managed even to imagine, even in the lurid descriptions of the end of our world scattered throughout the Bible.

Only through such purgative fires might we find ourselves transformed into less material, more spiritual-type worlds, perhaps on the model of the originating depth of our present universe that our physicists still seek to describe when they talk of a background-independent state or stage of the present universe, independent, that is to say, of space-time structures and the gross bodies that manifest these – there, at that spacetime-less depth or height of this universe, to share more fully in the time-lessness, the eternity of God. So that the faith of Jesus will never have triumphed in any fulfilment-age of this poor earth-world of ours after all. And we shall simply have to continue on our tragic way through this earth that is our very own world, allowing God to make of it as much a paradise as even God could make of it, in face of our persistent and undiminished falling. With some lines of Belloc's poem ringing in our inner ears, lines written in a south-easterly gale (I think it was) on Battersea Bridge:

We shall not reach the granite pier and paven

To lie to wharves we know with canvas furled.

My little boat, we shall not reach the haven.

It is not of the world.

Finally, it surely becomes increasingly impossible, if only in view of our perennial and quite frequently criminal stupidity, to believe that our evolutionary arrival in this universe represents the crowning achievement of this unimaginably vast and awesome creation. Surely no grand Creator Spirit worthy of the title could be so remiss as to make to evolve such supernal wonder, only to have it crowned by this self-centred, short-sighted, endemically erratic and destructive brood. This is a matter that those dedicated advocates of the so-called anthropic principle should consider, those scientists, that is to say, who construct such persuasive arguments to the effect that this universe seems designed from the outset to produce our species, or something very, very like it. There must of course remain the possibility that self-styled *homo sapiens* in its presently evolved form is light years away from the admirable species it will yet become and prove to be, and then the anthropic principle may not seem so odd after all. But in view of the exponentially increasing efficiency with which we are killing off our own race and destroying our earthly habitat, that type of proposition must attract, in betting terms, very, very long odds indeed. A far safer bet would see this species itself return on extinction to the bosom of the Creator Spirit, there to live the eternal life that Jesus preached, lived and passed into from his cross, as we make way for some species at least a little less unworthy of the goodness and splendour of creation, and leave little or no trace of our self-destruction behind in a universe vast enough to erase it.

And then there would be the question as to what part the prophet and son of God, Jesus of Nazareth, might be thought to play in the revelation of God's reign in any other section of this far flung universe, either presently or in the future, with species more intelligent and, more appositely, wiser than ours? To which the only answer must be this: especially in view of what our kind did to Jesus two thousand years ago, and no doubt would do again if Jesus were to knock on the doors of most of our present-day Christian churches, it is simply and strictly speaking not a question that we should think ourselves in the least bit fit to answer.

And yet, and yet, in spite of all of that, it still remains true that for any member of this errant race, the prospect of paradise both here and hereafter is, and will always remain, but a breath of the spirit within, and a flick of the will away. For that Creator

Spirit still breathes through the prophet and son of God, Jesus of Nazareth, through the true followers of Jesus, and through all of creation, and still breathes strongly enough to turn over a new leaf in the most hard-bound book of human life.

That we will all end up equally alright in the end, no matter how soon or how late we will have left the opening of our hearts to the benign reign of God, and the turning of our swords into ploughshares in order to take our full creative part in forging the paradise that is always possible on earth; that is the picture that Jesus paints with characteristic clarity of imagery in one of the best known of his parables, the parable of the labourers in the vineyard, or as it is more popularly known, the everyman a penny parable. (Matthew 20:1-16) Labourers who wish to be hired for the day by the owner of a local vineyard appear in the marketplace, some at 6am, others at 9, others at 12 noon, and some at 3pm; and even at 5pm, just one hour before stopping time, a group of men appear in the marketplace, probably the kind of men who are a burden to family and society alike, having been pushed out the door by their long-suffering wives and having loitered along the way, hoping to God that they would not meet anyone who would want to hire them at that late hour. But the same vineyard owner arrives on the scene and hires them also. And, typically enough, those who were last in to work were first up to the pay-desk where the steward, to their great surprise, gave them 'everyman a penny'; well a denarius actually, a good day's pay in those olden times: exactly the same amount as that agreed with the earliest arrivals.

Now the ones who had worked assiduously since dawn and had 'borne the burden of the day and the scorching heat' naturally thought that a far more substantial sum of money awaited them at the pay-desk. And when they also received everyman a penny they complained bitterly about the utterly unjust equalisation policy of the vineyard owner. Only to be told that he could do as he wished with his own largesse. To which he added the cryptic question to them, 'Is your eye evil because I am good?' The RSV version of the Bible translates that phrase with the bland, 'Do you begrudge my generosity?', thereby inexplicably losing all the power of the imagery of the evil eye. For that more powerful imagery can open the eye of the reader of this parable to a much larger picture. A picture in which these men who worked hard through tough times and conditions, hoping perhaps to buy the vineyard some day, and add other vineyards, make very sure that those who cannot or will not work so hard will never experience life as good as the money these hard-nosed money-makers can enjoy. Then the reference to the evil eye, the evil spirit, can suggest that we are once again in the presence of those whose lives are ruled by Mammon; and of all that follows in terms of a policy of securing and enhancing life at the expense of others, and enforcing such a policy with violence economic or, where necessary, military, thereby keeping in motion the crushing wheels of man's extreme and apparently unending inhumanity to man.

It is the unalterable and indomitable will of the Creator Spirit that everyman, whether evil-eyed or good, receive the full and endless *shalom*, if only at the end of their little dust-bound day. Whether or not they believe in and keep faith with this one true God during their earthly lives. For no work of everyman can earn this divine largesse; it is pure gift, pure grace. And equally none can deter God from creating and renewing paradise daily and forever, through human death itself. All that everyman can do, if the penny does not drop in this age of earthly creation, is to set up and keep faith with false gods; and then everyman is condemned to live in the hell that is inevitably co-created together with such idols as reproduce everyman's worst features, when everyman could all along be living in paradise: everyman a penny everyday. And we self-declared followers of Jesus of Nazareth must take a very large share of the blame for creating a false image of the Father of Jesus, the one we rightly call son of God, lord and messiah; and thereby preventing humanity at large from escaping from the hell it alone creates for itself. For so long in all the mainstream Christian churches, in our preaching, our ways of living and our high theologies we have presented as the one true God one who sent Jesus to torture and death in order to satisfy for human sinning some unremitting divine justice. And then for good measure we have had God, cast in our own worst image, create hell in some age or place at present unknown to us, in which all poor foolish people who sin and happen to remain unshriven should be tortured for eternity.

Without even noticing how a divinity so portrayed could lend its insidious and all the more powerful example and impetus to an ethos of the self-punishing, deprivation, suffering and death, the hell on earth visited by human beings on other human beings, all the way from modern magdalen laundries and latter-day Christian crusaders back to the ancient killing fields round the world in which the partnership of conquistador and priest added what they called pagan kingdoms to the ersatz kingdom of God that they took themselves to be expanding, in the name of Jesus, on earth.

And yet, for all that, like a treasure hidden in a field in another of the parables of Jesus, and despite all the weeds that we his self-declared followers have sown in it and in the world at large ever since it was written, the Bible contains the true picture of how the one true God reigns and runs God's vineyard, the world, according to the life and preaching of the prophet and son of God, Jesus of Nazareth.